PRIME MINISTERS
AND THE RULE BOOK

PRIME MINISTERS AND THE RULE BOOK

AMY BAKER

Politico's
PUBLISHING

First published in Great Britain 2000
by Politico's Publishing
8 Artillery Row, London, SW1P 1RZ, England

Tel 0171 931 0090
Email politicos@artillery-row.demon.co.uk
Website http://www.politicos.co.uk

A catalogue record for this book is available from the British Library

ISBN 1 90230 139 0

Printed and bound in Great Britain by St Edmundsbury Press.
Cover Design by AdVantage.

CONTENTS

FOREWORD
by
Lord Butler of Brockwell

To my mind, Amy Baker's project illustrates excellently the benefits of cooperation between academics and government.

Questions of Procedure for Ministers, now *The Ministerial Code*, has evolved over
more than fifty year. Successive hands, including Prime Ministerial hands, have
amended and added to it. Successive Secretaries of the Cabinet and their Staffs
have acted as editors. But the document's development has not previously been
logged or described. What I like particularly about Amy Baker's work is that she
sets changes in the guidance in the context of external events.

My successors in the Cabinet Secretary's office will, I believe, find this book
very useful. In the past, there would have been a Historical Section within the
Department which could have undertaken such research. Now, for most Departments, such services have had to be treated as luxuries and have been squeezed
out. So academic access serves the practitioners as well as the general fund of
knowledge.

On one aspect, as Amy Baker acknowledges in her final chapter, I disagree
with her treatment. Her characterisation of the Ministerial Code as a rulebook
— let alone elevating it to be part of the constitution — gives it, in my view, an
absolutist quality which has never been intended. It is lore, not law — a compendium of good practice, not a set of rules. Observance of it guides Ministers in
what has come to be regarded, over many causes célèbres, as proper conduct as
well as efficient government. But it is neither comprehensive nor absolute. Ministers are accountable to Parliament, not a piece of paper.

However, disagreements between academics and practitioners are neither un-
common nor undesirable and this disagreement does not diminish the value of
the research. Future Ministers and Cabinet Secretaries, among others, should be
grateful for this thorough and scholarly piece of work.

Lord Butler of Brockwell GCB, CVO
Autumn 1999

PREFACE

What guidance there is for Ministers on standards of conduct, as well as on procedural matters, is contained in *Questions of Procedure for Ministers*. In the context of the British constitution, *QPM* is a youthful document, dating from 1945 (although elements of it are older). [It] has no particular constitutional status, but because it is issued by [the] Prime Minister … it is in practice binding on all members of the Government.

First Report of the Committee on Standards in Public Life ('The Nolan Report')
(Cm 1850-1, HMSO May 1995, p.48)

Questions of Procedure for Ministers ('QPM'), recently re-titled the *Ministerial Code*, has always struck me as a rather mysterious phenomenon. It is very difficult to encapsulate precisely what it *is* in a short definition, as it has so many levels of significance within our political system which have also changed and developed through time. On the face of it, it is a compendium of rules and practices that have been written down and pasted into the document from time to time, following various accidents and hiccups that have occurred within the Cabinet system. It is updated periodically by senior officials and issued on behalf of the Prime Minister, with his or her approval, to every new Minister on appointment. However, the importance of *QPM* is much deeper and more complex than its appearance, as a Government guidance document, would suggest. It has been used internally for a variety of purposes and amended for various reasons for over half a century. As a confidential Cabinet paper, it had little external significance as its existence was not common knowledge and it was only declassified after thirty years. Yet, when the document was first published as part of the Conservative administration's 'Open Government Initiative' in May 1992, *QPM* was very quickly propelled into the public arena by journalists and politicians as *the* authoritative set of rules and principles for ministerial office.

Anyone who has read *QPM* may wonder why I have chosen such an obscure subject for detailed study. On first reading, it comes across as a dry document that deals with miscellaneous, and mostly mundane, practical day-to-day issues relating to the smooth operation of the Cabinet system. However, what may seem obscure is actually extremely important. *QPM* is the only official guidance document that exists within the British Constitutional framework on the internal organisation and workings of the Cabinet system and standards of ministerial conduct.

There were two compelling reasons for embarking upon this project. Firstly, the absence of any research into the genesis of this document, seemed to me, to be a notable gap in our common historical knowledge. This book seeks to fill that gap by tracing the historical evolution of the text from its origins in 1917, when the Secretary of the War Cabinet drafted a short set of confidential notes outlining basic Cabinet procedures for Ministers to follow, to its present form as a publicly available rulebook containing a comprehensive set of rules and principles relating to ministerial conduct and Cabinet procedures. Since May 1992, Ministers have been judged and criticised on the basis of this Government text, without any real understanding of why or how that text had been drafted and updated during its existence, for over fifty years, as a confidential document.

Anyone who wishes to gain a better understanding of what *QPM* has become, will be interested to know why it originated and how it has developed. However, it was remarkable to discover, at an early stage of this project, that even the drafters of this document in the Cabinet Office, who have access to all the files, lacked a collective memory of its growth and development. It seems that *QPM's* mutation into such a 'big player' in the wider political system was never anticipated, and consequently, its evolution was not internally documented. Sir Robin Butler, the former Cabinet Secretary, expressed a personal interest in the results of this project and I am extremely grateful to him for helping to make it possible. Without the grant of privileged access to certain public records, and without the release of the full set of revised editions of *QPM* — this book would be extremely thin and based largely on speculation.

The second reason for conducting this research was to discover not only how the text itself has changed, but how the document has functioned within the workings of government, and how those functions have changed at different times since 1945, particularly since its publication in May 1992. It is interesting, in relation to the question of *QPM's* constitutional significance, to see how members of the government have perceived its status and importance at any given time, and how that perception differs from the views of many external observers who have commented on the subject since *QPM* was first made publicly available. This history of the document reveals its changing power and status within central government as a confidential Cabinet paper. However, since its publication, it has had a much wider impact on the political system and I address the question of its status and importance as a published document in my concluding chapter.

The *Ministerial Code* will continue to evolve and change through periodic revision, and it will be interesting to observe how its status and importance develops into the next century. However, I hope that this book not only helps to de-mystify what the *Code* is, and how it functions today in the workings of govern-ment, but also that it contributes to the debate about the direction of its future development. So far, *QPM* has grown organically with no real plan or purpose. With an understanding of what it has become, we can ask the important ques-tion of what its primary purpose should be and how it could serve that purpose more effectively. This study will be of interest to anyone who has any use of *QPM,* which includes members of the government and Parliament, particularly members of select committees, as well as journalists and academics. However, it will also be relevant to students of post-war political and administrative history who have a special interest in the operation of the Cabinet system and the regu-lation of ministerial conduct.

ACKNOWLEDGEMENTS

I am grateful to Gresham College for making this project possible by funding my research and publishing the results. I am most grateful to Professor Peter Hennessy for sharing his vast knowledge on the subject and for all his support and encouragement.

I would also like to thank Professor Robert Blackburn, Alan Robinson, Dr Lars Mossesson and Dr Peter Levin for their valuable contributions, suggestions, ideas and advice. During the course of my research I conducted several interviews with former and serving senior civil servants, politicians, academics and members of the judiciary. I would like to thank all of them for their interesting comments and insight into the role of *Questions of Procedure for Ministers* within the Cabinet system. I would also like to thank those who took the time to respond to my enquiries in writing.

I owe special thanks to the Cabinet Office, particularly the former Secretary of the Cabinet. Sir Robin Butler and his former department were extremely helpful and assisted enormously by granting privileged access to public records. In addition, I have made extensive use of the Public Record Office at Kew and I am grateful to all the staff for their help.

Amy Baker

INTRODUCTION
by
Peter Hennessy

The original idea for a study of this kind came from Sir Robin Butler during his time as Cabinet Secretary. We talked about it on several occasions including the day we lunched together in York with Professor Rod Rhodes on 7 September 1992 a few hours before Sir Robin was to deliver his Frank Stacey Memorial Lecture on 'The New Public Management: The Contribution of Whitehall and Academia'.[1] *Questions of Procedure for Ministers* had been published by the re-elected Major administration just over three months earlier after what Sir Robin later referred to as 'an agitation ... in a good cause' on my part.[2]

I was a few weeks away from meeting my first set of students as the recently appointed Professor of Contemporary History at Queen Mary & Westfield College, University of London, having forsaken my previous career as a journalist. Sir Robin had said, more than once, how interested he would be to discover what events and episodes had triggered the various additions and amendments to the document since it was put together in its modern form in Mr Attlee's time. He suggested it might make a good project for one of my students. It has.

Amy Baker developed an interest in it as an undergraduate on my 'Cabinet and Premiership' course. She made it the subject of her thesis when taking QMW's MA programme in Contemporary British History. Thanks to the intellectual entrepreneurship of Gresham College and its then Provost, Professor Peter Nailor (who had a special feel for all matters governmental), Amy Baker was funded by the Council of Gresham College to produce this study. Sir Robin Butler, without whose internal support I could never, I suspect, have persuaded even the open government-minded Mr Major to publish the then current edition of *QPM,* extended that support by stimulating a flow of still more declassification short of the standard thirty years without which *Prime Ministers and the Rulebook* would not have been possible.

The importance of this volume is for each reader to judge. My own assessment of its centrality to the conduct of government would be this:

— Historically, their versions of *QPM* and the uses to which they put them are a revealing and indispensable element in any study of the Downing

Street stewardships of the eleven Prime Ministers who have occupied No.
10 since 1945.

– An historical study of *QPM* is a way of mapping changes in the shared view of
what constituted the proper conduct of Cabinet government *and* proper individual Ministerial behaviour (shared in the sense that this was usually a blend
of past practice, the official Whitehall view and the wishes of the current pre-
mier).

– The book also represents an important and revealing case study of the 'coral-
reef' nature of much of British constitutional practice — how a cluster of guidelines can grow and harden, first into expectations, then into conventions and ultimately into a code if not quite into a fully-fledged constitutional artefact.

– It is also the study of the potential of open government. Without Mr Major's
wish to publish (and the endorsement of his Cabinet to do so), *QPM* would
have remained the preserve of insiders and scholars, released only after thirty
years to the far from rapt gaze of a minute public. Since 1992, by contrast, it has
become a constant presence in the lives of Ministers and those who seek to call
them to account either in Parliament or through the media. *QPM* has escaped
from the Cabinet Secretary's office, the Ministerial safe and the university seminar room. It is now public property; part of the current political process.

Amy Baker is *QPM's* explainer and cartographer. Until she completed this work,
nobody — not even its guardians in the Cabinet Office nor her teachers such as
myself — had anything but a fragmentary knowledge of its precise genesis and its
incremental mutation. Anyone who belongs to, or aspires to, the political class or
the permanent Civil Service (or thinks that both need careful watching), will need
to familiarise themselves with Amy Baker on *Prime Ministers and the Rulebook*.

Peter Hennessy
Queen Mary and Westfield College, University of London and Gresham College,
Autumn 1999

1   Sir Robin Butler, 'The New Public Management: The Contribution of Whitehall and Academia',
    The Frank Stacey Memorial Lecture delivered at the Annual Conference of the Joint Universities
    Council, University of York, 7 September 1992.
2   Sir Robin Butler, 'The Themes of Public Service Reform in Britain and Overseas', *Policy Studies*,
    Autumn 1995, Vol.16, No.3, p.4.

In memory of Professor Peter Nailor,
Provost of Gresham College, 1928–1996,
the patron of this book

Chapter One
ATTLEE'S DIRECTIVES FOR A LABOUR GOVERNMENT

No Cabinets before or since have been more businesslike.

Sir David Hunt, 1987 [1]

The very first version of the prime ministerial rulebook for Ministers was issued by Clement Attlee in August 1945. Never before had Ministers been handed, on appointment, a consolidated version of prime ministerial directives for general guidance during their term in office. The Cabinet Secretary, Sir Edward Bridges, had taken the initiative during the run-up to the General Election, of appending the important prime ministerial directives on procedure that had been issued over the previous five years, to the Secretariat's *Notes on War Cabinet Procedure*.[2] The updated document, retitled *Questions of Procedure for Ministers,* was circulated to all Ministers on their appointment, after the approval of the new Prime Minister had been obtained. Following his experience in the War Cabinet[3], Attlee was acutely aware of the importance of procedure and the Cabinet Secretary's idea of producing a consolidation of directives (which effectively became a prime ministerial rulebook, although it was never referred to as such) proved to be a useful means of instructing colleagues to adopt efficient, businesslike practices.

At this stage, the scope of *Questions of Procedure for Ministers* was limited to notes on procedure and did not cover ministerial conduct — a matter which Attlee preferred to leave to the good sense of his colleagues. The document contained practical instructions, drafted specifically for the Labour administration and suited to Attlee's own style of government, indicating that Attlee never intended to establish a permanent, non-party code for Ministers, as it was later to become. His own editions were certainly never invested with any formal status within the Cabinet system. The very idea of a prime ministerial rulebook was a novel concept and Bridges, the Cabinet Secretary, had initially feared that any kind of prime ministerial guidance 'might look like an attempt to teach Ministers their business.'[4] However, by the late 1950s some amendments were made to *QPM* in response to ministerial enquiries regarding correct procedure and conduct, suggesting that Ministers came to appreciate the value of an internal reference manual to the 'dos and don'ts' of the Cabinet system.[5]

It was only after the establishment of a Cabinet Secretariat in 1916 that strict rules of procedure were formed and codified. Procedure became the responsibility of the Cabinet Secretary, to enable him to establish some continuity of practice within the Cabinet Office, which would not be disturbed on every change of government.[6] Sir Maurice Hankey, the first Secretary of the Cabinet, had drafted the original *Rules of Procedure* in 1917 for circulation to all Ministers, which remained relatively unchanged through successive governments up to the Second World War. Until this point the document had usually been submitted to the Cabinet on a change of government for incoming Ministers to collectively approve and re-affirm the rules.[7] This practice appears to have gradually lapsed under Hankey's secretariat,[8] and was never re-established by his successor, Sir Edward Bridges. It is interesting that no post-war Prime Minister before John Major[9] (who consulted his Cabinet about the decision to publish *QPM*),[10] has ever submitted the document to Cabinet for collective approval.

Before 1945, Prime Ministers did not contribute to the drafting of the text, nor were they invited to do so. Whilst preparing a revised version of the document in 1942 for Churchill's War Cabinet, Bridges stated in a letter to the Prime Minister's Principal Private Secretary, John Martin, that 'I hardly think it is necessary to show this document to the Prime Minister since, in effect, it only summarises existing procedure or rules of long standing'.[11] However, during the 1945 update (for the incoming government after the General Election) Bridges also annexed a consolidation of prime ministerial directives from the last five years which he felt would be of use to the new Cabinet. This was presented to Attlee who quickly re-asserted the Prime Minister's control over Cabinet business by issuing a constant stream of directives relating to procedure. By the time *QPM* was next revised in 1946, there had been so many directives that the Cabinet Office amalgamated the 'Prime Minister's annex' with the main text. In response to a proposal by the Prime Minister's Private Office to update the standing instructions about ministerial broadcasts and speeches, Sir Norman Brook (who was an additional Cabinet Secretary, alongside Bridges, at that time) suggested that 'it would be convenient to take this opportunity of issuing a revised *and consolidated version* of the various directives which the Prime Minister has issued from time to time on points of procedure'.[12] Once the two memoranda had been merged, every amendment to *QPM* (with the small exception of paragraph 58 (iv), 1949[13]) that was made during Attlee's premiership, stemmed from a prime ministerial directive. Through regular updating, the document soon became a fairly comprehensive rulebook suited to Attlee's businesslike style of premiership.

Attlee's predecessors had probably showed little interest in involving them-selves with the process of drafting or amending these rules of procedure for two reasons. Firstly, *Instructions to the Secretary* (as it was re-titled in 1919)[14] was not an inspiring document. It dealt with the rather tedious details of when to submit a memorandum for the Cabinet, the recording and circulation of 'conclusions' (re-lating to the Cabinet Minutes) and other administrative matters which were re-ally only the concern of the Cabinet Secretariat. These rules did not impinge on the Prime Minister's ability to shape the structure of the Cabinet system or set the agenda of Cabinet business. Nor did it restrict a Prime Minister's personal style. Secondly, Prime Ministers felt little need or desire to constrain the Cabinet system by creating a written rulebook for Ministers. If it was necessary to give instruction to Ministers, it could be done verbally or through a minute.

Attlee was a stickler for procedure though and very aware of the importance of administrative detail. His Principal Private Secretary, Lawrence Helsby, de-scribed him as 'orderly, regular, efficient and methodical to a degree that put him in a different class from any of the Prime Ministers who followed him'.[15] Attlee believed that 'the most important of all the Prime Minister's functions is to give a firm lead in Cabinet so that decisions can be taken quickly'.[16] His Government certainly needed to be efficient and decisive if it was to achieve and sustain its ambitious plans to create a 'Welfare State'. But Attlee was also influenced by his experience of both Ramsay MacDonald and Winston Churchill as Prime Min-isters and a determination to develop more efficient working methods for his own Cabinet. He felt that MacDonald was 'constitutionally averse from taking decisions and entirely incapable of understanding the proper use of committees and experts'.[17] As Deputy Prime Minister during the War he was often frustrated with the way Churchill chaired the War Cabinet, allowing endless discussions when many Ministers had not read the memoranda and had little knowledge of the subject under discussion.[18] He had once said quite bluntly to Churchill that 'a monologue is not a decision'.[19] Whilst chairing his own Cabinets, Harold Wilson recalls that Attlee was 'savagely cruel in rebuking, in very few words, any Minister who didn't know the subject adequately, had not been briefed [or] hadn't read the paper, particularly if it was his own.'[20] *Questions of Procedure for Ministers* presented itself as a useful means of laying down the ground rules which represented Attlee's view of how Cabinet government should operate.

With modern Cabinet procedure still in its youthful development, Attlee had much more scope to mould the system to suit his own working methods than any Prime Minister would have today. Although the office of Prime Minister re-tains much of its flexibility and freedom to organise the structure, agenda and allocation of portfolios, the scope for *procedural* innovation has become much more restricted as the system has become increasingly institutionalised around the Cabinet Office. For example, it can be argued that it was easier for Margaret Thatcher to work outside the system, rather than attempt to actually re-design the long established decision-making procedures. Although Tony Blair has more recently attempted to restructure and reorganise the Cabinet Office 'to create a focus for [the Labour administration's] drive to modernise government', the Cabinet Office will essentially continue to serve the Prime Minister and his Cabinet Ministers in order to assist the Cabinet reach collective decisions.[21] Part of the importance of *QPM* today is that it functions as a compendium of these 'long established' procedures and ensures a basic level of continuity through successive administrations. *How* decisions are made is more important, constitutionally, than most of the decisions themselves, and it is largely through the evolution of *QPM* that the British Cabinet system has developed an (internally) 'agreed' procedural framework. When Attlee entered the doors of Number 10, there were no formal written rules, apart from the Cabinet Secretary's brief notes, which left him with a wide discretion to create his own. Within six years he had expanded the Cabinet Secretary's notes on procedure almost three-fold (from 23 paragraphs to 65 paragraph on his last update in 1949).[22]

Attlee aimed to improve the efficiency and coordination of the Cabinet system partly through reform and partly through a process of tightening up existing procedures. He had a full experience of the problems of modern government from his posts within the inter-war Labour administrations and Churchill's Coalition during the Second World War,[23] and had given a great deal of thought to the question of internal reform.[24] His directives on procedure were designed to ensure that his reorganisation of the committee system worked efficiently and effectively. Detailed guidance was issued to committee chairmen in 1946 to encourage good chairmanship, and further guidance on the matter emerged in 1949.

Good chairmen were seen as the key to good government, as they were in a position to keep the discussion focused so that decisions could be made quickly. Attlee himself has been remembered for his own chairmanship qualities. Macmillan regarded him as one of the best chairmen he had ever experienced, both for his capacity to listen and for his decisiveness, 'At the end he would sum up shortly, succinctly and decisively'.[25] Attlee clearly felt that his own methods provided the best model for his committee chairmen. Whilst describing his own approach he stated that, 'to go through the agenda you must stop people talking — unnecessary talk, unnecessary approval of things already agreed, pleasant byways that may be interesting but not strictly relevant. And you shouldn't talk too much yourself, however good you are at it'.[26] His formal instructions, issued in *QPM*, were not too dissimilar and have a very distinctive 'Attlee flavour' about them:

> ... the Prime Minister wishes the Chairmen of committees to keep the following points in mind:
>
> (a) Discussion should be kept to the point; irrelevance or repetition should be checked.
>
> (b) Conclusions should not be framed in a way which will require further discussions by Ministers, if that is not necessary. Sometimes, when a policy decision has been taken, there is a tendency for a Committee to regard itself as responsible for its detailed working out or the supervision of its execution. While that may sometimes be appropriate, it can usually be left to the Ministers departmentally concerned.
>
> (c) The dilatory process of referring a question from one Committee to another should be avoided as far as possible.[27]

These instructions were revised slightly in 1949 as the committee system itself had begun to consume enormous amounts of ministerial time due to the sheer number of committees that existed. After an internal official review, sparked by several complaints from Ministers,[28] Attlee was forced to concede that the Cabinet system was becoming overloaded and that in future all business should be resolved at the lowest possible level.[29] The next edition of *QPM* included the following paragraph:

> Interdepartmental questions should be settled as far as possible between officials, or failing that between Ministers, of the Departments directly concerned. They should not be allowed to drag on. Where colleagues have to be consulted, but only two or three are directly concerned, agreement can often be reached by correspondence or by personal meetings; much time can be saved by personal contact. Failing agreement recourse can be had to the Prime Minister, Lord President or Chancellor of the Exchequer. This will often make it unnecessary to take the matter to a committee.[30]

At first glance, this amendment appears to rub against the traditional grain of collective decision-making by the Cabinet. An interdepartmental dispute could be resolved by direct appeal to one member of a triumvirate — the Prime Minister, the Chancellor of the Exchequer or the Lord President — without going through the Cabinet system. However, Attlee recognised that the sheer volume of government business in the post-war period made it essential to limit the number of issues that went to Cabinet or committee. He was a great believer in the paradox of democracy, as he once explained, 'Democracy means government by discussion, but it is only effective if you can stop people talking'.[31] Minor decisions or arguments simply had to be kept out of the Cabinet system entirely, to enable the Cabinet to deal effectively with the volume of important issues on the agenda. Some people, most notably his successor, Winston Churchill, believed that this emphasis on efficiency went too far. As Macmillan recalls of Churchill (with a note of sympathy), he did not 'regard Cabinet as a board of a company where the various executive directors should try to accomplish their own business with as little trouble as possible, scarcely sharing in the discussion of the problem of their colleagues'.[32] However, Cabinets since the 1970s have had to resort to Attlee's formula to cope with the increasing workload of modern government.

Proceedings in the Cabinet were to be kept just as tight — if not tighter, because Attlee was actually able to ensure that these meetings were short and sharp. Harold Wilson remembers his 'business-like control of [Cabinet] proceedings and his utterly clear capacity for summing up decisions'.[33] To achieve productive meetings Ministers needed to come prepared, with a defined set of issues to discuss. Memoranda were not only to be circulated two clear days in advance (a procedure that was established by Hankey) so that Ministers had an opportunity to read them, but they were also to be 'short and clear', so that Ministers might *actually* read them. He offered Ministers some guidance on how to draft the Attlee 'model memorandum' in QPM:

> The model memorandum explains at that outset what the problem is, indicates briefly the relevant considerations and concludes with a precise statement of the decision sought.[34]

The scope of Attlee's *QPM* extended beyond decision-making procedures — which are of constitutional significance — to include an assortment of other little 'problem-solving' instructions which the Prime Minister or his officials considered important enough for circulation in the general handbook. As a result, it became an odd mixture of working constitutional arrangements and 'housekeeping practicalities'.[35] Attlee even created a 'miscellaneous' section containing some instructions which could only have been intended for the duration of his own Government. For example, it included guidance on the need for Ministers to make sure they consult the Trades Union Congress at an early stage of formulating industrial policy or making decisions which would affect them; an indication that *QPM* could have developed along party political lines, radically changing with each new government. Due to the odd mixture of directives that were included in *QPM*, the entire document soon became a repository for 'miscellaneous' guidance for Ministers, ranging from important questions of what business should go to the full Cabinet, to the little practical details of attending Cabinet on time and making sure those meetings were not disturbed by messengers. It was not intended to function as a 'surrogate' constitution, but simply as a useful consolidation of the Prime Minister's directives.

Leak-proofing the Cabinet was certainly a priority on Attlee's list of 'practical-problems-to-solve' and virtually every leak created ripples of unease. Newspaper cuttings containing 'leaked' information were often kept by the Cabinet Office to record the extent of the problem,[36] and Attlee regularly sent out directives on the importance of 'secrecy'. Attlee's personal press adviser, Francis Williams, recalled (in an interview with Kenneth Harris) that when Hugh Dalton unwittingly leaked some details of the Budget to *The Star,* Attlee's reaction was one of complete amazement because 'anybody in his senses had chosen to talk to a *journalist*'.[37] Harris notes that Attlee's comment on the subject, when interviewed by Granada Television some years later, was 'His trouble was he *would* talk'.[38]

There were some serious leaks from the Labour Government long before Dalton's inadvertent *faux pas,* which had already triggered a growing subsection in *QPM* on 'Precautions against unauthorised disclosure'. The first directive on secrecy was circulated in November 1945, following a Parliamentary Question by Winston Churchill on the premature disclosure in the Press of the proposals for a National Health Service. Churchill's query concerned Attlee greatly, particularly as it followed other recent leaks of Cabinet level discussions[39] and he sought to encourage Ministers to set a high example within Government by telling them that 'No Government can be successful which cannot keep its secrets'.[40] Leaks continued to be a problem though, and in April 1946 Attlee appointed the Lord Chancellor to enquire into the source of leaks. His work began immediately, and rather unexpectedly, as a leak regarding the Atomic Energy Bill appeared in the Press that very day.[41]

The need for maintaining the secrecy of Cabinet proceedings has always been publicly defended by successive governments as being a vital support to the traditional constitutional doctrine of collective responsibility; it allows 'free and frank' discussion between Ministers as they need not fear the consequences of voicing their individual opinions. However, *QPM* does not set out the constitutional doctrine of responsibility to Parliament; it merely emphasises the political expediency of internal solidarity within a 'leakproof' Cabinet. Lord Salisbury delivered a classic expression of the traditional doctrine of collective responsibility in 1878:

> For all that passes in Cabinet every member of it who does not resign is absolutely and irretrievably responsible and has no right afterwards to say that he agreed in one case to a compromise, while in another he was persuaded by his colleagues...It is only on the

principle that absolute responsibility is undertaken by every member of the Cabinet, who, after a decision is arrived at, remains a member of it, that the joint responsibility of Ministers to Parliament can be upheld and one of the most essential principles of parliamentary responsibility established.[42]

The difference between this exposition and the text of *QPM* is quite striking. There was certainly no mention in *QPM* of upholding 'the most essential principles of parliamentary responsibility'. Both collective responsibility and the need for secrecy were expressed in terms of gaining tactical advantage over the Opposition. For example, paragraph 33 of the 1949 *QPM* states that leaks 'damage the reputation of the Government, impair the efficiency of its administration and assist its opponents.' Paragraph 31 states that 'the *method* adopted by Ministers for discussion among themselves of questions of policy is essentially a domestic matter, and is *no concern of Parliament of the public'*. [My emphasis]. Guidance on the practical application of collective responsibility was originally inserted into the appendix to the 1945 edition of *QPM,* containing the first consolidation of prime ministerial directives, and was not deleted (although the text was slightly rephrased) until *QPM* was redrafted for publication in 1992. So, whilst the purpose of the constitutional convention may be to ensure responsible government, the only apparent aim of the instructions in *QPM* was to enforce a culture of secrecy in order to avoid embarrassing disclosures of information.

The emphasis on setting down practical working methods, rather than the principles of public office, has been a format that all Governments (prior to the publication of the document in May 1992) have followed. The careful avoidance of defining constitutional terms and absolute obligations in *QPM* clearly illustrates that no Government has wished to 'write' a Constitution for the British Cabinet system. Attlee's reluctance to create a constitutional document was clearly expressed in February 1949 following the Lynskey Tribunal. The Tribunal was set up after John Belcher, a Parliamentary Under Secretary to the Board of Trade, was accused of receiving gifts and hospitality, made to secure favours in the application for licences from his department. After the Parliamentary debate on the Lynskey Report, it was felt necessary to give some clarification of the role of Parliamentary Under Secretaries. Much to Attlee's horror, the Cabinet Secretary, Sir Norman Brook, drafted a directive which set out their constitutional position in Government. Attlee's Principal Private Secretary, Lawrence Helsby, gently explained to Sir Norman that, '[The Prime Minister] feels that practice may have outstripped strict constitutional doctrine and that the draft lays too much emphasis on the latter ... My impression, for what its worth, is that there is really no difference of any substance as to the constitutional doctrine and the

PM's views would probably be met by some change in the emphasis designed to give slightly more prominence to current practice as distinct from theory.'[43] Attlee also rejected the idea of issuing rules on the acceptance of gifts and hospitality, stating in Parliament that 'Generally, this matter is one that can be safely left to be solved by the good sense and integrity of Ministers and civil servants'.[44]

One important practical issue, which first featured in the appendix to the 1945 edition of *QPM* and has significantly increased in importance to the present day, was the effective presentation of government policy to the media. Technological developments in the media, particularly the rise of television broadcasting, greatly affected the 'public' conduct of central government. Party discipline needed to be tightened, collective responsibility reinforced and coordination improved, to cope with the growing omnipresence of increasingly critical journalists. Clear instructions were given on speeches and broadcasts,[45] which were expanded in 1946[46] to include guidance relating to interviews, and letters and articles in the Press, in an attempt to prevent embarrassing gaffes by individual Ministers. For example, Ministers were instructed not to receive payments for Press articles, interviews or contributions to party publications and were asked to 'bear in mind that an interview granted to a representative of a single newspaper or agency may arouse jealousy and thus hostility in the rest of the Press'.[47] So whilst Ministers were to remain the judge of their own personal conduct, they had little discretion over how they were to present their policies and opinions, and more importantly, how they presented the Government. As a general rule, Ministers were discouraged from attracting media attention during Attlee's premiership, and were warned that 'their relations with the Press are always liable to be the subject of Questions in Parliament'.[48]

Not all of the instructions emanating from Number 10 were welcomed by Ministers though, and unpopular rulings were particularly resented if they were incorporated into *QPM*, as this ensured that they would be lasting. The practice of submitting the document to the Cabinet for its approval had ceased by this time, leaving Ministers with little opportunity to complain and giving the Prime Minister a wide discretion. Attlee discovered that the behaviour of individual Ministers could be regulated in a less direct manner by formulating a general rule for *QPM*. For the individual concerned though, this did not always make the 'medicine' easier to swallow. In November 1948 a directive was issued on the 'Assistance of the Law Officers'[49] which caused 'particular embarrassment to the Foreign Office'[50], although it is not stated in the files which Minister was being targeted. The directive stated that it was desirable for Ministers to make 'full use of the experience of the Law Officers' when formulating policy. This ruling seems to have been established to make a particular point, as it caused great inconvenience to departments who 'would sooner be left with the discretion to decide, in accordance with long-established usage, when to rely on the advice of their departmental lawyers and when to seek an opinion from the Law Officers'.[51] Attlee also annoyed Ministers when he declared that members of the Cabinet could not speak at by-elections — the reason being that their absence would be an inconvenience.[52] However, this instruction was relaxed on the suggestion of Sir Norman Brook, to state that Ministers should not *normally* speak at by-elections, before it was incorporated into *QPM*.[53]

Although it appears that, under Attlee, the Cabinet Secretary was no longer responsible for drafting new rules of procedure, Brook (who had replaced Bridges as Cabinet Secretary in 1947) continued to exercise some influence over what went into *QPM*. Relaxing Attlee's ruling on by-elections was just one example. Sir Norman Brook was also concerned with misunderstandings over the powers of Ministers to stand-in for absent colleagues and the increasing public expense of ministerial visits abroad — many of which he felt were unnecessary. One example was the Minister of Labour, George Isaacs' suggestion that he should study, on the spot, the system of wages regulation in force in Holland and Scandinavia. Through negotiations with Leslie Rowan[54] revisions were made to *QPM* to reflect these points. Rowan had a quiet word with Attlee on the matter, who agreed that Ministers should be prevented from 'joy riding' at the public expense.[55]

By the time Attlee called for a General Election in 1951, he had succeeded in implementing the majority of his reforms, both within central government and in the country as a whole. Many of his reforms were to survive intact through successive Conservative administrations — but one of the first changes to occur in October 1951, when Churchill returned to Number 10, was a severe cull of *Questions of Procedure for Ministers*. The 'Board of Directors' had disbanded and the 'Good Chaps'[56] were back in office.

Chapter Two
CHURCHILL AND THE RETURN OF THE 'GOOD CHAPS'

If you have ten thousand regulations, you destroy all respect for the law.
Winston Churchill [57]

Churchill was reinstated as Prime Minister just a few days before his seventy-seventh birthday in October 1951. He did not have the energy of his first premiership and it seemed to those around him that he came to office with a desire to relive the past rather than direct the future.[58] He certainly had no grand visions of reform[59], as Attlee had in 1945, and was suspicious of most of the reforms that his 'socialist' predecessor had implemented.[60] The revamped *Questions of Procedure for Ministers* was probably suspect too in Churchill's eyes, as no other Prime Minister had ever felt it necessary to create a written set of rules for Ministers. For the duration of Churchill's previous premiership[61] the only 'rules' for Ministers, as we have seen, were contained in a short set of notes on procedure from the Cabinet Secretary; now it was a lengthy consolidation of prime ministerial directives from a Labour Government. Even if the document had emanated from a Conservative government, it is still likely that he would have found the very *idea* of a prime ministerial rulebook distasteful and contrary to the principles of collective government. Churchill had a very different style of government and preferred to rely on the common sense of his colleagues within his Cabinet. As part of the general drive to revert back to the status quo of 1945, the rulebook was culled to the bare minimum of rules of procedure and was then left unchanged for over seven years of Conservative Government.

Sir David Hunt, who served both Attlee and Churchill as a Downing Street Private Secretary, recalls that the contrast between the style of the two Prime Ministers was enormous. He stated in a televised interview that 'You simply cannot imagine the difference between them'.[62] In his memoirs he recorded that 'While Attlee had a great power of decision, Winston Churchill, on subjects in which he took little interest, affected horror when his advisers pressed for a decision', he would say, "This is a democratic government. These matters must be decided by the Cabinet as a whole; I cannot possibly settle them on my own authority".'[63] However, whilst Churchill may have professed a concern to ensure collective discussion within Cabinet, which he clearly considered more important than the speed of decision-making, the testimonials of his colleagues suggest that his idea of collective discussion was actually a monologue from himself. As Lord Woolton recalled, 'in the last years of his ministerial life he distilled all [his] experience at Cabinet meetings for the benefit of his colleagues ... he talked to us about the things that he thought important for the country, but about which the Cabinet Secretariat had been given no notice and about which, of course, there were no papers'.[64] He had a far more relaxed approach to the workload of government than Attlee, and despite Attlee's efforts over the past six years to introduce businesslike procedures into the Cabinet, Churchill instantly reverted back to practices which were more akin to a gentleman's club. He did not like the cold formalities of business, nor did he like working with unfamiliar faces, particularly during his last premiership.

As his Joint Principal Private Secretary, John Colville, recalled, he had a 'habit of working in bed in the mornings when there was no Cabinet meeting ... ministers, generals and civil servants were received in his bedroom, his working papers spread before him on a large broad bed-table, a cigar continually having to be relit from a huge box of matches with blue and white tips, one of his 'young ladies' sitting patiently beside him with dictation book and pencil, his red-ink pens and blue-ink pens — and the gold pen used to sign documents — constantly lost in the debris before him. There might be a cat curled up on the blankets at his feet, but, cat or no cat, there was always Toby the budgerigar, who flew around the room making countless dry, and therefore easily removable, messes wherever he chose to alight.'[65] His methods were self-indulgent and slightly eccentric, but with no *fixed* rules of procedure to conform to within the British constitutional framework, the Prime Minister could (and may still) choose whatever working methods suited him best.

The status and importance of *QPM* today stems largely from its history; it has withstood the test of time and experience and has gained the approval of several Prime Ministers from the two main political parties. However, during the early 1950s, the permanent, non-party nature of *QPM* was yet to be fully established. The change of government in 1951 highlighted the fragile status of the rulebook, the significance of which seemed to fluctuate according to the workingstyle of the Prime Minister of the day. When the document was first submitted to Churchill for his approval, the text consisted mainly of new rulings drafted under a Labour government. As a youthful document which had been largely shaped during a Labour administration, Churchill was perfectly entitled to reject it in its entirety and revert back to the more modest *Instructions to the Secretary* — and to have done so would probably not have been frowned upon by officials at that stage. It was certainly not assumed by the Secretary of the Cabinet, Sir Norman Brook, that Churchill would reissue the document in its new Attleean form. Although, the fact that *QPM* was not entirely rejected by Churchill suggests that some of the rules, at least, were essential to the smooth-running of the Cabinet system, regardless of which particular political party or Prime Minister was in power. To take one example, Churchill approved the inclusion of rules and procedures governing ministerial absenteeism, which were drafted to prevent any difficulties arising as a result of the increasing number of trips abroad that were required of Ministers. Although Attlee had issued the initial directive detailing procedures for obtaining permission to be absent and the arrangements that should be made for the department whilst the Minister was away, his instructions were just as relevant to the new administration and were, therefore, incorporated in full into the new edition of *QPM*.

It appears, from the correspondence in the file CAB 21/2778 at the Public Record Office in Kew, that Churchill was never shown the 'unedited' version of Attlee's 1949 *QPM*. Senior civil servants were well aware of the contrast between the style of Churchill and his predecessor and of Churchill's deep suspicion of Attlee's reforms. To increase the chances of gaining the Prime Minister's approval of *QPM*, the Cabinet Secretariat (with the support of David Pitblado, who was a Joint Principal Private Secretary to the Prime Minister alongside Colville) culled the rulebook to remove most of, what might be described as, Attlee's conspicuous 'fingerprints'. Sir Norman Brook also took the extra precaution of trawling the files to establish which rules within *QPM* had already been approved by Churchill during his last premiership.[66] The rules which had not yet been cleared by him were marked up for the Prime Minister to examine. The revised proof which was submitted to him was significantly shorter than the 1949 edition, yet both Brook and Pitblado still seemed uneasy about how the new Prime Minister would react to the document, and endeavoured to assure him that it was both neutral and necessary. Pitblado stressed that the Number 10 Private Office had already 'examined [*QPM*] carefully in the light of the directions you have issued at various times, particularly those parts of the statement which are of special concern to No. 10' and that Sir Norman Brook had 'taken account of some of [their] suggestions.'[67] Although the 1949 edition had been culled by 19 paragraphs (a third of its length), the public records also indicate that senior officials were concerned that *QPM* was still too lengthy for a Prime Minister, who had been accustomed to issuing very short procedural guidelines. The war-time notes on procedure had consisted of only 19 paragraphs in total. Brook added in his covering note to Churchill that he had, 'condensed the print as much as [he could]; but, being intended as a work of reference, it is inevitably rather long'.[68]

The final proof was not circulated until six months after the Conservative government had been appointed. Although this was partly due to the preparation of the document by officials *before* submission to the Prime Minister, there was further delay by the Prime Minister after it had been submitted. It may have been one of those matters that Hunt found impossible to turn Churchill's attention towards. After a fortnight without a reply from Number 10, Sir Norman Brook felt it necessary to write a reminder to Pitblado to 'invite the Prime Minister's attention to this' so that the new version could be circulated to Ministers, who had been raising questions of procedure in Cabinet.[69] In contrast, Attlee had approved his first edition of *QPM* within a month of his appointment as Prime Minister, and had issued an update within his first nine months.

In preparing a revised proof of *QPM* for Churchill, the Cabinet Office was effectively creating a 'non-party' version of Attlee's rulebook. Attlee had tailored the document very much to his own style and the needs of his own Labour administration — and succeeding Prime Ministers may have followed suit, had the Cabinet Office not intervened. However, it would have defeated the original object of the document, if every Prime Minister had been allowed to 'hijack' the rulebook for their own purposes. As we have seen, Hankey had drafted the very first guidelines in order to establish some *continuity* of procedure which would enable the Cabinet Office to organise business without being disrupted too much on a change of government.[70] The bare essentials, such as when to submit a memorandum for Cabinet or a Ministerial committee were therefore retained, whilst those instructions which reflected Attlee's personal style were simply struck out and dispensed with. For example, his lengthy and detailed notes on improving the speed and efficiency of central government decision-making were not considered essential or 'conventional'; they fleshed out the bare bones of procedure with his own style, which was a matter for each individual Prime Minister to determine for themselves.

Sir Robin Butler has described the 'revision process', which senior officials usually undertake during the run-up to a General Election, as being primarily a matter of 'scissors and pasting'.[71] In 1952 the majority of the text was subjected to the 'scissors', although certain parts of the text were retained or redrafted for greater conciseness. Attlee's 'Miscellaneous' section, which he had attached to his 1949 edition, is likely to have been cut out by officials without too much hesitation as it consisted mainly of guidance specific to a Labour government. Senior officials would have been reluctant to waste Churchill's time with rules that he would never approve, such as Attlee's instructions relating to ministerial consultation with the Trades Union Congress. Officials may also have regarded the guidance for drafting a memorandum as being overly detailed for the Conservative government, as most of this section was either deleted or shortened. It is likely that this was viewed as far too stringent on the need to curb unnecessary discussion, which for Churchill was all part and parcel of the democratic process of airing views and opinions. Attlee's guidelines for committee chairmen, which were scrapped in 1952, had even included a bar on unnecessary attendance at committee meetings; Ministers were to be dissuaded from 'attending meetings for the purpose of making Departmental points which have no important bearing on the main issues under discussion.'[72] Any senior official who knew Churchill would have suspected that he would not have agreed to the retention of such a rule and deleted it without question.

During the 1952 review, only a few new rulings were 'pasted' onto the 1949 version; these consisted of directives from Attlee's last year in office, which had been filed away with the intention of incorporating them in the next edition, and which received approval from Churchill. The most significant additions were rulings on policy presentation and procedures for obtaining permission to be absent from the United Kingdom. The presentation of policy was considered to be of great importance to Churchill and if anything excited his interest in *QPM*, it is likely that the paragraphs dealing with the media and the House of Commons did. He was renowned as a great orator and had delivered many memorable speeches in Parliament. His popularity with the general public had also been enhanced by his stirring radio broadcasts during the war, which conveyed the Prime Minister's voice directly into people's living rooms. At the time this had been a relatively novel method for a British Prime Minister to mobilise national support,[73] and it proved to be enormously effective. Although, as John Colville remarked, Attlee and Churchill 'belonged to a generation which considered that a politician should make his mark in the House of Commons,' rather than through the media,[74] the advances in media technology, particularly television broadcasting, were becoming difficult to ignore. The 1951 Election was the first to receive television coverage and the ruling that ministerial broadcasts were to be kept to a minimum was deleted from *QPM* in 1952.[75] A new ruling, allowing greater freedom to broadcast in foreign countries, was drafted by Attlee after strong complaint by the President of the Board of Trade, Sir Hartley Shawcross, that *QPM* was too restrictive.[76] This was inserted into Churchill's *QPM* with a paragraph stating that, 'broadcasting by sound and television is a useful instrument for conveying the British point of view to people in other countries'.[77]

Churchill disliked television for himself but did attempt to come to grips with it by arranging a private screen test held at Number 10. However, the private film only reinforced his aversion to T.V., by convincing him that he did not possess the appropriate skills for it.[78]

Attlee's ruling that press articles and interviews should be kept to a minimum was also erased, probably because it was becoming impossible to sustain. Technological advances not only facilitated new 'mediums' of reporting, such as television, it also enabled faster reporting and wider networks of communication. Politicians were more frequently confronted with reporters of one type or another, demanding a statement, on the spot, on a particular policy or event. This was one area of politics where 'common sense' could not be relied upon, a point demonstrated by Hugh Dalton when he leaked some budget details to a journalist. Discipline needed to be tightened if a government was to maintain its authority by defending consistent lines of policy. This is an area of *QPM* that has continued to expand, highlighting the increasing importance of presentation to every government in the post-war era.

The 1952 'cutting and pasting' exercise had transformed *QPM* once again. Whereas Labour Ministers had been presented with a comprehensive Government 'business manual', the newly appointed Conservative Ministers simply received a few basic instructions on procedure and guidance on policy presentation (to which Churchill drew special attention in his covering note to Ministers). However, although the growth of *QPM* was stunted during the 1950s, it was not stopped and the importance of the document was soon revived under the premiership of Harold Macmillan.

Chapter Three
MACMILLAN STANDARDISES CONDUCT

Profumo does not seem to have realised that we have — in public life — to observe different standards from those prevalent in many circles.

Harold Macmillan [79]

Anthony Eden was the only post-war Prime Minister who did not issue an up-dated version of *QPM* during his premiership. After the rulebook was signifi-cantly down-sized at the beginning of Churchill's premiership, it appears to have been neglected by the Conservative administrations for several years. The public records for this period contain only scant references to *QPM* and offer no explanation for the lack of periodic revision. Consequently, it is difficult to assess the perceived status and importance of the document within govern-ment during these years. Eden is unlikely, however, to have taken any personal initiatives to codify Cabinet procedures. The testimonials from his colleagues confirm that his style of premiership was very much 'hands on', indicating that he probably preferred to issue oral instructions rather than circulate directives for incorporation into the rulebook. David Dutton has observed that, 'in a cu-rious way [Eden] sought to ape Churchill [in his style of government], even to the extent of conducting some government business from bed'.[80] Although, in contrast to his predecessor, he would be constantly on the telephone to one Minister or another, issuing instructions, questioning, criticising and generally harrying his colleagues about their departmental work. Robert Rhodes James states that Eden's personal minutes 'give a less accurate record than in the case of Churchill's Governments ... [because] Eden conducted so much of his busi-ness as Prime Minister in private meetings with individual Ministers or on the telephone, to which his colleagues were inordinately attached'.[81] Macmillan recalled that he kept 'sending me little notes, sometimes twenty a day, ringing up all the time'. Over the Christmas weekend in 1955, Selwyn Lloyd (who had recently been appointed Foreign Secretary) counted a total of 30 telephone calls from Chequers.[82]

The escalating crisis over the Suez Canal dominated the last five months of Eden's premiership and is likely to have been a further reason behind the failure to update *QPM*. On the 26th July 1956 Colonel Nasser nationalised the Suez

Canal Company, leading Eden to become involved in a mission to regain British and French control of the company, which culminated in secret collusion with Israel to invade the Canal Zone. There is no evidence to suggest that the Cabinet Office even attempted to draw Eden's attention to updating the rulebook during this difficult period, which may have been partly due to a fear of Eden's unpredictable temperament and partly due to the sheer pressure of other work during the unfolding crisis. William Clark (then a Downing Street Adviser on Public Relations) recalled that, 'the private secretaries sometimes refused to take things up with him because they knew it would worry him and cause an explosion. Always at the back of everything was the fear that he would lose his temper and we should be sworn at'.[83] However, it is slightly more curious that there was no attempt to revise *QPM* immediately after Eden's appointment as Prime Minister, and the omission may be indicative of the Prime Minister's personal lack of interest in the document.

When Macmillan took over, he was left with the difficult task of picking up the pieces. Repairing the damage of the 'Suez debacle' was his most pressing task,[84] but he also wanted to restore a good working relationship with the Cabinet and improve working methods. He entered Number 10 with a desire to modernise the country and the Cabinet, and he began by restoring a sense of 'quiet, calm deliberation' in the Cabinet room.[85] Ministers were once again mostly trusted to run their own Departments as Macmillan asserted his authority from a more comfortable distance than his predecessor. Like Attlee, he 'knew how to run the Cabinet in a quick, businesslike way',[86] but Rab Butler, his arch rival for the Premiership, felt that although he was 'very good' he was 'exceeded [only] by little Attlee, who had the habit of biting people in the pants'.[87]

Once a degree of 'normality' in the Cabinet had been re-established and Macmillan's Government was stable, the Cabinet Office began preparing a draft revise of *QPM*. After six years of neglect it was quite out of date, particularly the section on television broadcasts. Macmillan was beginning to overcome his initial aversion to television in 1958 and to realise its advantages, just as Eden had during his own term in office. Eden had once stated that he 'attached first importance to television as a medium'[88] and, as Anthony Sampson notes, Macmillan 'was well aware...that the new medium gave him a unique chance to by-pass the Press lords and project himself — and nobody else — to the nation.'[89] Significant changes had occurred in the world of television since the last issue of *QPM* in 1952, which Anthony Sampson describes quite succinctly:

> Television added to the personal predominance. In the four years since 1955, the proportion of homes with TV sets had increased from forty per cent to seventy per cent

and, after the beginning of commercial TV in September 1955, television reporting became more intense and dramatic; the old 'fourteen-day rule' [prohibiting TV discussion of any subject that was being debated, or likely to be debated, in the House of Commons in the next fortnight and] which limited topical discussions had been discarded, and both channels wanted big names with big news. They wanted a peripatetic Prime Minister, and were contemptuous of little-known Opposition spokesmen. Apart from the official party broadcasts, politicians were dependent on the invitations of news-minded producers, and the Prime Minister could always make news.[90]

The advent of commercial television (and some pressure from Anthony Eden) precipitated an all-party agreement on the use of television broadcasting by the Government, and the Opposition's right of reply.[91] These notes, which were incorporated into the revised *QPM*, explained that Ministers could only broadcast by invitation. It was agreed that party political broadcasts would be allocated on a quota basis and that ministerial broadcasts would occasion a right of reply if controversial, although Ministers could appear in a news report without risking a right to reply. As Ministers were still learning how best to use television to present government policy, *QPM* ruled that the Prime Minister's approval must be sought before any type of broadcast was given, even if Ministers intended to take part in a programme in a purely private capacity.[92] However, this initial caution towards ministerial appearances on television was soon relaxed when it was found to be both impractical and unnecessary to consult the Prime Minister on every occasion.[93]

Just as television had the potential to build a Minister's reputation, it could also be his downfall. Eden certainly felt that the cameras turned on him during the Suez Crisis[94], and Macmillan once, rather caustically, described television cameras as 'that hot, pitiless probing eye', always lurking in the background, especially in airport lounges, waiting to catch you at your worst. He recalled that, 'After fourteen hours of travel you get off the airplane, wanting only a shave and a bath — oh no, you are cornered. The lights in your eyes, the cameras whizzing. You put up your hand to shade your eyes and the next day there you are in the *Daily Clarion* looking weary, old, worried, over a caption which implies you are past it'.[95]

Ministers could no longer avoid being in the limelight, and misconduct was invariably picked up by journalists as a newsworthy item. Towards the end of the 1950s a section of the British public was beginning to reject strict 'universal' values for a more 'free' society, yet still expecting high standards from those in public office. For example, Ernest Marples attracted attention to himself whilst Minister of Transport in January of 1960, as he held a position of senior partner in a firm of contractors (Marples Ridgway and Partners) which had obtained a contract worth £250,000 from the government. Lord Kilmuir, the former Lord

Chancellor, was similarly criticised in September 1962 for his chairmanship of the Board of Plessey. In the same month, Basil Di Ferranti, Parliamentary Secretary to the Minister of Aviation, created a stir as it was revealed that he had a shareholding in a family company that covered almost every aspect of the work of the Ministry of Aviation. The Government were clearly sensitive to the risk of fuelling bad publicity and were careful to inform the Press, in February of that year, that Rab Butler (then Home Secretary) had withdrawn from the Cabinet discussions on the proposed merger between Courtaulds and ICI, to prevent a conflict of interest arising from his shareholding in Courtaulds.[96]

In response to the close scrutiny of ministerial affairs by the media, the new edition of *Questions of Procedure for Ministers* in 1958 contained more than its title suggested. Tucked at the back of the document, Ministers received their first taste of a formal code of conduct on private interests. Despite the existence of a 'generally accepted' ruling that Ministers should avoid conflicts of interest (a rule that can be traced back to Gladstone, see below), Ministers had never before been issued with formal written rules on their appointment to office, which they were expected to abide by *to the letter*. Conduct was no longer a matter of common sense and personal judgement, to which successive Prime Ministers had preferred to leave it. General standards were now to be enforced.

The section on shareholdings and directorships, which was incorporated in 1958, was actually drafted by Winston Churchill's post-war administration and circulated in *Hansard* for general reference in 1952.[97] There are few clues as to what motivated the drafting of this code, or indeed if Churchill personally initiated the project. It is more likely that his senior officials decided to 'tidy-up' the files, such as the Precedent Book,[98] so that when they were consulted on such matters, they could give clear and consistent advice to Ministers. However, it was never included in *QPM* for two reasons. Firstly, this was considered to be simply a handbook for the administration of the Cabinet system, and secondly (and more importantly) because it was widely believed that Ministers did not need to be *instructed* how to behave; matters of propriety were thought to be well understood. The 1952 guidelines were simply a consolidation of the rules which had been formulated over the period of half a century and expressed in the Commons from time to time. It was issued in *Hansard* after Sir Waldron Smithers (Conservative MP for Orpington) had 'asked the Prime Minister what regulations govern the continuation of salaried service with a private company on appointment to ministerial office'.[99]

Gladstone is believed to have been the first Prime Minister to rule that Ministers must not hold directorships whilst in office, and his diaries show that he expected strict adherence from his Cabinet colleagues. His diary entry for 31st October 1892 states, 'Directorships: Action and emolument should be suspended during terms in office. This is to be made known.'[100] On the 14th August 1893, he wrote to Lord Rosebery: 'We have been rather vigorous in two points of economy. (i) Directorships not to be held by members of the Cabinet. (ii) Law Officers deprived of private practice.'[101] Palmerston was the first Prime Minister to state simply that Ministers should not accept presents.[102] Successive Prime Ministers made various statements in the Commons to refine or simply restate the general position on conflicts of interest.[103] The attitude of most Prime Ministers, however, was that the principles of conduct in public office need only be expressed orally from time to time, as Ministers could be trusted to act on their own judgement in each circumstance.

Churchill accepted that the rules governing conflicts of financial interests ought to be codified. However, he did not think it appropriate to regulate the acceptance of gifts in the same manner. Several questions relating to this were raised within the Commons following the provision of free travel facilities to and from the United States, for the Prime Minister and Foreign Secretary, by the Cunard Company. Churchill echoed the views of his predecessor, Clement Attlee, in his reply to a Question in the House by George Wigg (Labour MP for Dudley), by stating that 'No specific regulations have been laid down: but it is *well understood* that no Minister or public servant should accept gifts or services which would place him under an obligation to a commercial undertaking'[104] [my emphasis]. He later added that 'I think it would be a great mistake to try to lay down detailed rules and regulations, which have not been found necessary in the past, by question and answer at this period of our discussions'.[105]

There is no evidence that Macmillan was any more enthusiastic about setting down the rules of conduct than his predecessors. His administration simply responded to the growing need for clarity on these issues. By the late 1950s it was plain that Ministers were not as familiar with the general principles as Churchill had assumed. Instead they were constantly asking senior civil servants whether they could accept the various gifts that were being showered upon them by lobby groups, business interests and foreign representatives. Derek Stephen, Private Secretary to Sir Norman Brook, felt particularly 'uneasy' that *QPM* said 'nothing about the question of Ministers accepting gifts from firms' because 'the few cases that came up during the course of 1958 suggests to me that it might *not* be clearly understood that no Minister should accept gifts or services which would place him under an obligation to a commercial firm. If it was so well understood I doubt whether one, at least, of these cases would ever have been referred to us.'[106] The 'good chap theory' of self-regulation, which relied on rules of honour, was clearly no longer working when the Chancellor of the Exchequer, Derrick Heathcote Amory, had to *ask* whether he could accept a Chiltern spin dryer, from Chiltern manufacturers, as a thank you offering for reducing the purchase tax in the Budget in 1958! Yet, just a few months later, a Minister was given permission to keep a set of 'rather attractive drinking glasses', as he had already broken one and it was agreed that they could not possibly be sent back.[107]

The Chief Whip, then Edward Heath, voiced his concern to the Cabinet Secretary, Sir Norman Brook, after he became aware that a number of companies were offering large hampers of wines and spirits to Members of Parliament, and he suspected that some Ministers had accepted.[108] Brook agreed that it was time to clarify the rules for Ministers if allegations of impropriety and public criticism were to be avoided. *QPM* was revised in 1959, so that these rules could be included without delay. There was a further update in 1963 which included guidance on the acceptance and exchange of gifts from foreign representatives. These were drafted by the Treasury in 1961 to 'ensure greater uniformity of practice' and to avoid the 'risk of apparent discourtesy' to foreign representatives through blanket refusals.[109] The development of detailed regulations governing the acceptance of gifts was relatively swift in comparison to the gradual evolution of the rules relating to directorships and shareholdings. Only a decade after Churchill had warned of the 'great mistake' of trying to 'lay down detailed rules and regulations', *QPM* offered comprehensive written guidance on gifts and hospitality.

The acceptance of gifts was not the only aspect of 'conduct' which concerned Macmillan. Several long-established rules of propriety were codified and incorporated into *QPM* during his time in office for various reasons. For example, the rule that a Minister should not ask a civil servant to attend or take part in a party political conference was incorporated in 1958. This was prompted by a committee of enquiry rather than a particular event. In the wake of the controversy surrounding the Masterman Report,[110] the Government had announced its decision to lift restrictions on the political activities of certain grades within the Civil Service in March 1953.[111] The Government's reforms actually went further than the Masterman Committee had originally recommended. Whereas the Committee had suggested that only very junior civil servants be given complete political freedom, the Government proposed to create an 'intermediate level' of civil servants who could also engage in political activity subject to the approval of their employing department.[112] The senior Civil Service would remain completely non-political. As a precaution against any confusion, a new paragraph was inserted into *QPM* to ensure that Ministers were well aware that rules governing their relations with senior civil servants remained unchanged, in particular, the rules relating to party conferences.

The rule prohibiting the use of official resources for party-political purposes was another long established convention that was suddenly added to the guidance in *QPM* in 1959[113] and 1963.[114] Again, it was inserted as a precautionary measure, for the run-up to the application for membership of the European Economic Community, rather than a response to a particular breach. The Director General of the Central Office of Information, T. Fife Clark, was concerned that Ministers would use the large number of forthcoming official occasions as a platform for party political speeches on Europe, and spark public criticism.[115] Although his fears turned out to be unfounded, guidance was, nevertheless, inserted into the next update of *QPM* in 1963 to rectify the omission.

Macmillan is perhaps best remembered as the great would-be 'Moderniser' in Government, and his application to join the EEC was just one illustration of this. It is slightly surprising that there is little trace in *QPM* of his efforts to modernise Cabinet procedure, particularly as he was the first Prime Minister to show a serious interest in tackling the problem of ministerial overload. In 1957 he established a committee of enquiry into the burden on Ministers,[116] under the chairmanship of Lord Attlee. Following the Committee's report, Macmillan circulated a directive summarising the key recommendations. The report had not made any radical suggestions, but it did propose that Ministers adopt more efficient working methods. For example, Ministers were instructed to insist on brevity in departmental minutes and correspondence in order to reduce the amount of material for reading, and were advised to discontinue the practice of personally meeting Commonwealth visitors at the airport.[117] Although Macmillan returned to the subject of ministerial overload in a Cabinet meeting some five years later, his directive on the efficient transaction of government business was never incorporated into *QPM*. This may have been to avoid repetition as many of the Committee's proposals were already covered by the document. Attlee's instructions, which were incorporated in the late 1940s, on settling business at the lowest possible level and ensuring brevity in memoranda for Cabinet and Cabinet committees, had become standard guidelines in *QPM*. However, the failure to incorporate any new suggestions to reduce overload meant that the problem was never really tackled, and appears to have been a missed opportunity by Macmillan.

The only recommendation from the Committee's Report which found its way into *QPM* concerned greater delegation to junior Ministers (referred to as 'Parliamentary Secretaries' in *QPM*). But even this ruling was not a direct result of the report on ministerial overload. Instead it was prompted by internal squabbling between officials and junior Ministers some years later, and was not inserted into *QPM* until 1963. As a result of these (unspecified) difficult relations between Ministers and officials in the Ministry of Labour in 1962, Sir Lawrence Helsby, the Permanent Secretary to that department, wrote to Sir Norman Brook for advice. The files were duly trawled for any notes on the 'constitutional position' of junior Ministers, but the only documents to be found were two directives issued by Attlee in the late 1940s.[118] Quite unusually, the essence of these directives from a Labour Prime Minister were distilled into two new paragraphs for *QPM* during a Conservative Government.[119] Although a draft of the new instructions was submitted to the Prime Minister for his approval before incorporation into the rulebook, it is unclear whether the Cabinet Secretary felt it necessary to draw Macmillan's attention to Attlee's original directives, which had formed the basis of the new paragraphs.[120] Brook did, however, suggest that Helsby point this out to the Minister of Labour, John Hare, and advised him to '[tell your Minister] that you had ascertained that in my view the constitutional position set out in that paper was no less applicable today under a Conservative Government than under the Labour Government 13 years ago'. However, Brook added a word of caution, by asking Helsby to 'consider whether [it] would be helpful [to show the Attlee directives, as] it is possible that it might have the opposite result'.[121]

Although Macmillan had decided to carry on as Prime Minister following the Profumo Scandal, he was struck down by trouble with his prostate in the autumn of 1963. As a result, he resigned through ill-health in October 1963, leaving a rather unusual *QPM* to his successor, Sir Alec Douglas-Home. The addition of rules of conduct, which codified the ethics of public office, sat rather strangely alongside the more familiar notes on administration and media management. There was no distinction between the two as regards status or importance — all were thrown together to produce a miscellany, which Peter Hennessy has described as a 'a mix of immutable principles and housekeeping practicalities'.[122]

Despite the allegations of misconduct that were made against certain Ministers from time to time,[123] there was still a general consensus (at least amongst politicians) that there was no need to create strict regulations for Ministers, which were accorded a 'quasi-legal' status. Ministers were still, on the whole, seen as 'good chaps', and those who were not would be held to account by Parliament. Although the most serious aspect of ministerial misconduct during the Profumo affair was John Profumo's lies to Parliament, it was the security risk which appeared to cause most concern to the administration. The recent spate of spy scandals had dominated the headlines and caused much embarrassment for the government.[124] However, apart from Profumo, the only other Minister who had been implicated in a spy scandal (and was subsequently cleared by the Radcliffe Tribunal) was Thomas Galbraith.[125] From the government's perspective, therefore, these affairs raised questions of security, rather than ministerial conduct. As a result, the only impact of Profumo on *QPM* was the inclusion of new procedures for security which emerged after the publication of the Denning Report on Profumo. The new paragraphs stated that Ministers were now to be briefed by the Security Service, MI5, on appointment and asked to sign a declaration after reading the relevant provisions of the Official Secrets Act. Ministers were also warned not to show Parliamentary Private Secretaries any documents that were graded secret or above, except where the Prime Minister had given his 'personal' authorisation.[126]

Douglas-Home had a very different approach to the conduct of his colleagues. In his biography of Lord Home, D.R. Thorpe states that his 'administration was the last example of a certain style of government', although he notes that, 'It is easy to categorise this as amateurism, to see Home as the most hands-off Prime Minister since Baldwin'.[127] In contrast to Macmillan, Home was reluctant to issue standard guidance in response to specific cases, preferring instead to allow room for discretion. For example, when the issue arose of allowing a Minister's wife to accompany him on official business trips abroad, William McIndoe (the Private Secretary to the Cabinet Secretary, Sir Burke Trend) noted, with a degree of frustration, in a minute to Trend that, 'As you know, the Prime Minister is disposed to interpret the rule [relating to the travelling expenses of wives] with greater latitude than his predecessor'.[128] He explained, in a separate correspondence, that he had asked Malcolm Reid (a Downing Street Private Secretary) whether the Prime Minister would wish to seek advice on the Assistant Postmaster General's (Raymond Mawby) slightly 'marginal' request that his wife accompany him on an official trip to Italy. McIndoe noted that 'his reply was that the Prime Minister would almost certainly not want any advice, because his normal inclination was to grant requests of this kind and he would probably feel the more inclined to do so at the present time, when the Postmaster General [Reginald Bevins] was having difficulties enough'.[129]

The Cabinet Office foresaw problems with this approach, as they were aware that Permanent Secretaries were expected to advise and then defend (if necessary) their Ministers on matters of propriety — a task made more arduous in the absence of consistent 'rules'. McIndoe warned Trend that 'No. 10, despite their knowledge of the Prime Minister's inclinations, would do well to keep Ministers and their Private Secretaries up to the mark in this respect, because if they do not and a visit subsequently provokes public criticism, they will have very little in writing with which to justify the Prime Minister's decision.'[130] He further added that the Postmaster General, Bevins, would need to establish that in this present case Mrs Mawby's accompanying her husband satisfied the test of public interest, as set out within the current instructions in the Precedent Book, which were as follows:

'The test of public interest will be satisfied not only if the Minister is unwell and needs his wife to look after him but also if her presence on an official tour overseas is very desirable in order that she may act as his hostess, and give help in the unofficial social contacts which ease the despatch of public business'.[131]

As a civil servant seconded from the Commonwealth Relations Office, McIndoe would have been well aware of the problems that tended to arise. In the run-up to the 1964 General Election, the Cabinet Office drafted a revised version of *QPM* which included guidance on the travelling expenses of wives as well as other expenses, *despite* the Prime Minister's aversion to such rules.[132] Douglas-Home's defeat in the Election may have seemed quite convenient to the drafters of *QPM*, who knew that their amendments would now be 'automatically' approved by the new Prime Minister, Harold Wilson. However, it did not take Wilson long to discover that *QPM* could be very convenient for his own purposes.

Chapter Four
HAROLD WILSON'S INSTRUMENT

As the new ministers were almost all without Cabinet experience, it was a good time for reform.

Harold Wilson [133]

The General Election in 1964 brought Labour back into power after thirteen years out of office with Harold Wilson as the new Prime Minister. Despite the Government's small majority of only four seats, there was a mood of optimism in the country. Harold Wilson had promised that a new Britain was going to be forged in the 'white heat' of a 'scientific revolution', [134] which, coupled with his energy and enthusiasm, created a feeling that things were really going to change. Wilson's dynamic 'Kennedy-style' campaign [135] in the run-up to the election had sharply contrasted to the rather lacklustre campaign of Sir Alec Douglas-Home. There had been more media coverage of the 1964 election than in any previous contest and Wilson made the most of it, particularly television broadcasts. Douglas-Home had shied away from the cameras as much as possible, serving only to reinforce his image of being a rather 'aloof' aristocrat who presided over the 'fag-end' of a Conservative administration, steeped in scandals. [136]

One of Wilson's first tasks as Prime Minister was to approve and reissue *Questions of Procedure for Ministers,* which the Cabinet Office had revised in preparation for the new government. The document had not only been elevated in status as an essential reference manual to guide Ministers through the increasingly complicated tasks of modern government, it was of particular importance to the new and largely inexperienced Cabinet team. Sir Burke Trend, the Cabinet Secretary, presented Wilson with the revised draft of *QPM* on his first day in office with a covering letter which stressed the importance of its speedy circulation. His note to the Prime Minister illustrated the status which *QPM* had then acquired, as he described it as 'an entirely non-party document, which codifies the general principles of ministerial conduct as they have evolved over many years'. He went on to state that, 'it has the authority of a good many Prime Ministers, of different party complexions; and it is revised, in the light of changes in practice, at regular intervals.' [137] It is curious that Trend chose to diminish the status of the document in a public interview, given in 1986, by claiming that *QPM* was nothing more than 'tips for beginners — a book of etiquette'.[138] It was clearly of much greater importance to the Cabinet (and indeed to the Secretary of the Cabinet himself) than a 'book of etiquette' as the majority of the rules contained within the document had, by this stage, crystallised into continuing conventions.

A comparison between Sir Burke's covering letter to Wilson and that drafted by Sir Edward Bridges (then Secretary of the Cabinet) for Attlee nineteen years previously, highlights the degree of change in *QPM's* status. In his note to Clement Attlee, Bridges simply stated that 'Prime Ministers have found it necessary to issue notes of guidance to Ministers on particular points of procedure' and emphasised that it could be 'amended as you desire'.[139] It is significant that Wilson was not invited to do the same. Although *QPM* was still regularly 'updated', it had become too important to the smooth operation of the Cabinet system to be dramatically revised at the whim of a new Prime Minister. Wilson, however, did not wait to be 'invited' to amend the document. Aware of the inexperience of his colleagues (and perhaps influenced by his experience of Attlee's frequent revisions), he seized his opportunity to make significant changes.

During his first term in office, Wilson adopted Attlee's businesslike approach to Cabinet government. In a radio interview in 1964 he had said that 'if elected, I intended to run No. 10 not only as a chairman, but as a full-time managing director or chief executive, for my incoming team would have almost no Cabinet or administrative experience.'[140] Wilson himself was very well qualified for the post of Prime Minister; he had experience as a wartime civil servant and occupied a range of ministerial posts during Attlee's administrations. As Peter Hennessy has remarked, 'nobody was better prepared on paper for No. 10 than Harold Wilson.'[141] His experience as a civil servant gave him a keen awareness of how the bureaucratic system worked and, perhaps more important to the new Prime Minister, was his knowledge of how to *use* the formal Cabinet system to his advantage.

Wilson's first edition of *QPM* was issued within three days of the formation of his Government. He approved the draft that Sir Burke had presented to him, which had been revised in the light of changes during Douglas-Home's administration. He did, however, make one change of his own. Wilson wanted to establish a new practice whereby if departmental spending estimates differed from the Treasury's estimates, both were to be quoted in a Cabinet memorandum; a rule which he states dated back to Attlee's Government.[142] In his subsequent updates of the document, many of the amendments made were a result of his personal initiative. Although the changes were made in a piecemeal fashion, Simon James has observed that collectively they 'added up to a major change in the operation of the system'.[143] Wilson strove to make the Cabinet system more efficient and centralised, with a disciplined Cabinet team; he aimed to tighten the purse strings for official expenses and clamp down on internal security and confidentiality. In addition, the Government's public image was to be carefully packaged for the media under the direction of two former Lobby journalists, Trevor Lloyd-Hughes, and later, Joe Haines.

To make the Cabinet system more efficient, Wilson began by tightening up the rules of procedure for preparing and circulating Cabinet memoranda. It was to be stressed in *QPM* that the Cabinet Office would not normally accept a memorandum involving expenditure for circulation to the Cabinet or to a Ministerial Committee unless it had been discussed with the Treasury first and an estimate of expenditure had been agreed in advance.[144] When the work 'overload' on the Cabinet increased as the 1960s lengthened, bad habits tended to creep in. Wilson recognised that it was essential to reinstate sound practices if the government was to cope effectively with the volume of business.

Wilson continued to tighten up such procedures after his return to office in 1974. For example, during his second term a requirement was added that the Cabinet Office should always be given seven days' notice of any business to be submitted to Cabinet, even if it was to be raised orally.[145] Cabinet memoranda were to include more information as well, such as an estimate of manpower required by a proposal or any accommodation problems that might arise.[146] Such issues were to be discussed with the Civil Service Department (which had been established in 1968) and the Property Services Agency respectively *before* the substance of the policy could be dealt with by the Cabinet. Following the UK's entry into the European Economic Community in January 1973 (during Heath's premiership), it also became necessary to indicate any impact a proposal might have on the UK's obligations as a member of the European Economic Community and to clear all proposals with the law officers in order to prevent the risk of judicial review through the courts.[147] This was to allow many of the questions of implementation to be ironed out beforehand, enabling the Cabinet to focus purely on the political merits of each proposal. Wilson also established a rule that White Papers and similar documents were to be submitted to the Cabinet Office one month before publication, so that they could be cleared either by the full Cabinet (and according to Wilson's memoirs this was done 'paragraph by paragraph')[148], or an appropriate ministerial committee. This, presumably, was to ensure that collective responsibility was maintained for all policy proposals.

In many respects, the tightening up of these procedures was a response to the growing problems of 'ungovernability' in the 1970s that academics such as

Anthony King had been expounding.[149] Whilst the 'power' of modern government was subject to more constraints, such as the European Community, the globalising economy, the oil price explosion after 1973 and the problems of 'stagflation', the pressures of government business mounted, particularly at Cabinet level. Government business had increased in volume and complexity, making greater demands on ministerial time with an increased volume of material to read and committee meetings to attend.[150] Ministers were also required to travel more frequently for international meetings and summits and were constantly under scrutiny from the media. A further pressure came from the courts as the 1960s saw the advent of increased judicial activism in the field of administrative law. Against this background, a new section appeared in the 1969 edition of *QPM* entitled 'Consultation of the Law Officers',[152] which stressed the need to resolve any potential legal difficulties arising out of policy proposals, before the Government committed itself to any 'critical decisions'.[153]

The development of the Cabinet committee system enabled a greater volume of business to be despatched at Cabinet level, but for it to work effectively it was essential that committees took decisions with the same authority as the full Cabinet. Wilson noted in his memoirs that there was a 'tendency' in the 1960s 'for a defeated Minister almost automatically to seek a re-run at Cabinet, even if he was in a minority of one. This threatened to congest the work of the Cabinet, and to weaken the authority of the committees and their chairmen.' Consequently, he 'had to direct — and make public that no appeal to Cabinet could hope to succeed unless it had the backing of the chairman of the committee.'[154] Simon James has used the experience of the Netherlands as an illustration of the 'impossibility of operating without such a rule'. As a result of the unlimited right of appeal to Cabinet that the Dutch Ministers enjoy, 'Cabinet Ministers meet two or three times a week, while each of its dozen committees meets on average, only six times a year. Dutch Prime Ministers compensate by creating ad hoc groups of three or four people who decide key issues, such as policy on terrorism and the government's socio-economic policy, to the annoyance of other colleagues.'[155] However, the formalisation of the rule in *QPM* may not have simply been a matter of efficiency — it also conveniently enhanced Wilson's potential to manipulate and control the committee structure, enabling him to steer certain policy decisions.

Wilson strongly denies that he 'fixed' the membership and chairmanship of committees,[156] but the testimonials of his colleagues shed a rather different light on his approach. On receiving the new instruction regarding appeals to the Cabinet, Richard Crossman wrote in his diaries that, 'The whole note is very interesting and if you had standing committees with permanent members who worked as a team, as a microcosm of the Cabinet, it would be satisfactory. But if half the awkward decisions are shoved outside into these special MISCS [miscellaneous Cabinet committees], Harold can get his way and in my view Cabinet Government can be frustrated.'[157] Barbara Castle also complained of Wilson's manipulation of the committee system in her diaries. She wrote, 'there are a lot of 'MISCS' of whose existence some of us don't even know! There is a MISC 205 [on monetary policy], of course, which Dick [Richard Crossman] hasn't cottoned onto yet; another MISC dealing with Rhodesia, of which I am not a member (even the circulation of the Rhodesia telegrams is 'restricted' so that I can't get hold of them). I've just discovered there is a Nuclear MISC — heaven knows who's a member of it! The documents belonging to MISCS are usually Top Secret.'[158] Castle admits that Wilson tended to bring 'the conclusions of these inner discussions to Cabinet for final ratification', but by that stage in the decision-making process that it was often 'very difficult for the rest of the Cabinet to change them. All that one can do is to decide whether the near *fait accompli* makes the continuation of one's membership of Cabinet impossible.'[159]

Wilson's desire to be the 'managing director' of his Cabinet was apparent through the number of Cabinet procedures which now required the Prime Minister's permission, or at least consultation with his Private Office, before Ministers could take action. No previous Prime Minister had formally required such a high degree of centralisation around Number 10 and only Tony Blair, since then, has gone further. For example, policy presentation was closely monitored by Number 10 and appointments of parliamentary private secretaries, special advisers and all public appointments required the personal approval of the Prime Minister. Above all, Wilson placed a particular emphasis on the long standing rule that Ministers abide by the doctrine of collective responsibility and support all decisions of the Government, even if they personally disagreed with them. This ruling was temporarily relaxed for the run-up to the referendum on membership of EEC in 1975, but never deleted from the pages of *QPM*. Whereas previous Prime Ministers had confined their guidance on collective responsibility to a couple of paragraphs, Wilson reminded his Ministers of its importance throughout *QPM*, particularly in the sections relating to the presentation of policy and security.

The presentation of policy was an important issue for the new Prime Minister, who recognised that image and appearances could have a powerful impact on public opinion. He himself was adept at giving interviews and was a skilful performer on television. Crossman remembers how 'brilliantly he handle[d] the Lobby. He [was] a kind of further education lecturer and they [ate] out of his hand when he explain[ed] everything very sensibly, rather pedestrianly, in a style which they [felt] at home with.'[160] Wilson's very first edition of *QPM* contained new guidance on dealing with Lobby correspondents both 'on' and 'off the record' which had been drafted in the Cabinet Office during the run-up to the 1964 General Election, on the suggestion of John Groves, who was the Deputy Public Relations Adviser at Number 10.[161] However, it was in the next update that he had an opportunity to insert detailed guidance on media management and formally establish procedures which centralised control of policy presentation.

The 1966 edition of *QPM* made it clear to Ministers that all speeches and broadcasts were to be cleared with Number 10 in advance. The Prime Minister was to be sent 'up-to-date particulars' of their public speaking engagements 'in order to co-ordinate the presentation of the Government's policies'[162] — and, no doubt, to ensure that everybody was toeing the line. The Chief Press Secretary at Number 10 was to coordinate all contacts that Ministers made with the press, particularly the lobby correspondents, and the broadcasting authorities. Ministers were required to present him with their proposals for a Ministerial broadcast[163] and consult him before arranging a briefing with the Lobby.[164] In the 1976 update, it was added that Ministers should also allow the Press Secretary time to comment on the content and timing of Government announcements. Ministers were required to consult each other, if they intended to speak on matters which were the responsibility of another Department,[165] and to consult the Prime Minister 'before any mention [was] made of matters which either affect the conduct of the government as a whole or are of a constitutional character.'[166]

The new instructions governing Ministers' relations with the Press were issued after Anthony Howard, a journalist from *The Sunday Times,* caused the Government some concern. Howard was appointed by *The Sunday Times* in January 1965 and given the title 'Whitehall Correspondent', despite the fact that he was not a member of the Lobby. He publicly criticised the Government's heavy use of the Lobby and established his own style of journalism which aimed to 'publish the secret matters of politics'.[167] After talking to a few Ministers he wrote a revealing piece on the internal politics of Whitehall. There was a swift response from the Principal Private Secretary at Number 10, Derek Mitchell, who decided to 'tighten up the instructions to Ministers — and Departments — on the rules governing relations with the Press and to mount a blockade against Anthony Howard personally'.[168] Ministers were instructed not to make 'excessive use' of the 'Lobby conference channel' and were to 'use the Information

Branch of his Department' when arranging a Press conference.[169] The reason behind this was to ensure that, in future, a Press Officer was always present when a Minister gave a briefing.[170]

Wilson's approach to media management appears to have caused some concern to Edward Heath, who served as Prime Minister for one term between the Wilson administrations. Heath publicly criticised Wilson's gimmickry and manipulation of the media and wanted to run his government in a way that provided a complete contrast. In his manifesto, *A Better Tomorrow,* Heath attacked Wilson's 'cheap and trivial style of government' where 'decisions have been dictated simply by the desire to catch tomorrow's headlines'. He promised 'a new style of government' which would 're-establish our sound and honest British traditions in this field'.[171] Clearly this included a new approach to the media as Heath removed all the sections on policy presentation from Wilson's *QPM* before issuing it to his new Ministers, with a note that they would be incorporated at a later date after careful study and revision.[172] Heath wanted to establish a serious dialogue with the media on a more open and honest basis, and began by appointing a former Foreign Office official, Donald Maitland, as his Press Secretary — a striking contrast to the former *Sun* journalist, Joe Haines.[173] Heath's biographer, John Campbell, states that the new Prime Minister 'set his face deliberately against anything that smacked of "image-building" and tried to change the Lobby system 'in favour of on-the-record briefing'.[174] However, his honourable efforts were to prove ultimately unsuccessful. Campbell explains that, 'The Lobby refused, insisting that they must retain discretion as to what was on the record and what was off it. There followed a tussle of wills between Downing Street and the Lobby ... until a compromise was agreed — daily briefings from Pym (Leader of the House of Commons) at the House of Commons and a weekly one in Downing Street — and the old system was resumed much as before'.[175]

Michael Cockerell notes that Heath experimented with the idea of prime ministerial television broadcasts as a more direct and open alternative for conveying information to the public, which would also enable him to by-pass the Lobby completely.[176] On 12th July 1971, following negotiations with the French President, Georges Pompidou, on Britain's third application to join the European Common Market, Heath staged a grand televised press conference at Lancaster House which proved to be very successful. However, Cockerell states that 'in the event the idea foundered when it was pointed out that the Opposition would inevitably demand equal air time in which to reply'.[177] Heath's attempt to scrap the traditional 'off-the-record' briefings had also backfired as he was criticised for, what appeared to be, an aloof and presidential style of leadership.

Cockerell quotes the opinion of James Margach, the Political Editor of *The Sunday Times,* who wrote, 'It was as though he blamed the machinations of the media for the failure of his policies'.[178]

Heath's guidance on policy presentation was finally issued in 1971 in a new edition of *QPM*. It is perhaps a testament both to the non–party nature of the document and to the absolute necessity of tight media management within modern government that very little had actually been altered. The bulk of the text from Wilson's 1969 edition was simply reinserted with a few minor amendments. For example, Ministers were advised that when pondering whether to accept an invitation to broadcast they should 'consider whether the proposed interview will provide an opportunity either to explain government policy or to clear up a misunderstanding.' If not, 'the Minister may well conclude that … his appearance on the news bulletin may be 'superfluous and debase the currency of ministerial appearances on radio and television'.[179] Much of Wilson's guidance on how to 'use' the Lobby was also deleted, but Ministers were still free to give unattributable briefings should they 'find it desirable'.[180] The only significant additions that Heath made to the document were paragraphs relating to travel arrangements by rail and air, which informed Ministers of the appropriate forms of transport for various official trips and reminded them of the need to consider costs in order to minimise their expenses.

As the frequency of ministerial trips increased, the need to economise on expenses charged to public funds became more important. Wilson was also careful to remind Ministers in his own instructions, that they must be able to account for and justify all their expenses on travel and hospitality.[181] Edward Short, Wilson's first Chief Whip, recalls that his 'puritan stinginess about the use of public facilities characterised the whole of Harold's premiership and was completely inexplicable to [the] official drivers, who had been accustomed to more lavish masters'.[182] Ministers were even given 'the strictest instructions from the Prime Minister that improvements and decorations in ministerial offices had to be kept to the bare essentials' — although Wilson did not go as far as to add this to *QPM*. Short remembers the surprise amongst Ministers on their return to office in 1974, when they saw 'the vast amounts which had been spent by the Heath Government on decorations and improvements in Downing Street, Chequers and elsewhere.'[183]

As with all administrations, Wilson faced the familiar problem of maintaining internal confidentiality and preventing 'leaks'. Edward Short recalls that 'each time a damaging piece of information was made public, the Prime Minister read the Riot Act to the Cabinet and constantly warned them that if they made notes in Cabinet they must not, in any circumstances, be taken out of the Cabinet room. This homily was repeated whenever he saw anyone writing'.[184] During Wilson's second term in office new instructions were incorporated into *QPM* to advise Ministers that even the release of 'isolated items of information' could lead to 'serious leakages of information', as the Press and broadcasting agencies were adept at piecing these snippets together from several sources. However, it was further added that 'in appropriate cases it may be in the public interest to communicate certain information in confidence to a responsible editor, lobby correspondent, etc., for the purposes of guidance; but this is permissible only when it is known that such confidence will be respected.'[185] It may seem unusual for a Prime Minister to actually suggest that his Ministers provide confidential information in certain circumstances — but Wilson was well aware that this could be an effective means of setting the agenda. He did not, however, appreciate it when Ministers leaked information which undermined his own agenda, and the diaries of his colleagues recall his constant frustration with leaks. Wilson set a bad example through his own conduct though, as he was known to be a serial leaker himself. Barbara Castle's diary records a Cabinet meeting in March 1968, when Wilson stated that he was 'livid about the stories that he [was] to wind up the DEA [Department of Economic Affairs] and told us that he had instructed Gerald Kaufman [then a press officer] to brief the press to the contrary.' He warned the Cabinet that he had been 'collecting 'finger-prints', to which Jim Callaghan angrily replied, 'Your fingerprints were clearly there'.[186] Richard Crossman observed that as far as Harold Wilson was concerned 'anything he tells a journalist is briefing and anything any other Minister does is leaking'.[187]

The Chief Whip found that close scrutiny of Minister's business diaries was often very revealing during a leak investigation and 'always insisted on having copies of their schedules [as] on more than one occasion they disclosed a contact between a Minister and a reporter at the appropriate time.'[188] This procedure was swiftly formalised by a new ruling in *QPM* which stated that 'Ministers in charge of Departments should arrange to send the Chief Whip on each Monday morning an up-to-date list of the speaking engagements of all Ministers in the Department, both of an official and of a party nature, since engagements of a party political character may be used for the presentation of the Government's policies.'[189]

Wilson's rule against taking notes in Cabinet (which did not find its way into *QPM*) was intended to prevent ministerial diary-keeping as much as leaks. He was well aware that several Cabinet Ministers were keeping records for their diaries or memoirs and became concerned when he heard rumours that Ministers were signing contracts with publishers whilst in office.[190] An internal committee on ministerial publications, established in 1967 to consider the issue, suggested in its report that all ministerial publications be sent to the Cabinet Secretary for his view on whether it complied with the convention of collective responsibility. If not, it would either be edited accordingly or refused permission to publish. The report further suggested that Ministers should sign an undertaking to comply with this procedure.[191]

Wilson later discovered that this had not resolved the issue as Richard Crossman's diaries were published after his death in 1974, despite being refused permission by the Cabinet Secretary, Sir John Hunt. The Crown served a writ on the publishers, but lost its case for an injunction to stop publication. Lord Widgery, the Lord Chief Justice, stated in his judgement that he could 'see no ground in law which would entitle the court to restrain publication of these matters'.[192] This was an unsatisfactory conclusion for the Prime Minister and the Cabinet Office and led to the establishment of an external committee of enquiry, chaired by Lord Radcliffe, to propose clear procedures for the future.[193] The report[194] recommended a stringent but voluntary code of practice which was accepted in full by the Government. The new code required Ministers to sign an undertaking to submit works intended for publication for prior approval of the Cabinet Secretary. Although the majority of the Cabinet signed, Tony Benn and Roy Jenkins refused on principle[195] — and Tony Benn's diaries note, without explanation, that the Prime Minister himself did not sign.[196] The code of practice effectively became mandatory following its incorporation into the 1976 edition of QPM. Benn recalls that Ministers were instructed to conform to the principles of the Radcliffe Report, and also advised to leave testamentary instructions for their executors to follow the recommended procedures — a small precaution to prevent a repeat of the Crossman affair. Wilson bluntly emphasised the point in a Cabinet meeting by remarking to his Ministers, 'Don't keep a diary, and if you do keep a diary, don't die. The Government must have a view.'[197]

Although QPM is binding on all Ministers, a senior civil servant who served during the Wilson administrations recalls that Wilson would occasionally amend QPM as a means of 'controlling' particularly troublesome Ministers such as Tony Benn.[198] Relations between Benn and Wilson were close when Labour was in Opposition, prior to Wilson's first premiership, but became increasingly strained during the Wilson administrations as Benn changed his political stance to become a prominent figure of the far left wing of the Labour Party. By 1969, Tony Benn was describing Wilson in his diaries as 'a small-minded man, who always gets to the least important part of the issue, suggesting ways of downing the Tories or embarrassing Heath ... when events call for a higher degree of States-manship'.[199] Ben Pimlott notes that 'it was during the 1973–4 miners' dispute that Wilson began to regard Benn, not merely as a boat-rocker, but as a serious threat to the Party's electoral chances'.[200] He nevertheless gave him a significant post, as Secretary of State for Industry, in his 1974 Cabinet, in order to placate the left, with the intention of neutralising him whilst he was there. He managed to ensure that Benn's draft White Paper on industrial intervention through a National Enterprise Board and planning agreements with leading companies, which he thought was 'sloppy and half-baked', never saw the light of day, by establishing a special committee of senior Ministers under his chairmanship 'to mastermind its re-drafting'.[201]

New rulings which were incorporated into *QPM* in 1974, particularly those relating to speeches and broadcasts, are likely to have been directed primarily at Benn, who would use the party's National Executive Committee as a platform for his own policy convictions. Wilson wrote in his memoirs that 'it became my duty in subsequent months to draw to the attention of certain Ministers the overriding requirements of this code of conduct [*QPM*], particularly the relationship to their membership of the NEC of the Labour Party and their subsequent committees.'[202] Speeches, press articles and party publications were all to be more closely monitored to ensure that they complied with the principle of collective responsibility. For example, paragraph 104 of the 1974 (October) edition stated that 'If a Minister intends to make a speech in which he deals with, or makes observations which bear upon, matters which fall within another Minister's responsibilities, that Minister must invariably be consulted.' The same rule applied to any written texts by Ministers, and it was further emphasised that 'Ministers would not normally be expected to have time for such writings whilst holding office'.[203]

Wilson's attempts to keep Benn in check by waving the rulebook at him every time he stepped out of line were not successful. Tony Benn refused to accept that *QPM* was binding upon himself or his departmental Ministers. His diaries record that he expressed his view on *QPM* to the Prime Minister in quite blunt terms. He notes that on 17th June 1974 he remarked to Wilson that, 'They have never been published. They have never been collectively discussed with me and I do not accept them.'[204] He went even further in his rejection of the document, by drafting his own 'departmental' version of *QPM* (in the same month) for his Ministers at the Department of Industry, creating a direct conflict with the Prime Minister's guidelines. His own minute concluded: 'We are still ourselves, Labour Party and trade union members, as well as Ministers; and our accountability is to our consciences, to the people, to the Party and to the Movement, as well as to the Government.'[205] According to Tony Benn's diaries, Wilson's view was that 'Ministers have no other existence than as Ministers'.[206]

Tony Benn was not the only Minister who caused concern through his behaviour in office. Lord Longford (who was at the time Lord Privy Seal) had also attracted the attention of the Prime Minister in 1965 by his rather indiscreet and controversial prison visits, which almost led Wilson to issue a code for Ministers' private behaviour. His visits to Pentonville Prison to see Nevin Craig[207] became particularly embarrassing when a fellow prisoner alleged, in a letter of complaint to two Conservative MPs that Longford was using his influence to secure preferential treatment for Nevin. Although the allegations were refuted by the prison staff, one of the MPs, Brigadier Clarke, raised the issue in the House of Commons in an adjournment debate.[208] Edward Short, the Chief Whip, recalls that 'Harold, always anxious to head off trouble, took an unexpectedly serious view … and decided to see Lord Longford with the Home Secretary [Sir Frank Soskice] and Sir Charles Cunningham, Permanent Secretary at the Home Office'.[209] In addition to this little talk, an instruction was circulated to Ministers, prohibiting visits to prisoners unless the consent of the Home Secretary and the Prime Minister had been given.[210] Lord Longford wryly remarked in his memoirs that 'one gained the impression that such visits were not desirable'.[211] Even the Chief Whip thought that this was 'rather exaggerating the importance of the matter'.[212] However, it was further discussed whether more general guidance on 'the need to avoid behaviour which might lead to gossip and innuendo damaging to the Government' ought to be included in *QPM*.[213] The Cabinet Secretary, Sir Burke Trend, felt that such guidance could 'never be so comprehensive as to prevent failures of judgement and common sense',[214] and the idea was eventually rejected as any new guidance was likely to be construed by Lord Longford as a further reprimand on his own behaviour.[215]

Longford, however, did not escape further censure, as just a few weeks later, he decided to accept an invitation to attend Christopher Craig's wedding — Nevin Craig's infamous brother who had (fairly recently) finished serving a life sentence for the shooting of a policeman. When Wilson was informed of this by his Principal Private Secretary, he wrote a personal note to Longford, urging him not to go through with the plan. In his letter he wrote, 'I know that it is in a remote place and that there is *some* hope that your attendance would not attract publicity. However, in view of the recent Adjournment Debate in which attention was drawn to your connection with Craig, I must tell you that I think it would be extremely unwise of you to go to this wedding. The fact is that anything you now do you may be thought to be doing as a Minister'.[216] No further action was taken though, as Longford thought it best, at the time, to simply 'comply with [Wilson's] wishes in regard to this particular matter' and keep a low profile.[217] He later wrote, in his autobiography, that 'this piece of action, or rather inaction, I regret more than anything I did or failed to do during my time in Cabinet'.[218] However, his inaction may have spared Ministers from renewed discussions on the possibility of drafting rules to restrict Ministers' personal choices and private conduct.

The allegations made by the Czech defector, Josef Frolik, in 1969, that Labour Members of Parliament had accepted money for spying throughout the 1960s, were perhaps more alarming to the Wilson administration. Will Owen, Tom Driberg and the Postmaster-General, John Stonehouse, were all named and accused of working for the Czech intelligence. Philip Ziegler states in his authorised biography of Wilson that the Prime Minister, 'was sceptical, the more so since MI5, in a moment of over-excitement, confused Will and David Owen and maintained that the latter was a spy'.[219] However, he adds that Wilson 'had no intention of blocking an enquiry'[220] and consequently, all were investigated by MI5. *The Times* (much later) reported Frolik as saying he 'knew of no other place in the world outside Austria and West Germany where infiltration of the Government apparatus, of Parliament; of the Trade Unions and of scientific institutions was so complete and on such a grand scale as in Great Britain'.[221] Will Owen, the Labour Member for Morpeth, was charged in 1970, but acquitted after a two-week trial. Both Driberg and Stonehouse (who had previously been Minister of State for Technology and Under-Secretary at the Ministry of Aviation) were also cleared of the allegations, but the story fuelled smear campaigns against the Labour Government. Ziegler notes that, although Stonehouse was not brought back into office in 1974, he 'caused a still greater furore when he faked his death by drowning in Miami … [He] eventually re-emerged in Australia and was tried and convicted on eighteen charges of theft and false pretences. It did not rebound to the credit of the government in which he had served'.[222]

It is probably no coincidence that after the Frolik stories (which arose against the background of the ongoing Cold War) *QPM* was expanded to cover security and intelligence matters.[223] The atmosphere during the Cold War was tense and rumours were rife. The Government was so anxious to avoid any possibility of Communist infiltration that Ministers were even required to investigate the status and country of origin of any foreign au pair girls employed within their household.[224] A note was circulated to all Ministers, alerting them to the increasing numbers of au pair girls arriving in the UK from Communist countries. They were warned that there was a 'potential security risk in the employment of such people in the homes of both Ministers and officials who have access to classified information'. The note explained that 'the presence of such a person in a household could be used by an intelligence service in ways which could be inimical to the interests of security in this country'. As a result of the security check, it was discovered that the Parliamentary Secretary to the Ministry of Technology, Peter Shore, employed an au pair girl from Yugoslavia. Although she was cleared by the Security Service, Peter Shore was advised to replace her, within three months, with a girl from a non–communist regime.[225]

Ever since 1945, the only security matters covered by *QPM* were 'precautions against unauthorised disclosures of information'. In March 1974, Wilson retitled the section, 'Propriety and security in the conduct of government business'. Although the specific guidance relating to the employment of au pairs was not incorporated into *QPM,* the new section included instructions to prevent the interception of telephone calls and also advised Ministers 'to take care to conduct themselves, both in public and private, in such a way as to avoid becoming involved in circumstances which could either damage the Government's good name by provoking scandalous speculation or be used against them as a means of pressure by hostile intelligence agents.' In addition, Ministers were discouraged from having 'direct contact with persons offering their services as intelligence agents.' If approached they were to 'offer no comment' and inform their Permanent Secretary of the approach.[226] These amendments were retained in subsequent updates for the duration of the Cold War. They were finally removed from *QPM* when it was redrafted for publication, although it is possible that they are still in circulation in a separate confidential manual on security matters.

To what extent a Prime Minister utilises *QPM* as a means of organising Cabinet business and disciplining ministerial colleagues depends very much on their style of government. Whilst every Prime Minister will develop their own personal approach to the job, it is interesting to note that the rulebook has accorded better with the working methods of the Labour Prime Ministers in the post-war period. This is not a suggestion that *QPM* is any way party-political, but merely an observation of the fact that Clement Attlee, Harold Wilson and more recently, Tony Blair, have all demonstrated a preference for government 'by the book'. This may, to some extent, be a reflection of Labour Party values and practices. The Labour Party established a constitution from its very beginning and has always valued detailed procedures for its internal operations and elections. Although the rules of ministerial office are made explicit in *QPM*, the process of amendment was far from fair or democratic, and was a bone of contention with Tony Benn for many years. The only written procedures for British Cabinet government were confidential and subject only to the Prime Minister's approval. Individual Prime Ministers had the discretion to make significant alterations to the rulebook if they chose to do so, without consulting the Cabinet and without any need to account to Parliament. For Wilson, this made it a useful instrument to organise and control his Cabinets.

Wilson's resignation in April 1976 provided an opportunity for the Cabinet Office to revise QPM yet again, and incorporate selected prime ministerial directives which had been issued since the last update in October 1974. In previous years, an update had not always been produced on the appointment of a new Prime Minister if their arrival had not followed a general election.[227] However, by the time John Major was appointed Prime Minister, following the resignation of Margaret Thatcher in 1990, it had become standard drill.

The 1976 revise was also a chance for the new Labour Prime Minister, James Callaghan, to suggest his own amendments to the document. Callaghan was not as bureaucratically-minded as his predecessor and did not involve himself greatly in the details of QPM's revision. However, after two years experience as Foreign Secretary, he was very aware of the increasing problem of gifts and hospitality from foreign governments and approved of the inclusion of further guidance on this issue in QPM.[228] These instructions were incorporated at a time when conflicts of interest were an issue again, particularly as Britain's membership of the EEC had dramatically increased the number of ministerial trips overseas. As Wilson recalled, 'in the period of just over two years from March 1974 to April 1976, there were thirteen official Head-of-Government visits abroad, and fifty-nine incoming visits' and these were only the 'Head-of-Government' meetings.[229] Foreign Office Ministers in particular, were frequently faced with offers of gifts or hospitality during the course of business. The revised QPM instructed Ministers 'not to overlook the possible foreign policy implications of such day-to-day matters as acceptances of offers of hospitality to prominent political figures visiting this country, social commitments of a similar kind, and public support for open letters, etc.'[230] They were advised to consult their Permanent Secretaries, when 'deciding whether to accept or to offer gifts', who would 'be able to advise them about the rules applicable to civil servants in analogous circumstances'.[231] It was further added that the general principles governing the acceptance of gifts also applied to gifts offered to a member of family. This was inserted after Bob Cryer (Labour MP for Keighley) had pointed out in a written question, that the guidance for Ministers were not as tight as those given to civil servants, and neglected to mention gifts given to families.[232]

Conflicts of interest in public life, particularly the receipt of gifts and hospitality, had once again become a sensitive issue following the report of the Royal Commission on Standards in Public Life. The Committee, chaired by Lord Salmon, had been established in the wake of the Poulson affair to enquire into the standards in public life generally. In its report, the Committee stated that Mr Poulson, a businessman involved in the construction industry, had 'succeeded in corruptly penetrating high levels of the civil service, the National Health Service, two nationalised industries and a number of local authorities'.[233] Although the affair had not involved government Ministers, Tony Crosland was briefly implicated in the Poulson case in January 1973. It was alleged that Crosland had accepted an antique-silver coffee pot worth £500 from Mr Poulson, whilst he was Secretary of State for Education and Science, after Poulson's firm had built a comprehensive school in Bradford. In fact, the coffee pot had been a reproduction worth only £40.[234] Nevertheless, the incident highlighted the potential dangers of accepting gifts. Although the Salmon report did not directly influence any new amendments to QPM,[235] the new guidelines on gifts were incorporated at a time when the standards in public life generally were being called into question.

As QPM is not normally updated between general elections, Callaghan's prime ministerial directives were not incorporated into the general rulebook until after the 1979 General Election, which the Conservatives won. On a change of government, the Cabinet Office generally has a greater discretion over the revision of the document, as the incoming Prime Minister who approves the revised draft, is unlikely to be aware of the internal procedural problems that the previous Government experienced. One significant amendment made during the 1979 update, formally increased the Treasury's influence in Cabinet decision-making. The revision established an exception to Wilson's ruling that appeals from members of Cabinet committees to the full Cabinet were not to be made without the consent of the committee Chairman, to allow Treasury Ministers an 'automatic right of appeal'.[236] This was made to ensure that the Treasury could enforce the rigid programme of restrictions on public expenditure which had been introduced following the 'IMF crisis' of 1976, by objecting to any committee decision which involved further expenditure.[237] To secure the loan from the International Monetary Fund, the Cabinet was compelled to accept cuts of £1.5 billion from the total public expenditure planned for 1977–8, and £2 billion from the total for 1978–9.[238]

The directives of the outgoing Prime Minister may not always be pertinent to the next administration. Callaghan's successor, Margaret Thatcher, did not suffer from the affliction of minority Government, and yet amongst those directives which senior officials selected for incorporation into *QPM*, were instructions which Callaghan had issued prohibiting dissent in the Commons from parliamentary private secretaries. When Callaghan was first appointed Prime Minister, he led a 'minuscule majority'[239] of two seats in the Commons which had whittled away by July 1976 after three defections,[240] leaving him with a minority Government. Loyalty from the Parliamentary Labour Party was therefore a priority concern as he struggled to maintain the survival of his Government for three years.

Dissent from Labour Members jeopardised the Labour Government's chances of survival. In January 1977, Callaghan was concerned by two instances of rebellion. On the morning of 11th January, a controversial clause of the Government's Social Security [Miscellaneous Provisions] Bill, to restrict unemployment pay for occupational pensioners between the ages of 60 and 65, was defeated in committee by eleven votes to five.[241] A week later, seven parliamentary private secretaries (three of whom were attached to Cabinet Ministers) abstained during a debate on defence.[242] The Prime Minister imposed a strict ruling that parliamentary private secretaries would be sacked in future if they voted against the Government. However, further problems were experienced with Tony Benn's PPS, Brian Sedgemore, in November 1978, when he referred to a restricted Treasury document, which he should not have seen, during a Select Committee enquiry. Tony Benn recalled that Sedgemore, a member of a general sub-committee of the Select Committee on Public Expenditure, 'had put a question to Denis Healey, who was giving evidence on EMS [European Monetary System]. He had asked, 'What about the secret Treasury paper?' quoting the number and referring to the fact that the paper warned of the need for deflation.'[243] As a result, he was promptly dismissed by Callaghan who imposed a further ruling that PPSs who serve on select committees 'should not do so [i.e. serve] in the case of inquiries into their own Minister's Departments and ... should avoid associating themselves with recommendations critical or embarrassing to the Government.'[244]

In effect these rulings restrained parliamentary private secretaries, who worked for the Government on an unpaid basis, in their capacity as Members of the House of Commons, representing their constituencies and scrutinising the executive. It has been clearly stated in every edition of *QPM* since 1945 that parliamentary private secretaries are not members of the Government, they remain private members, and as such they 'should be afforded as great a liberty of action as possible'. Although none of these points were deleted during the 1979 revision, the amendments that were made to the document clearly contradicted them. At the time of his dismissal, Brian Sedgemore complained to the Speaker of the Commons of 'interference by the Executive' in the right of backbench MPs to raise whatever came to their attention in the course of public questioning. He maintained that his work on the sub-committee to the Expenditure Committee related to his position as a Member of Parliament, and not to his position as parliamentary private secretary to Mr Benn.[245] Callaghan's firm handling of dissenting PPSs is perhaps understandable, given his difficult parliamentary position. However, it is curious that his directives were considered to be appropriate for incorporation into the general rulebook. It is also slightly ironic that these instructions were inserted into *QPM* for the benefit of the Conservative Party which defeated Callaghan's Government on a Motion of No-Confidence, and won the 1979 General Election with a comfortable majority of forty three seats. Mrs Thatcher did make use of the ruling though in 1986, when she dismissed Andrew Hunter, as Parliamentary Private Secretary to Lord Elton (Minister of State for the Environment), for voting against the Second Reading of the Shops Bill.[246] Although this individual act of rebellion had not threatened the survival of her Government, it had caused considerable political embarrassment, and the ruling in *QPM* is likely to have provided a convenient justification for his dismissal.

Chapter Five
THE THATCHER EFFECT

It is for each Prime Minister to decide how to run his or her Cabinet.

Nicholas Ridley [247]

Margaret Thatcher's unique style of premiership has been widely commented upon — not least by her former ministerial colleagues, who have both praised and complained of the way she managed her Cabinets. She was determined, before she even entered Downing Street, that she would run a 'conviction government', remarking in an interview that 'as Prime Minister I could not waste time having any internal arguments.'[248] She took a strong lead in Cabinet discussions and, as her position strengthened, she began to ignore the formal procedures which continued to be circulated in *QPM*, and increasingly conducted business through small ad hoc groups or bilateral talks.

On his resignation in 1986, following the Westland Affair (which erupted after an internal row between Leon Brittan and Michael Heseltine over the future ownership of the Westland Helicopter Company), Heseltine criticised the disintegration of traditional collective decision-making procedures and accused the Prime Minister of 'setting-aside ... the Constitution'.[249] As the constitutional boundaries for Cabinet government have never been clearly mapped out in Britain, others took a different view and some have vigorously defended Thatcher's style. Bernard Ingham, Thatcher's Chief Press Secretary, commented in his memoirs that, 'if Mrs Thatcher extended the frontiers of what is possible in a British system, so much more is there to be said for the quality of her leadership'.[250] Nicholas Ridley went further, to state that 'she was constitutionally always in the right',[251] as 'it is for each Prime Minister to decide how to run his or her Cabinet'.[252]

It is certainly true that British Prime Ministers have a wide discretion over the organisation and management of Cabinet business. However, whilst they are not constrained by a written constitution, they are restricted by certain conventions and greatly influenced by the procedures operated by the Cabinet Office. To some extent, *QPM* has become a further restraint on unconventional styles of government. By codifying procedures and practices, the document confers 'legitimacy' on these practices and consequently ensures that they crystallise into continuing conventions. Sir Kenneth Wheare defines the concept of 'constitutional conventions' to mean 'a binding rule, a rule of behaviour accepted as obligatory by those concerned in the working of the constitution.'[253] He contrasts this with a 'usage' which he describes as 'no more than a usual practice. Clearly a usage might become a convention. What is usually done comes to be what is done. [However] It is often difficult to say whether a particular course of conduct is obligatory or persuasive only'.[254] In a sense *QPM* clears up any uncertainty as to the status of an existing practice by establishing an 'obligatory' ruling and thereby accelerating the development of a 'usage' into to a hardened convention. Although Prime Ministers retain the authority to revise the document as they see fit, by this stage it had become easier to add to the existing rules than attempt to make any significant deletions. A former senior official who served under Thatcher stated that, 'it is like the Common Law. You have all the advantages of it being agreed and established and it is easier to build on that than to start from scratch'.[255]

Harold Wilson was able to use *QPM* as a management tool because he worked *through* the system and made many additions to the text. By contrast, Mrs Thatcher became increasingly frustrated with the formal channels of decision-making, which often delayed or obstructed her own policy wishes. Yet she did not dispense with *QPM* or attempt to re-write the rules for Cabinet government, and consequently she never seriously challenged the traditional operation of Cabinet government. Instead, she sought to by-pass the Cabinet system by channelling key decisions away from Cabinet and its formal committees, into ad hoc groups, where the membership could be 'chosen to suit her own thinking',[256] and bilateral discussions. Whilst she was not the first Prime Minister to hold meetings and discussions outside the formal committees of Cabinet (Wilson, Callaghan and Heath had also found them useful on occasions),[257] Thatcher expanded this practice to an unprecedented degree.

Although Mrs Thatcher did not always work within the parameters of the rulebook, significant amendments made during her premierships suggest that *QPM* nevertheless continued to be a useful means of regulating certain matters, such as policy presentation and private interests. The Cabinet Office continued to ensure that the administration operated smoothly and prepared revised editions of *QPM* for the Prime Minister to approve at the beginning of each administration. A former senior official working at that time recalls that amendments to *QPM* were 'initiated in the Cabinet Office, drafted there and then submitted to the Prime Minister for her approval'.[258] Although Mrs Thatcher did not directly involve herself in the process of updating *QPM*, as

Wilson had done, the Cabinet Office revised the document in the light of her own style and preferences, to ensure that her approval could be obtained for its re-issue and circulation.

When Mrs Thatcher entered Downing Street in 1979 as the first female Prime Minister in Britain, she had a workable majority of 43 seats in Parliament.[259] Her position in the Cabinet was not as comfortable though, as her views on the economy were only shared by a minority of her colleagues.[260] Although *QPM* never excited much interest from the Prime Minister, she ran her first Cabinet very much by the book, adhering closely to the traditional principles of collective decision-making. A former senior official who served under Thatcher recalls, 'it was a way of doing business put to her by the Cabinet Secretary, John Hunt,[261] who was [initially] a powerful man, and she was content to follow that route'.[262] Jim Prior recalls that 'she operated very strictly through the Cabinet committee system, with the Cabinet Office taking the minutes'.[263]

The revised draft of *QPM* in 1979 (incorporating Jim Callaghan's directives) was quickly approved for circulation to the new Ministers, and issued under a lengthy covering note from the Prime Minister, which emphasised the importance of the document and drew out the key points. In her note, Thatcher wrote that she attached 'the highest importance to the principles enunciated in the memorandum concerning collective and ministerial responsibility. They must inform all our work, in departments, in our collective deliberations and in our public activities.'[264] Thatcher was keen to run an organised and efficient Cabinet and reportedly warned her Ministers early on to 'pull their socks up' over inadequate preparation for Cabinet meetings.[265] Nigel Lawson recalls that Thatcher herself, 'always did her homework on the subjects for discussion, almost as if she were about to sit an examination'[266] and was clearly frustrated when others had not.

QPM was (quite unusually) formally revised on a couple of occasions during her first term in office. The normal practice during previous administrations was to wait until the next general election to amend the document. Between elections, senior officials would normally make a note of revisions to be made and flag up directives from the Prime Minister for incorporation during the next update. However, in June 1980 Ministers received a note from the Cabinet Secretary, then Sir Robert Armstrong, informing them of three revisions which had been made to *QPM*. These included a redrafted paragraph 4 which emphasised the importance of Cabinet meetings by stating that 'Cabinet meetings take precedence over all other business except meetings of the Privy Council'. Requests for permission to be absent were only to be made 'in the most exceptional circumstances, and should be made at the earliest opportunity and by personal minute to the Prime Minister'. The rules for junior Ministers regarding permission to be absent were simultaneously revised. It was now unnecessary for them to gain the Prime Minister's approval, so long as they had permission from the Ministerial Head of Department, the Foreign and Commonwealth Office and the Chief Whip. In addition, paragraph 88 on appointments by Ministers was redrafted for greater clarity.[267] Three months later, Ministers received a similar note detailing a further amendment. The revision concerned the budgeting of ministerial visits overseas and was to make Ministers accountable for their expenditure on official visits abroad. The new ruling instructed Ministers to arrange for the returns of their visits to be sent three times a year to the Civil Service Department, so that a central record of costs could be maintained.[268]

When *QPM* was fully revised following the General Election in June 1983, a significant amendment was made. A lengthy new section was inserted entitled 'Changes in ministerial responsibilities' which outlined the Prime Minister's authority to allocate ministerial functions. Although it is unclear precisely what motivated this amendment, codification of the Prime Minister's powers arguably strengthened her position in Cabinet. The first paragraph of this section informed Ministers that:

> The Prime Minister is responsible for the overall organisation of the Executive and the allocation of functions between Ministers in charge of Departments. Her approval should therefore be sought where changes are proposed that affect this allocation and responsibilities for the discharge of ministerial functions. This applies whether the functions in question are derived from statute or from the exercise of the Royal Prerogative, or are general administrative responsibilities.

One incident that may have triggered this new section was the reorganisation of Ministry of Defence by the Prime Minister in May 1981, which caused a degree of controversy.[269] Mrs Thatcher removed the old structure which consisted of one Minister of state and three parliamentary under-secretaries, representing the Army, the Navy and the Air Force, after the Under-Secretary for the Navy, Keith Speed, had publicly criticised the Government's proposed cuts in Britain's naval strength. Speed was dismissed and a new structure was established of two Ministers of state, one for the Armed Forces and one for defence procurement, and two under-secretaries. *The Times* reported that the move was 'seen to be attempting to stifle inter-service squabbling at a time of cuts in defence expenditure, to prevent other embarrassment such as that caused to the Government by Mr Speed's outburst.'[270] A statement clarifying the Prime Minister's powers over the organisation of the Executive may have been drafted to prevent any future internal criticism of changes implemented by her.

The new edition of *QPM* also included detailed instructions on the preparation of business for the Cabinet, reflecting Thatcher's earlier insistence that her
colleagues arrive at Cabinet thoroughly primed for the meeting. The revised text
stated that, 'Memoranda should be circulated in sufficient time to enable Ministers to read and digest them, and to be properly briefed on them'. The importance of upholding the 7–day advance circulation rule for all memoranda prepared for Cabinet committees, and particularly those prepared for Cabinet was
stressed:

> To ensure that the 7–day rule is complied with in the case of Cabinet memoranda,
> drafts will have to be received by the Private Secretary to the Secretary of the Cabinet
> early in the afternoon (certainly not later than 4.00 p.m.) of the Wednesday, eight days
> ahead of the Thursday Cabinet, at which the memoranda is to be discussed.[271]

However, just as Ministers were issued with tighter instructions on Cabinet
procedure, Margaret Thatcher began to change her style. After victory in the
Falklands War, her personal popularity had risen,[272] and the General Election
had produced a landslide majority for the Conservatives of 144 seats. Mrs
Thatcher gained the confidence to assert her authority in Cabinet and conduct business her own way. She reshuffled her Cabinet and moved Nigel
Lawson, Geoffrey Howe and Leon Brittan, who were all 'convinced supporters
of [her] new brand of conservatism'[273], to the three main offices of state: Chancellor of the Exchequer, Foreign Secretary and Home Secretary — to bolster
support for her policies in Cabinet. As time went on, she chose to conduct
more business through small ad hoc groups or by striking bilateral deals with
Ministers. Jim Prior has stated that 'the formal Cabinet committees were very
much down-graded' and that her small groups were 'dominated by her cro-
nies'.[274] When Michael Heseltine was Secretary of State for the Environment,
his policy proposal for investment in decaying inner-city areas following the
inner-city riots of July 1981 was effectively blocked by the Prime Minister in
an ad hoc group stacked against him.[275] Nigel Lawson recounts a similar experience as Chancellor of the Exchequer, when he attempted to place the issue
of joining the ERM on the Cabinet agenda. Mrs Thatcher, who was opposed
to the idea, set up an ad hoc group to discuss the question. Lawson recalls that
as the meeting was outside the formal Cabinet system, it had no constitutional
significance; therefore, 'even though an overwhelming majority came out in
favour of joining the ERM at that time in November 1985, no decision to do
so was taken'.[276]

The Prime Minister's methods clearly contradicted the written guidance in
QPM, which each Minister received on appointment to office. Paragraph 3 of

the document, which first appeared in Attlee's 1946 edition of *QPM*,[277] made it clear that:

> Cabinet and Cabinet Committee business consists, in the main of:
> (i) Questions which significantly engage the collective responsibility of the Government, because they raise major issues of policy or because they are likely to occasion public comment or criticism.
> (ii) Questions on which there is an unresolved argument between Departments.

However, her ministerial colleagues did not initially object to her increasingly unorthodox style. Many recall in their diaries and memoirs, that her style was 'highly convenient' in the short term. Jim Prior has written of the 'obvious advantages for those few on the "inside track", who came to regard meetings with other colleagues as increasingly unnecessary and time-wasting.'[278] Nigel Lawson's account notes that, 'Most of the time it [was] comforting for them to feel that all they need[ed] to do [was] strike a deal with the Prime Minister and not have to bother overmuch about persuading other colleagues'.[279] It was only later, when some Ministers became aggrieved that their own policy proposals were repeatedly blocked, or that their advice was continually undermined by Thatcher's entourage of personal advisers (as Lawson was by Sir Alan Walters) that criticism grew. Michael Heseltine, Nigel Lawson and Geoffrey Howe all indicated in their resignation statements that Mrs Thatcher's style was a central factor which contributed to their decisions to resign. Her removal from office in 1990 and the appointment of John Major as her successor, marked an immediate return to the traditional procedures of decision-making.[280]

Although the rules regarding Cabinet and Cabinet committee business in *QPM* clashed with Thatcher's preferred methods of decision-making, guidance on other matters in the document very much accorded with her style. Nicholas Ridley has noted that, 'one quality which attracted her admiration was being good at "presentation". Those who got a consistently good press, or who excelled on television, found their futures assured.'[281] Thatcher was always concerned to ensure that the government's policies were communicated effectively, and indeed, no modern Prime Minister could afford to ignore the sections in *QPM* relating to media management and policy presentation. In contrast to Wilson's instructions, which focussed primarily on the need to consult Number 10 before making speeches or announcements, Ministers were offered very practical guidance under Thatcher, on tactics for securing the most effective presentation of their policy decisions. For example, the 1983 edition of *QPM* informed colleagues that, 'it is often the practice of Ministers to give separate radio and television interviews after [a press conference] in order to secure the most effective presentation of their views or announcement.'[282] Lengthy advice on broadcasting was also inserted during this update.

As regards invitations to broadcast, Ministers were instructed that they 'should as a rule respond positively, subject to their being satisfied that they will be given an adequate opportunity to explain Government policies and measures. In the interests of effective coordination of the presentation of Government policies, Ministers should ensure that the Number 10 Press Office is informed of their intentions. This will enable them to use broadcasting opportunities to best advantage and to avoid duplication with colleagues. The Chief Press Secretary at Number 10 is available to advise and help Ministers in securing their objective of propounding Government policies.'[283] Mrs Thatcher was also concerned, as a former senior official recalls, 'to be consulted and to have things cleared with her in advance',[284] and Wilson's rulings regarding prior consultation with Number 10 were left intact.

Whilst Ministers were, on the one hand, being encouraged to use every possible means of presenting policies to Parliament and the public, they were also reminded, in a new paragraph inserted in 1987, not to use official facilities for publicity and advertising which was 'essentially party political'.[285] The codification of this long-standing convention did not arise through a particular incidence of ministerial misconduct (although Ministers were also accused of breaching the convention),[286] but was instead the result of the Greater London Council's propaganda campaign to save itself when faced with abolition. The GLC claimed that they had acted quite legally under section 142 of the Local Government Act 1972 which permitted local authorities to spend money on advertising jobs and for general publicity. However, as the Under-Secretary for Environment, Sir George Young, pointed out when answering a parliamentary question, the Act itself had been 'drafted at a time when there was a general observation by councillors of all parties that funds [were] not to be used for blatant party propaganda'.[287] The controversy led to a pledge from the Environment Secretary, Patrick Jenkin, to prevent local authorities from using ratepayers' money for party political propaganda and to the establish a committee of enquiry into the conduct of local authority business.[288] The Cabinet Office submitted a memorandum to that committee, clarifying the conventions in central government, which was circulated to all departments and referred to in QPM.[289]

Thatcher had a strong sense of moral values from her upbringing and expected a high standard of conduct in public life from all of her colleagues. As a senior official who served under her observed, 'she knew what the rules [relating to private interests] were and expected them to be followed rigorously by her

Ministers'.[290] These rules were tightened up during the 1983 update and again in 1987, as a result of the recent insurance losses and internal scandals at Lloyd's of London (and the potential for application for judicial review on the grounds of bias due to a pecuniary interest — which I shall discuss in detail later on), of which many Conservative MPs and Ministers were 'names'.

The reputation of Lloyd's was greatly damaged by a string of business scandals that arose during the late 1970s and early 1980s.[291] Following the Sasse affair in 1978, more scandals erupted in 1982 as two managing agencies, Christopher Moran and Alexander Howden, were charged with discreditable conduct and a third agency, Posgate & Denby, were found to have accepted unauthorised 'stop loss' policies.[292] The lack of regulation of the insurance markets was criticised in the media and in Parliament, and several calls for external supervision of Lloyd's were made. After the Fisher Report, commissioned by Lloyd's to enquire into the matter, the Lloyd's Act was passed in 1982 to improve the insurance market's powers of self-regulation. The Act contained clauses which aimed to prevent conflicts of interest arising within the market by requiring Lloyd's brokers to divest, within five years, their interests in managing agents, and by further requiring managing agents to sell-off their interests in members' agents, which introduce new 'names'.[293]

As a result, *QPM* was also tightened up to prevent a more serious potential conflict of interest arising for Ministers. The new guidance instructed that the Prime Minister, Chancellor of the Exchequer, Secretary of State for Trade and Industry, Ministers in the Treasury dealing with taxation and Ministers in the DTI dealing with insurance, were prohibited from becoming members of Lloyd's, and those who were already members were to suspend underwriting for the duration of that office.[294] All other Ministers who were members of Lloyd's were urged to withdraw from active participation. They were further advised that they would be required to suspend underwriting selective risks if they those risks were in areas of business over which their department had responsibility.[295] Ministers could only continue with a connection with Lloyd's whilst in office, if they obtained the Prime Minister's permission to do so,[296] and an internal register of Ministers who were members of Lloyd's was to be kept by the Cabinet Secretary.[297] After further Lloyd's scandals in the mid-1980s, which culminated in the PCW affair, the Government intervened by establishing a committee, chaired by Sir Patrick Neill QC, to recommend further regulatory reforms.[298] During the next update of *QPM* in 1987, the guidance for Ministers was substantially tightened up once again to prevent any potential conflict of interest, or even a hint of one, from arising.[299]

Although not related to Lloyd's of London, there was a suspicion that the Prime Minister herself had breached the rules of conduct in January 1984, by failing to declare a conflict of interest between her son's business interests and her public functions. In March 1981, during her official visit to the Gulf, the Prime Minister had made strenuous efforts to secure contracts for Britain as part of her 'battling for Britain' campaign. As a result of her lobbying, a contract for £300m to build a university in Oman was awarded to Cementation Ltd. However, it was later revealed that her son, Mark Thatcher, had been in Oman at the same time acting on behalf of Cementation Ltd, the only British company that was seeking the contract.[300] Mrs Thatcher refused to answer questions in Parliament on whether she knew of her son's commercial interests at the time, stating that it was not relevant to the Oman contract.[301] This attracted heavy criticism, including public criticism from the former Prime Minister, Edward Heath.[302] When the Conservative-dominated Select Committee on Members' Interests declined to investigate the allegations, 20 Labour MPs withdrew from the *Register of Members' Interests* in protest.[303] The allegations were finally published as a minority report by Dale Campbell-Savours (Labour MP for Workington), a member of the select committee on Members' Interests,[304] but no further action was taken. *QPM* had been amended in 1979 to include instructions on gifts given to family members,[305] but did not expressly mention conflicts of interests arising out of family interests until 1987,[306] after a review of the possible grounds for legal challenge of government action had been conducted. Unsurprisingly, the document was not revised as a direct result of the allegations against the Prime Minister.

QPM was revised in the light of particular events which had caused embarrassment to the Government though. For example, the Westland Affair[307] led to the codification of the long-standing rule that the advice of the law officers 'must not be disclosed outside the Government without their authority'.[308] This amendment was triggered by the political damage caused by the leaking of part of the Solicitor-General's letter to Michael Heseltine (then Secretary of State for Defence) by Colette Bowe, Director of Information at the Department of Trade and Industry. Extracts of the confidential letter were sent to the Press Association on 6 January 1986, with the approval of the Ministerial head of department, Leon Brittan. The leak became particularly embarrassing when it was revealed that it was done with the knowledge, if not express approval, of both the Prime Minister's Private Office and Press Office. Following pressure from Parliament and a critical report from the Select Committee on Defence, the rule regarding the confidentiality of the law officers' advice was restated in the Government's response to the committee's report.[309]

The events leading to the prosecution of Clive Ponting, an assistant secretary at the MOD, under Section 2 of the Official Secrets Act 1911, caused considerable political embarrassment which damaged Thatcher's high reputation after achieving a British victory in the war over the Falkland Islands. However, the affair also led to the incorporation of two of the most constitutionally significant paragraphs in *QPM* — one expressing the convention of individual ministerial responsibility and the other outlining the proper relationship between Ministers and senior civil servants.

The affair began in May 1982 during the Falklands crisis, shortly after the British Task Force attacked the *General Belgrano*, a former US 1930s cruiser which formed part of the Argentinian surface fleet, even though it was outside the Exclusion Zone. The Leader of the Opposition, then Michael Foot, raised a question in Parliament on the circumstances which led to sinking the ship.[310] The issue was taken up by Tam Dalyell (then Labour MP for West Lothian)[311] who launched a personal campaign lasting two years, to discover the truth. The pressure of repeated enquiries sparked an internal investigation under Michael Heseltine, the Defence Secretary, who assigned the task of gathering highly sensitive information to Clive Ponting. Having conducted a full investigation into the facts, Ponting was then asked to draft replies to parliamentary questions on the subject. Ponting favoured open and frank replies, and drafted a very full answer to a PQ from Denzil Davies (Labour MP for Llanelli). After intervention from the junior Minister, John Stanley, Heseltine persisted in refusing to reply to any of Tam Dalyell's detailed questions, which Dalyell regarded as a breach of his individual ministerial responsibility. According to Ponting, John Stanley had argued all along that the department should have claimed that all the information was classified and could not be released.[312] Heseltine attempted to justify his position with the following statement, which was given in evidence to the Foreign Affairs Committee in November 1984:

> It was apparent to me that if we were to move down the route of following the detailed analysis which was being requested of the Ministry in questions to me, we would end up with yet more requests for yet more information ... it was quite apparent to me that the more information that we provided the more it would fuel yet more demands for yet more information.[313]

Clive Ponting felt unable to support the deliberate misleading of Parliament, and sent two documents to Tam Dalyell, which were passed on to the Foreign Affairs Committee who were conducting an investigation into the issue.[314] As a result, he was prosecuted by the Government, but acquitted by the jury who accepted his 'whistle-blower' defence. The outcome of the trial concerned the

Government, as it upset the traditional understandings of the role of the Civil Service. A memorandum on the responsibilities of civil servants in relation to their Ministers was therefore drafted by Sir Robert Armstrong (the Cabinet Secretary and Head of the Home Civil Service) to clarify the issue, and circulated in *Hansard*.[315] Far from settling the matter, the Armstrong Memorandum (as it became known) sparked further controversy and led to a critical report from the Treasury and Civil Service Committee (TCSC),[316] which forced the Government to reappraise their understandings of the constitutional position of civil servants, as set out by Armstrong.[317] The Memorandum was revised in 1987 to reflect the new position after lengthy debate, and the 1987 edition of *QPM* asked Ministers to read the Government's responses to the various select committee reports on the matter.[318] Extracts from the revised Armstrong memorandum and the Government's response to the TCSC were incorporated into *QPM* during the 1991 update.[319]

A further, very significant outcome, was achieved by the TCSC many years later. Following another inquiry into the role of the Civil Service, conducted by the TCSC in 1994, the Government accepted a proposal recommended by the select committee, for a new Civil Service Code. The Government indicated, in its response to the select committee, that the new Code would 'apply to all civil servants, summarising the constitutional framework within which they work and the values they are expected to hold'. In addition, the Code would incorporate 'a new, independent line of appeal to the Civil Service Commissioner in cases of alleged breaches of the Code or issues of conscience which cannot be resolved through internal procedures'.[320]

Ministers also found themselves increasingly embarrassed by defeats in the courts, which necessitated the drafting of an internal guidance document on judicial review for senior officials and the inclusion of tips for Ministers in *QPM*. The judiciary had become increasingly active in the field of administrative law both during and since the Wilson administrations, and by the 1980s the Government was being bombarded with challenges. Applications for leave to apply for judicial review against central government were increasing steadily,[321] yet the majority of senior civil servants and Ministers lacked a knowledge of basic legal principles and often found themselves unprepared for challenges when they arose. The Treasury Solicitor, Sir Michael Kerry, publicly admitted in the early eighties that the situation was becoming problematic. In an article published in 1983, he wrote, 'The Crown has lost too many cases in the courts recently ... New cases are continuously coming to the attention of myself and my colleagues in which senior administrators show a surprising ignorance of elementary legal principles. Furthermore, a number of recent cases in the public eye have shown a lack of appreciation of the impact of legal consideration on administrative problems involving either considerable financial loss or embarrassment to Ministers'.[322]

In 1982, for example, the Secretary of State for the Environment, then Michael Heseltine, refused to hear representations from local authorities before imposing rate-capping. Brent London Borough Council and others successfully challenged that refusal in the courts,[323] compelling Heseltine to consult and re-make his decision. In his article, Sir Michael Kerry wrote that, 'the Department did not take into account the possible legal implications of refusing to hear representations while the decision taking process was in train.' The Secretary of State for Social Services, Norman Fowler, was similarly publicly embarrassed when forced to delay and then revise the implementation of his department's policy on entitlement to board and lodging payments to welfare claimants in 1985 as a result of a challenge through the courts.[324] The aim of the policy was to prevent so-called 'holidays on the dole', and was introduced as part of the Government's commitment to reducing public expenditure on social welfare. However, it was held, by both the Divisional Court[325] and the Court of Appeal,[326] that the Secretary of State had acted *ultra vires*. Even Margaret Thatcher was faced with a legal challenge, when she decided in 1984 (in her capacity as Minister for the Civil Service) to ban Trade Unions at G.C.H.Q, without first consulting the Civil Service unions. The case went to the House of Lords,[327] and although the Government won on the grounds that national security issues were non-justiciable, the Law Lords stated that the exercise of the Royal Prerogative (previously immune from review) was open to review by the courts if justiciable.[328] This judgement increased the possibility of yet more applications for review against central government departments in the future.

Sir Michael Kerry's article sparked an internal study into the number of successful legal challenges against the government and possible ways to prevent further government defeats in the courts.[329] A pamphlet was produced by the Cabinet Office for circulation throughout departments in March 1987, entitled *The Judge Over Your Shoulder,* which offered practical tips for senior officials to avoid legal challenge of government decisions and actions.[330] The 1987 edition of *QPM* was also revised to include instructions to Ministers, reminding them of the need to consider possible applications for judicial review when taking decisions, and to consult the Law Officers accordingly.[331] A new ruling was also inserted requiring Ministers to 'cover any issues on which departments have been advised that there may be a risk of challenge in the courts by means of application for judicial review' in their memoranda before submitting it for Cabinet or Cabinet committee.[332]

In order to prevent legal challenges arising out of the knowledge or suspicion of a Minister having a pecuniary interest in an issue on which he has made a decision, Ministers were also reminded, in a new paragraph, that a direct pecuniary interest could render that decision void in the courts. This guidance was inserted into the section entitled 'Ministers' Private Interests', and gave Ministers a brief summary of the position in law. Ministers were warned that in such situations they may be required to 'give up a particular holding of shares (but a disposal in advance of an unfavourable decision would be very dangerous); or preferably to delegate to another Minister to whom no such apparent conflict of interest could apply'. Delegation of a decision was also advised 'in cases of exercise of non-statutory powers (e.g. placing a contract) or other influence where the risk of conflict of interest exist or might reasonably appear to exist'. If the Minister decided, nevertheless, to exercise the non-statutory power himself, 'he should first consult the Legal Advisers in his Department in cases where the exercise of those powers have a direct effect on the rights and duties of citizens'.[333]

The majority of the revisions made to *QPM* during Thatcher's premiership indicate that the document, although elevated in status, continued to function primarily as an internal compendium of practical guidance for Ministers, rather than as a formal code or surrogate constitution. Although important and long-standing conventions and practices were being codified in *QPM*, it was usually in response to ad hoc incidents which had caused great political embarrassment, in order to avoid a repeat. However, regardless of the motivation behind the new instructions inserted into *QPM* during the 1980s, the end result was that *QPM* was gradually being transformed into a much stricter and more precise formal rulebook which Ministers were increasingly expected to abide by. The rules of conduct for Ministers had been significantly expanded and tightened up, and important guidance had been included on the law relating to pecuniary interests in administrative decision-making. Two key constitutional conventions, governing individual ministerial responsibility and the proper relationship between Ministers and civil servants, had also been codified for permanent reference. In contrast to the instructions relating to the presentation of policy, the rules of conduct, administrative law and constitutional conventions were not just 'practical guidance' — they were important rules relating to public office with which Ministers were obliged to comply if they wished to continue in office. As a confidential document, *QPM* was only intended to guide and support Ministers, and was enforced at the Prime Minister's discretion. However, publication of the document was to give it a very important new function, creating the very first official public yardstick of ministerial conduct and the operation of cabinet government.

Chapter Six
JOHN MAJOR GOES PUBLIC

John Major has been given far too little credit for what he has done to shed light on the working parts of government. This ... is partly because of the unglamorous nature of the important constitutional documents which he has — for the first time — made public.

Sarah Hogg [334]

The results of the Conservative Party leadership election in November 1990 were slightly surprising, to say the least. A new Prime Minister emerged, underwhelming in character (at least in public), only forty-seven years of age, who had not spent long in office and whom the majority of the general public had heard little about.[335] As a journalist remarked on the day of his appointment, 'even a few months ago most people would have been hard pushed to name Mr Major as the Chancellor of the Exchequer'.[336] John Major was elected the new leader of the Conservative Party after gaining 185 votes against Michael Heseltine's 131, and Douglas Hurd's 56.[337] Although he was two votes short of the required majority, Heseltine and Hurd withdrew in favour of him when the results were announced. His first comment to his colleagues when they convened for Cabinet echoed the general surprise, 'Who would have believed it?'[338]

With the appointment of John Major, there was an immediate change in the style and conduct of business at Cabinet level, which Ministers noticed from the moment they sat round the Cabinet table for their first meeting.[339] Chris Patten remarked that, 'We got the summing up at the end of Cabinet, rather than at the beginning';[340] another colleague added that, 'when he sums up, he does so making people feel that they have been consulted.'[341] Senior officials also noted and welcomed the change. Within Major's first month, one remarked with 'a huge grin' that, 'Discussion is allowed; argument even'.[342] Sir Charles Powell, who had been close to Margaret Thatcher as her Foreign Affairs Private Secretary and continued to serve under Major,[343] explained why senior officials warmed to his style. 'John Major is more disposed to listen to his Cabinet colleagues than Mrs Thatcher was ... [Her] idea of chairing a meeting was to sit down, announce what the conclusions were going to be and challenge anyone to fight her. John Major is quite different, he's a natural chairman. He likes to hear points of view and then he will draw his conclusions. That's why, on the whole, officials love him because he chairs an orderly meeting and you can write the minutes quite simply. I used to have to invent the minutes of Mrs Thatcher's meetings because otherwise government couldn't have got on.'[344]

John Major not only returned to the spirit of *QPM* by restoring a sense of collegiality in Cabinet, he also abided by the letter of the document. The traditional procedures for Cabinet decision-making and conducting government business within the formal Cabinet committee system were strictly followed and even the use of ad hoc ministerial committees declined. Lord Wakeham (then Lord Privy Seal) confirmed, in a lecture delivered at Brunel University in 1993, that 'the move towards the use of the use of *ad hoc* groups...appears to have been halted except perhaps as a means of ensuring the speedy resolution of problems that emerge, for example between two Ministers with different responsibilities in a particular subject area. Indeed my impression is that the balance has shifted back towards greater reliance on Standing Committees'.[345]

QPM was updated and reissued by the Cabinet Office, on behalf of Mr Major, within two months of his appointment — a process which had become standard drill by this stage. The change of Prime Minister provided an early opportunity for the Cabinet Office to revise the document in the light of issues that had arisen since the last update in 1987. However, some of the amendments made during this redraft suggest that this was also an opportunity to reassert certain conventional practices that had lapsed under Thatcher's premiership. For example, there had been a growing tendency during the 1980s for Ministers to put forward their policy proposals by way of a personal minute to the Prime Minister, rather than submitting a memorandum for the Cabinet. This practice was encouraged by the Prime Minister herself, who would often 'ask a particular Cabinet colleague to prepare a paper on a particular issue just for her, not for the Cabinet'.[346] In order to encourage a return to the normal practice of submitting memoranda for collective consideration, the 1991 edition of *QPM* informed Ministers that, 'proposals for consideration in Cabinet or a Cabinet Committee should normally be circulated as a Committee paper.' However, it was added that, 'If for any reason they are circulated as minutes addressed to the Prime Minister, they are subject to the same requirements as circulated papers.'[347]

Sarah Hogg and Jonathan Hill,[348] policy and political advisers to John Major respectively, wrote that 'in Chris Patten's view, the most difficult aspect of John Major's legacy from Margaret Thatcher was her particular style of leadership. The system ... had got used to being driven at breakneck speed, with no regard for holes in the road, or even corners.'[349] Formal procedures for ensuring collective consideration of major decisions were increasingly ignored and the formal Cabinet system was often by-passed at the crucial stages of decision-making.[350] Hogg and Hill hint at Major's concern to restore collective procedures in their account of his premiership, *Too Close to Call,* by stating that, 'the bits of procedure which require Ministers to put their policy proposals to Cabinet committees for clearance are amongst the most important.'[351]

The guidance on publishing White and Green Papers was also redrafted in 1991 to place a greater emphasis on the need for collective consideration of policy proposals before publication. Ministers were instructed to, 'consider whether [the White or Green Paper] raises issues which require full collective ministerial consideration, and, after consulting the Cabinet Office as necessary, seek clearance through the appropriate Cabinet Committee.' They were further warned that, 'any Command Paper containing a major statement of Government policy should be circulated to the Cabinet before publication ... even when no issue requiring collective consideration is required.'[352]

Several new paragraphs appeared in the 1991 edition as a result of issues which had arisen during Thatcher's last term, and which had been noted and filed away for inclusion in the next update of *QPM.* The rules regarding private investments were tightened up further after embarrassing allegations had arisen in the late 1980s of impropriety in the financial affairs of certain Ministers. Cecil Parkinson caused a stir regarding his private financial dealings in November 1989, when City rumours fuelled media speculation that Parkinson, then Secretary of State for Transport, was involved in insider dealing. The affair led to the inclusion of guidance on a rather obvious point of law, as Ministers were reminded in a new paragraph that they were bound by the provisions of the Companies Securities (Insider Dealing) Act 1985 'in relation to the use or transmission of unpublished price sensitive information'.[353] The rumours surrounding Parkinson appear to have been sparked by the making of a documentary, commissioned by Channel 4, which investigated alleged City share irregularities, and which mentioned the Minister by name.[354] Before the programme was actually transmitted, an article about it appeared in *The Scotsman.*[355] Cecil Parkinson vigorously denied the rumours by issuing the following statement to the Press Association through his solicitors, Peter Carter-Ruck and Partners:

> In the light of rumours this morning, following a report in today's *Scotsman,* we are instructed on behalf of the Rt Hon Cecil Parkinson MP to state:
> 1. There is no foundation whatsoever for rumours that Mr Parkinson has been engaged in any insider dealing, nor in any share dealings of whatsoever nature.
> 2. On Mr Parkinson's appointment as a member of the Government, in accordance with established practices, his funds were transferred to his stockbrokers to deal

with his cash and any investments they might make on an entirely discretionary basis, in which he played on part whatsoever.

3. That the rumour that he might resign as Minister of Transport is totally without foundation.

4. In the event of a repetition of any of these baseless rumours, he will not hesitate to sue.[356]

The scandal quickly fizzled out when a statement was issued by Channel 4 the following day to stress that their programme in no way suggested that Cecil Parkinson was guilty of any illegal activities.[357] However, the seriousness of the wider allegations made in the programme led to further questions in the House of Commons regarding the extent of insider dealing generally.[358] Dale Campbell-Savours (Labour MP for Workington) asked the Prime Minister more specifically whether there were any safeguards covering Ministers (and former Ministers) and price-sensitive information, and whether any breaches had occurred in the period 1982–88.[359] In response, Mrs Thatcher stated that the rules for Ministers included, 'advice that Ministers should scrupulously avoid speculative investments in securities about which they have, or may be thought to have, early or confidential information likely to affect the price of those securities,' and that she was not aware of any breaches. These guidelines had existed through successive governments and were incorporated into *QPM* in 1958 under Harold Macmillan.[360] However, the Parkinson affair prompted the incorporation of a new paragraph clarifying the legal position, which was inserted alongside the well-established instructions to which the Prime Minister referred in her written answer.[361] This was not only to prevent further allegations causing embarrassment to the Government, it was also to avoid a repeat of the panic which was caused in the stock market.

The new guidance on investments emphasised that Ministers must not only avoid an actual conflict of interest, they should also avoid any *apparent* conflict. Unfounded allegations could be just as damaging as a truthful revelation of financial impropriety. Ministers were advised to review all of their investments upon assuming office and told that 'if it seems likely that any of them might give rise to an actual or apparent conflict of interest, they should be disposed of.'[362] It was added as a further precaution that, 'if Ministers have substantial investments covering a wide range of interests, such that it might be difficult to judge the likelihood of actual or apparent conflict of interest, they should consider, as an alternative to disposal, transferring the investments to a blind trust, i.e., a discretionary trust under which the Minister is not informed of changes in investments or of the current state of the portfolio.'[363] In order to safeguard any Minister who was subsequently the subject of allegations, Ministers were also asked to record 'whether or not they consider any action necessary and the nature of any action taken.'[364]

The tighter rules were drafted in an attempt to avoid, or at least minimise, 'sleaze' allegations in the vulnerable climate of mass privatisation and sophisticated lobbying. The media were always eager to detail the investments and directorships held by Ministers and MPs in the hope of unveiling a scandal. The investments of Cecil Parkinson for example, whilst he was Secretary of State for Transport, were deemed to be the 'most prolific' by *The Guardian*. The newspaper noted that they included Babcock International and Tarmac and Sears Holdings, which were involved in potential private motorway schemes that Mr Parkinson was in a position to award.[365] Parkinson did, however, follow the rules by placing all of his interests under the supervision of a firm of stockbrokers, when first appointed to the Government in 1979.[366]

Frequent media reports of former Ministers securing jobs with privatised firms, after they had been involved in the privatisation of that particular piece of the former public sector, led to allegations of 'privatisation sleaze'. Concern grew over the absence of rules covering former Ministers and business appointments, as a stream of Ministers secured City jobs shortly after leaving office.[367] Norman Tebbit was the first to arouse criticism when he secured an appointment as a non-executive director of British Telecom plc in 1987, after having been responsible for the privatisation of BT during his spell at the DTI. Sir Norman Fowler was then appointed a non-executive director of the National Freight Corporation, a privatised haulage group, after having encouraged the privatisation of NFC in 1982 as Secretary of State for Transport. Lord Walker followed the trail of ex-Ministers to the City when he secured directorships with British Gas plc, the merchant bank N. M. Rothschild and Smith New Court (a City securities house 30 per cent owned by Rothschild). The former Energy Secretary had been responsible for the privatisation of British Gas in 1986, which was handled by N. M. Rothschild. In June 1990 Lord Young stirred controversy when he was appointed an executive chairman of Cable and Wireless, only a year after serving as Secretary of State for Trade and Industry, with responsibility for telecommunications policy. It was reported that he was first mooted as the successor to Lord Sharp at Cable & Wireless when he left the DTI in July 1989, but the idea was postponed in order to avoid allegations of a conflict of interest.[368] Nigel Lawson, the former Chancellor of the Exchequer, also made headlines when he was appointed a non-executive director of Barclays Bank in 1990.

News of Lord Young's appointment to Cable & Wireless sparked fierce criticism from the Opposition spokesman for Trade and Industry, then Gordon

Brown, who demanded a full inquiry and called for former Ministers to be subject to rules similar to those applicable to former civil servants. Under the Civil Service rules, senior civil servants were required to seek approval from an advisory committee for their first job, and any others within two years of leaving the Civil Service, which could recommend a waiting period of up to two years. Permanent secretaries were additionally subject to an automatic waiting period of three months before taking outside employment.[369] David Winnick (Labour MP for Walsall North) introduced a Ten-Minute Rule Bill which sought to establish a five-year waiting period for Cabinet Ministers before they could take up appointments from companies they had helped to privatise.[370] Although Mrs Thatcher did not publicly submit to the pressure — defending the status quo by referring to Lord Wilson's statement as Prime Minister, that 'These matters are best left to the discretion and good sense of the individuals concerned'[371] — *QPM* was redrafted to contain guidance on the matter for Ministers. No formal rules were established, but Ministers were strongly advised that 'they should naturally avoid any course which would reflect adversely on their or the Government's reputation for integrity or the confidentiality of its proceedings'.[372]

In addition to further guidance on avoiding financial conflicts of interest, Ministers also received stricter instructions regarding conduct and statements that might conflict with Government policy. Collective responsibility has been increasingly insisted upon by successive post-war Prime Ministers as a necessary mechanism for the survival of government in a disciplined party system. However, previous guidelines for Ministers had only covered speeches, broadcasts and statements made in their ministerial capacity. By 1991, the guidelines had expanded their reach into Ministers' private lives. In 1979 a new paragraph was inserted to warn Ministers that association with pressure groups 'can give rise to misunderstanding about the Government's position'.[373] This was redrafted in 1991 to establish detailed restrictions on Ministers' private associations with non-public bodies. The new paragraph stated that, 'Ministers should take care to ensure that they do not become associated with non-public organisations whose objectives may in any degree conflict with Government policy and thus give rise to a conflict of interest.' They were advised not to accept invitations to act as patrons of pressure groups or other non-public organisations. Association with charities was deemed permissible, so long as Ministers ensured that, 'in participating in any fund-raising activity, they do not place themselves under obligation as Ministers to those to whom appeals are directed'.[374]

Conduct and statements made by Ministers in their capacity as a representative of a constituency was also further restricted by a detailed new paragraph on deputations. This paragraph expanded upon a general ruling, which had been in-corporated into *QPM* in 1969 under Harold Wilson, that 'Ministers should not take part in any public representations (or in deputations) to other Ministers; but they are free to make their views about constituency matters known to the re-sponsible Minister by correspondence or by personal interview, provided that this is not given publicity'.[375] The new paragraph, inserted in 1991, expressed concern over the particular problems which arose over 'views expressed on plan-ning applications and certain other cases involving exercise of discretion by Min-isters (e.g. on school and hospital closures, highway or power station enquiries) in which representations intended to be taken into account in reaching a deci-sion may have to be made available to other parties and thus may well receive publicity'. In order to avoid any embarrassment, Ministers were asked to 'confine themselves in such cases to representing the views of constituents rather than ex-pressing a view themselves' and when it was unavoidable to express a view they were advised to 'eschew criticism of Government policy' and 'make sure that the views they are putting forward are ones expressed in their capacity as constitu-ency MPs. Finally, Ministers were warned that, 'once a decision has been an-nounced, it should be accepted without question or criticism'.[376]

A new list of considerations for Ministers to take into account when draft-ing a memorandum for the Cabinet also appeared in the 1991 redraft of *QPM*. Ministers were instructed that, in addition to the existing requirements (such as including an indication of costs, manpower requirements or accommoda-tion problems in any policy proposal) 'Papers should where appropriate, [also] cover the impact on business and the impact of the European Convention on Human Rights. Proposals with value-for-money implications should state what is to be achieved, by when and at what cost. Papers should also cover presentational aspects and, where appropriate, a draft announcement or state-ment should be attached.'[377]

These new requirements highlight the growing complexity of Cabinet busi-ness, which has necessarily led to modern Cabinets adopting the function of a body of approval and review rather than decision-taker. As Lord Wakeham com-mented in his Brunel lecture, 'The increasing use of Cabinet as a reporting and reviewing body rather than a decision-taker is … an irreversible consequence of the complexity of modern government'.[378] Proposals could only be approved by the full Cabinet after the details had been finalised and all possible implications had been fully examined. If a memorandum did not contain all the necessary in-formation, time would be wasted by having to refer the matter back to the origi-nating department, or to a committee of the Cabinet, for further consideration.

The need to consider the European Convention on Human Rights *before* implementing a policy proposal, illustrated the growing pressure on the UK government from both the domestic courts and the European Court on Human Rights, to comply with their obligations under the Convention. The preamble to the Single European Act (signed by the 12 Member States in 1986) also emphasised the importance of adhering to the ECHR by expressing the common objective, 'to work together to promote democracy on the basis of the fundamental rights recognised in the Convention'. Although the UK had not incorporated the Convention into domestic law, the English judiciary were increasingly willing to construe legislation in accordance with the ECHR,[379] and the frequency of defeats before the European Court on Human Rights,[380] which were heavily reported in the media, could cause extreme political embarrassment. Since the Single European Act came into force, the European Court of Justice has also been more willing to apply the Convention to Community law.[381]

In 1987 the Cabinet Office produced a circular entitled *Reducing the Risk of Legal Challenge,* which highlighted the need to consider the impact of the ECHR when preparing legislation or formulating policy proposals. The guidance stated that 'the Government is obliged to give effect to judgements of the European Court of Human Rights and decisions of the Committee of Ministers concerning violations by the United Kingdom. Important changes in law and practice have been required as a result'. It also noted that 'a consistently high level of applications and decisions concern the UK'. Senior officials were therefore advised that 'any memoranda submitted to a Cabinet committee, or accompanying a Bill submitted to the Legislation Committee, should include an assessment of the impact, if any, of the European Convention on Human Rights on the action proposed'.[382] This was one of many internal circulars (including *The Judge OverYour Shoulder*) which had resulted from the general review, conducted in the early 1980s, into the level of litigation being brought against the Government.[383] The guidance on preventing legal challenges by way of an application for judicial review was immediately incorporated into the 1987 edition of *QPM* — however, it was not considered necessary, at that time, to also include the guidance relating to the ECHR.

One notable case which caused particular embarrassment for the UK government in the late 1980s was the *Spycatcher* lawsuit, which concerned the publication of Peter Wright's book, based upon his experiences as an MI5 officer. The lengthy and complicated litigation which arose during the *Spycatcher* affair, culminated in an embarrassing defeat for the Government. The European Court ruled that when the UK upheld the injunctions against *The Guardian* and *The*

Observer,[384] they breached Article 10 which guarantees freedom of expression and information. The court stated that once the book by Peter Wright, *Spycatcher,* had been published in the United States in July 1987, it could no longer be described as 'secret'.[385] The ruling was not only embarrassing for the Government, it also had serious implications for a key section of the Official Secrets Act 1989, which bound former members of the security and intelligence services by an absolute duty of confidentiality.[386] The Official Secrets legislation had been amended in 1989 in the light of the *Spycatcher* affair to allow no exceptions to the duty of confidentiality and to make it an offence to publish protected information, even if it had already been disclosed without permission.[387] Following the European Court judgement, it seemed that editors and journalists could publish confidential information obtained from former intelligence staff, if the information had already been made public abroad.

Just a month after the 1991 version of *QPM* was issued, the House of Lords reaffirmed, in case of *R. v. Home Secretary, ex parte Brind,*[388] the accepted principle that the Convention should be taken into account where domestic legislation is ambiguous. However, they also determined that 'where Parliament had conferred on the executive an administrative discretion without indicating its precise limits, to presume that it must be exercised within the Convention limits would be to go far beyond the resolution of ambiguity'.[389] In other words, the Law Lords were refusing to apply the Convention to the exercise of an administrative discretion by a Minister, on the grounds that discretionary powers were unambiguous. Following this decision, Lord Lester of Herne Hill QC began lobbying the Government, to secure an official statement which expressed the duty on officials to comply with the Convention when discharging their public functions.[390] Although the initial replies to his questions were 'circumspect, [and] carefully worded to avoid any suggestion that they might be liable in domestic law for a failure to comply'[391] with the ECHR, the Government finally expressed a duty on civil servants to comply with the Convention in the new Civil Service Code, which came into force on 1 January 1996.[392] The Government further stated that *QPM* would be brought into line with the Code when it was next revised,[393] and that "It is expected that Ministers and Civil Servants will comply" with the guidelines in these documents.[394] The new version of *QPM,* entitled *Ministerial Code,* issued by Tony Blair in July 1997, now states that Ministers have a duty 'to comply with the law, including international law and treaty obligations, and to uphold the administration of justice'.[395]

It is interesting that the guidance relating to Ministers' constitutional obligation of accountability and their proper relationship with civil servants, which resulted from the Ponting affair, was not actually incorporated into the text of the document until 1991. Thatcher's revised *QPM* in 1987 merely referred Ministers, in her covering letter, to the Government's response to the various select committee reports which investigated the issues. The reason for this delay is not clear, and we are not likely to find out until the public records for that year are released. However, there are several possible explanations. It may have been the case that the Cabinet Office was not, at that time, convinced that such guidance needed to be codified for permanent reference — or there may have been reluctance to reduce such important obligations to a few written paragraphs. On the other hand, Mrs Thatcher may have personally opposed the incorporation of formal guidance on these points. Whatever the explanation, the important point is that the formal incorporation of these key conventions in *QPM* marked the beginning of a new phase in the document's history. Since 1991, guidance on important unwritten parts of the British Constitution relating to Ministers and the conduct of central government, have been inserted into *QPM*. These changes, coupled with publication of the document, have significantly transformed the functions of *QPM* in the British political system. Previously it had been no more than an internal guidance document, but since May 1992, *QPM* has become a public set of rules and standards by which Ministers can be judged.

John Major's decision to redraft and publish *Questions of Procedure for Ministers* in 1992, along with a published list of ministerial Cabinet committees, was a significant step towards a more open and transparent system of government. As Sir Robin Butler has publicly acknowledged, the 'prime mover' behind this decision was Professor Peter Hennessy, who lobbied the Conservative Government for the release of this information for many years.[396] Undeterred by Mrs Thatcher's consistent refusals to release the document, Professor Hennessy sent a copy of Australia's equivalent to *Questions of Procedure for Ministers,* entitled *Cabinet Handbook* (first published in 1983) to Mr Major in October 1991, in the hope that the new Prime Minister would follow the Australian practice. He also enclosed a copy of the annual report of the Department of the Prime Minister and the Cabinet in Canberra, which listed the membership of ministerial committees, the number of Cabinet papers discussed and the number of meetings held. In his covering letter, Professor Hennessy wrote, 'Recalling your commitment to openness in the Citizen's Charter, it occurred to me that, while the Cabinet Office and the Cabinet itself cannot be expected to create performance indicators for themselves in the manner of a public service or utility, a measure of disclosure about their working methods would sit well with the spirit of the charter.'[397] He received an encouraging reply from the Principal Private Secretary at Number

10, Andrew Turnbull, which stated, 'The Prime Minister was interested in the degree of publication by the Australian Government'.[398] In 1992 John Major made a firm commitment to publish both *QPM* and the composition of ministerial committees of the Cabinet by pledging to do so in the Conservative Party Manifesto, *The Best Future for Britain*.[399]

Before the decision to publish was announced, John Major put the matter to Cabinet for collective consideration. He was anxious to gain a consensus of approval before taking action, because once the document was published, it would be impossible to reverse that decision. A senior official serving at the time stated that 'he felt he had to consult them ... it was a collective government act'.[400] The Cabinet meeting itself was historic though, as this was the first occasion that any post-war Prime Minister has placed *Questions of Procedure for Ministers* on the Cabinet agenda. Ever since 1945, when Clement Attlee incorporated a consolidated version of his directives into the text, *QPM* has been regarded as a prime ministerial document, despite the fact that it has continued to be circulated as a Cabinet paper. John Major did not go as far as asking the Cabinet to approve the text of the document, however, as that very much remained the Prime Minister's prerogative. Consultation only took place to approve publication, and approval did not come easily. A senior official has commented that there was a lot of discussion before the collective decision was reached and that 'there were Ministers who thought it very unwise to publish'.[401]

QPM was also extensively restructured and redrafted in preparation for publication. Ironically, the document which provided guidance for Ministers on policy presentation and media management, had now itself become a major presentational issue for the Government. However, it is a testament to the stability of *QPM* that the majority of the changes made were largely cosmetic and did not fundamentally transform the nature of the document. The most striking difference between the published version of the document and its predecessor, was the improved and more 'user-friendly' structure. The text was completely reorganised to create clear and coherent sections, each covering different aspects of a Minister's job, for example 'Ministers and Cabinet Procedures' and 'Ministers and their Departments' etc.

Whilst the actual contents of the guidance were left intact (with the notable exception of the removal of the section relating to internal security), textual amendments were made in order to project a more positive image to the public. For example, the paragraph on collective responsibility was rewritten to offer more publicly acceptable reasons for the need for confidentiality of internal proceedings. Whereas the 1991 edition had suggested that disclosure could be 'embarrassing',[402] the new version justified the principle of confidentiality on the basis of 'national interest', the need to protect the 'privacy of opinions' and the 'security of Government documents' — political embarrassment was not mentioned.[403]

Notes on party political tactics were removed to give the document a more neutral and formal appearance. For example, a sentence relating to statements in Parliament was redrafted to remove the words 'advantageous presentationally', from the sentence 'where early release is sometimes advantageous presentationally', with the more straightforward word of 'required'.[404] The notes on the advantages of 'off-the-record' lobby briefings were also removed, although this, to some extent, reflected John Major's more open approach to lobby briefings. His Press Secretary, Gus O'Donnell, indicated in October 1991 that information from Number 10 could be attributed more precisely as 'Downing Street sources'.[405] During Mrs Thatcher's premiership, lobby briefings, held by her Press Secretary, Bernard Ingham, were wholly unattributable, or vaguely attributed to 'government sources'. *The Guardian* and *The Independent* had boycotted the Lobby system in protest, but rejoined in 1991 when attribution to Number 10 was permitted.[406]

As well as removing undesirable words and phrases, the document was also reviewed for any significant 'gaps' in the text. For example, mention of the Liberal Democrats had previously been omitted from the section dealing with arrangements for party political broadcasts[407] and the paragraph on accountability had failed to specifically mention select committees.[408] Further additions included more detailed discussion of the need to observe equal opportunities laws when making public appointments.[409] Overall, the language used in the redrafted version was much more formal, giving the text the appearance of official guidelines, rather than useful guidance. However, the drafters seem to have been careful not to vest the document with the appearance of a prescriptive code. A new introductory paragraph was written to replace the traditional covering letter from the Prime Minister, which would provide new colleagues with a brief overview of its nature and contents. The new paragraph contained a key clause effectively giving Ministers a 'get-out-of-jail-free card' (as a former student of Professor Hennessy's once put it)[410] by stating that, 'It will be for individual Ministers to judge how best to act in order to uphold the highest standards'.[411] As regards private interests, the new version read 'Ministers will want to order their affairs so that no conflict of interest arises'. The words 'will want' diluted the mandatory obligation of the previous edition which stated 'Ministers *must* order their affairs ...'[412]

However, once the document was published, the text was open to public criticism and substantial pressure was exerted on the Government by various groups, including high-profile committees of inquiry, to make specific changes to the text of *QPM*. Publication had unveiled to the electorate the long-established rules of procedure and conduct to which Ministers were expected to abide. Once these rules became transparent, external observers were not only able to scrutinise ministerial conduct more effectively, they were also able to scrutinise the internal rulebook itself. The whole process of revising and updating *QPM* was about to change quite dramatically.

Chapter Seven
NOLAN, SCOTT AND SLEAZE

[Sleaze] is the selfish use of public office for personal advantage. Sleaze is not necessarily financial and not necessarily illegal. Typically it involves bending the rules without breaking them. Sleaze is pernicious and degrading and has to be rooted out.

Lord Nolan [413]

The publication of *QPM* had immediate implications for the accountability of Ministers. One High Court judge has privately described *QPM* as a statement of the terms of ministerial office.[414] In many ways the public at large have treated it as such, by expecting either a valid explanation for the Minister's conduct, or a resignation, when the rules appear to have been breached. Those Ministers who had voiced objection in Cabinet to the publication of the document probably felt that their reservations should have been heeded. Journalists and MPs were quick to employ the published rulebook as a tool to scrutinise and judge the behaviour of individual Ministers, frequently 'hauling them up' for breaching the rulebook. A search of the *Justice Parliament* CD Rom has revealed that during the 1992–93 Parliamentary Session, 'procedure for Ministers' was mentioned by Members of Parliament 41 times.[415] This dropped to 15 mentions in the following session and dropped again in the 1994–95 session to 13 mentions, but in 1995–96 the statistic dramatically rose to 48 mentions as a result of the Nolan and Scott investigations. A search of *FT Profile* (UK News), an on-line database of all the national newspapers[416] and other news sources, shows that by the autumn of 1997, *QPM* had been quoted 334 times since 1st May 1992.[417] However, the most important consequence of publication was not the frequency with which *QPM* was publicly mentioned, but the context in which it was being referred to. *QPM* was being cited as an authoritative document which Ministers must abide by to the letter or resign — and allegations of failure to comply with *QPM* featured strongly in several of the ministerial resignations that were tendered during Major's final term.

Major's attempt to create an image of an open and honest Government appeared to backfire within just a few months, when the National Heritage Secretary, David Mellor, was accused of misconduct for accepting gifts and hospitality of significant value on two separate occasions.[418] The first allegation was not serious as it did not appear to involve a conflict of interest, but Mellor was nevertheless criticised after a revelation in the *Daily Mail* that he had accepted the loan of a chauffeur-driven Mercedes and the occasional use of a luxury Mayfair flat from Elliot Bernard, a property developer. Shortly after this story, it was revealed in court, during a libel case brought by Mona Bauwens against *The People,* that Mellor had also accepted free air-flights and a month's stay in Marbella for himself and his family from Mona Bauwens during the Gulf crisis. As she was the daughter of a prominent PLO member, their relationship stirred some public concern. The shadow Heritage Minister, Bryan Gould, was able to refer, in a letter to the Prime Minister, to paragraph 126 of the recently published *QPM*, to show that Mellor was clearly in breach of the rules of ministerial office. The paragraph laid down the rule that Ministers should not accept offers of gifts, hospitality or services which 'would, *or might appear to,* place him or her under an obligation'.[419] [My italics].

Despite the fact that the acceptance of the free family holiday at least 'appeared' to place Mellor under an obligation to Mrs Bauwens in view of her family connections, John Major defended his Heritage Secretary by stating, in his reply to Bryan Gould, that 'David Mellor took the view that the holiday which he and his family took with Mrs Bauwens at her expense was a purely personal matter which did not touch on his ministerial responsibility or place him under any obligation in respect of his ministerial duties.' This defence appears to be based upon the 'let out' clause in paragraph 127 of *QPM,* which allowed for individual interpretation of the gifts ruling by stating that it was 'primarily a matter which must be left to the good sense of Ministers'. However, many MPs journalists and academics alike were not prepared to accept a subjective application of such an important rule, and it was widely believed that Mellor had made a grave misjudgement. The highly respected historian of the Conservative Party, Lord Blake, told *The Times* that, 'If it becomes clear that David Mellor has breached those guidelines [in *QPM*] he should resign and he should do so without delay.'[420] Mellor did eventually submit to the pressure of public opinion, resigning from office on 24 September. However, he offered no apology for his conduct and explained that his resignation was a result of the press campaign against him.[421]

The Mellor affair was the first test of the effectiveness of *QPM* as a public code. As Lord Blake stated in his interview with *The Times,* 'There is no point in having guidelines if that means that they can simply be ignored'.[422] It was not enough for the Prime Minister to simply publish the guidelines, he was also expected to ensure that they were complied with. In addition, the Prime Minister also faced public criticism if the Government's interpretation of whether the rules had been breached or not was at variance with the views expressed in the media and in Parliament. Although Major personally wanted to keep Mellor in office, he found himself unable to defend him against the demands for his resignation. So although the rules had been made public and were open to external scrutiny, their enforcement continued to depend upon the Prime Minister's wishes (which are inevitably influenced by political factors) and the strength of his political position to carry through those wishes. The increasingly precarious Parliamentary position of John Major's Government during his final term (which gradually dwindled to a minority in the Commons in 1996)[423] meant that the Prime Minister had become even more vulnerable to Parliamentary and public criticism and consequently, less able to 'save' his colleagues in the face of criticism. Although, in theory, he continued to be the final judge of his colleagues' conduct, he was increasingly unable to enforce his decisions in practice.

It should be noted, however, that publication has proved beneficial to Ministers on occasions. Since the rules were made public, Ministers have been able to defend themselves more effectively when faced with allegations of misconduct if they can show that they have complied with the rules in *QPM*. For example, Michael Heseltine, then Deputy Prime Minister, admitted in July 1996 that whilst in office, he had taken part in multi-million pound share deals concerning the ownership and control of Haymarket publishing group.[424] He justified this by stating that he complied with the guidelines on shareholdings in *QPM* by placing his shares in a trust. He also stated that he was not obliged to completely dispose of his interest in the company because, although he and his family together owned a majority of the shares, he did not have a 'controlling interest' on his own. However, the trust set up for his shareholding does not seem to have been strictly in accordance with *QPM*, as the guidelines suggest Ministers establish a 'blind' trust for their investments, so that they are 'not informed of the changes in investments or the current state of the portfolio'.[425] Heseltine chose to reserve the right to tell his trustees when to buy or sell shares in the private company, and therefore left himself open to at least to the possibility of an apparent conflict of interest. The former Cabinet Secretary, Lord Armstrong of Ilminster,[426] confirmed that the purpose of the rule to set up a blind trust was to ensure that 'decisions are taken not by the ultimate shareholder but by the trustee of the blind trust'.[427]

However, attempts by Ministers to hide behind loopholes in the rulebook have often only served to highlight the fact that *QPM* was limited in scope, with many notable 'gaps'. Rules can only be enforced where they exist — so when *QPM* has been found to be lacking or simply unsatisfactory, there has been public criticism and pressure on the Government to amend the document accordingly. When Norman Lamont, then Chancellor of the Exchequer, was criticised for using £4,700 of public funds to contribute towards his legal expenses incurred by his action to evict a 'sex therapist' tenant, it was noted that the guidance within *QPM* did not specifically cover this point. Although paragraph 25 stated that, 'Ministers occasionally become engaged in legal proceedings primarily in their personal capacities but in circumstances which also involve their official responsibilities' — and advised Ministers to consult the Law Officers first for their view — the guidance did not state when it would be acceptable to use public funds.[428]

In Lamont's case, the action did not involve his 'official responsibilities' as Chancellor, but it was argued by senior officials that it had nevertheless 'impacted adversely on the office of the Chancellor and the conduct of official business'.[429] The Cabinet Secretary, Sir Robin Butler, and the Permanent Secretary to the Treasury, Sir Peter Middleton, and Sir Terence Burns (who replaced Middleton in May 1991) explained to the House of Commons Public Accounts Committee, that public funds had only been used to cover the costs of handling press allegations concerning Lamont's eviction — the costs of the actual eviction were paid for by the Conservative Party Central Office. Although the PAC accepted that the decision to use public funds had received 'high-level consideration', they recommended that there should be a review 'of the principles required to determine these distinctions' and added that this 'should lead to the issue of consolidated and clear guidance for the use of both officials and Ministers'.[430]

In response, the Government has revised paragraph 25, by making a very subtle textual change in order to clarify the position of Ministers when they face legal proceedings over personal matters. The new *Ministerial Code*[431] states that 'Ministers occasionally become engaged in legal proceedings primarily in their personal capacities but in circumstances which *may have implications for them in their official positions.'* [432] There has still been no clarification of when a Minister may use public funds, however. A senior official has explained that 'it was too complicated to actually state the legal position in the document, but the new draft was intended to make clear to Ministers that they must get advice from the Law Officers first … As for the issue of where the divide lies between the use of public and private funds, that is a matter for the Accounting Officer [i.e., the Departmental Permanent Secretary], who looks at each case individually and who is responsible to the Public Accounts Committee.'[433] It was noted, however, that John Major adopted a more cautious approach when he found himself in similar circumstances some months later. During his own libel actions brought against

Scallywag and the *New Statesman,* he was careful to make it absolutely clear to the media that he had paid for his own legal expenses.[434] The Prime Minister successfully sued both magazines following the publication of articles speculating about an alleged extra-marital affair with a caterer, Clare Latimer.

A further omission from *QPM* was noticed when the conduct of Michael Mates, a Parliamentary Under-Secretary at the Northern Ireland Office, came under scrutiny in the summer of 1993. Mates was criticised for making a gift of an engraved watch to Asil Nadir, shortly after the businessman had skipped bail and fled to Cyprus to avoid the fraud charges against him.[435] As *QPM* only covered the acceptance of gifts by Ministers, and the offer or exchange of gifts with Government members in other countries,[436] Mates could not be accused of breaching the rules, even though his conduct appeared to be improper for a person in his position. Peter Riddell commented in *The Times,* that although there was no rule against his actions in *QPM,* 'it was a stupid mistake for Mr Mates to make a gift with such a quaintly inscribed, and supportive, dedication to someone facing 13 charges of theft and false accounting and who had also been a large donor to the Tory party.'[437] The Prime Minister, however, defended the conduct of his colleague in a Commons statement by remarking that although he had made a 'misjudgement', 'it [was] not a hanging offence'.[438]

Although Mates did resign on this issue, Lord Lester remarked in an article in *The Guardian* in 1994 (following subsequent 'sleaze' allegations against politicians), that 'the present system is more like a colander than a code, with lots of holes where unscrupulous behaviour can seep through.'[439] Gradually some of these holes have been plugged as they have come to light and been subjected to criticism. For example, following the Mates affair, *QPM* was revised to expressly cover the offer the gifts.[440] However, the code, overall, was still not watertight — and as Lord Nolan observed, 'no set of rules can cover every circumstance'.[441] In his opinion, what was missing, was a clear set of ethical principles.

After a stream of serious 'sleaze' allegations against individual members of the Government in 1994 (and other MPs), John Major announced the appointment of an independent committee to examine standards in public life, chaired by the Law Lord, Lord Nolan. Public confidence in politicians was at a low ebb, as a 1994 Gallup poll revealed that 64% of the public believed that 'most MPs make a lot of money by using public office improperly'.[442] A *Sunday Times* journalist had compounded public fears in July 1994 by posing as a businessman and persuading two parliamentary private secretaries to ask questions in Parliament for the sum of £1,000 each. One unnamed senior Minister had remarked, in response to the revelation of their acceptance of the fee; 'Frankly, I would have thought that at least two-thirds of the Tory party and one-third of Labour MPs if they were in government, would have done what these chaps have done'.[443] Such comments only reinforced the general impression that the rules of public office were not clear, and each MP seemed to have his or her own interpretation of what was acceptable behaviour. Although the two parliamentary private secretaries in question resigned immediately,[444] the Government was also faced with embarrassing allegations against Jonathan Aitken (Chief Secretary to the Treasury)[445] for enjoying an undeclared weekend at the Ritz Hotel in Paris at the expense of Saudi businessmen,[446] and Neil Hamilton (Trade and Industry Minister) and Tim Smith (junior Northern Ireland Minister), for asking questions in Parliament (before they became Ministers) for cash payments without declaring this in the *Register of Members' Interests*.[447] It was further alleged, in the same month, that the Home Secretary, Michael Howard,[448] and the former Prime Minister, Baroness Thatcher,[449] failed to declare conflicts of interest arising out of family interests, whilst holding office during the 1980s.

It is interesting that the outcome of each case differed so remarkably. Before the implementation of the Nolan recommendations, there were no established procedures nor any special machinery within Parliament for investigating allegations and imposing disciplinary action. Consequently, no action was taken against Baroness Thatcher, and there was very little follow up to the allegations against Michael Howard.[450] Neil Hamilton and Tim Smith, however, were subjected to the new post-Nolan procedures for enforcing standards, and both were investigated thoroughly by the new Commissioner for Standards, Sir Gordon Downey, and then later by the Standards and Privileges Committee. Both were found to have breached certain Parliamentary rules.[451] Jonathan Aitken brought a libel action against *The Guardian* and *Granada Television* in response to the allegations made against him. However, the case collapsed after it emerged that he had lied to the High Court about his trip to the Paris Ritz.[452] Aitken was consequently investigated by the police and charged with perverting the course of justice and perjury.[453]

When the Prime Minister appointed the Nolan Committee (as it was to become commonly known), it is unlikely that he foresaw the significant constitutional changes that were about to take place. Simon Jenkins commented in *The Times,* shortly after the first Nolan Report was published, that the British Constitution (which he described as a 'curious box of tricks') had just biffed Mr Major in the face. He wrote, 'John Major and Sir Robin Butler thought they were smart in coming up with Lord Nolan ... Yet after three months, [he] has blithely begun to rewrite the British Constitution'.[454] As Jonathan Dimbleby stated in his introduction to Lord Nolan's Richard Dimbleby lecture, 'Public Life; Public Confidence', the Nolan Committee has 'fundamentally altered the rules governing the lives of our elected representatives'.[455] The changes made to the text of *Questions of Procedure for Minister,* in response to the Committee's recommendations (and in many cases by adopting those recommendations verbatim), marked a watershed in the history of the document. They not only transformed the nature of the document, through establishing a formal set of ethical principles for Ministers to abide by, they also significantly changed the traditionally exclusive and internal procedure for revising the document by establishing an independent, external input into that process. Although certain committees of enquiry had looked at *QPM* as part of their evidence whilst it was still a confidential document,[456] specific outside recommendations for the revision of *QPM* were unprecedented prior to the Nolan Report.[457] As a senior official remarked whilst discussing the impact of the Nolan Committee, 'publication has now limited the Prime Minister's autonomy over the document. It is now going to be a much more co-operative effort'.[458]

The Nolan recommendations affecting the text of *QPM* included a proposal to amend the introductory paragraph, which had been drafted for the first published edition in May 1992. The Committee expressed concern with the words, 'It will be for Ministers to judge how best to act in order to uphold the highest standards', as this gave the impression that Ministers made 'their ethical judgements in isolation'. The Committee pointed out that in reality, 'To remain in office they must retain the confidence of the Prime Minister and, in a question of conduct, that will involve the Prime Minister's own judgement of the ethics of the case'.[459] They therefore recommended this sentence should be followed by another declaring that, 'It will be for the Prime Minister to determine whether or not they have done so in any particular circumstance'.[460]

Of greater significance was their recommendation that 'a free-standing code of conduct or a separate section within *QPM*' should be created, which would clearly express the ethical principles that underpinned the document.[461] Although the Committee accepted that 'the precise wording of the new guidance will be a matter for the Prime Minister', they did provide a draft code of principles for the Government to consider.[462] The Committee also proposed that the title of the document be changed to *Conduct and Procedure for Ministers* 'to reflect its scope'.[463] As regards the rules on the acceptance of gifts and hospitality, they proposed that departments should keep a record of 'hospitality accepted by Ministers in their official capacity', as they do for gifts, and 'make these records available if asked to do so.'[464]

In response, the Conservative Government accepted the 'broad thrust' of the Committee's recommendations, and adopted the Nolan code of ethical principles subject to a few minor amendments.[465] However, they were not prepared to accept fully the recommendation regarding the position of Prime Minister, stating that this 'would....go too far towards suggesting that the Prime Minister's relationship with his ministerial colleagues is that of invigilator and judge'.[466] Instead, the new introductory paragraph reaffirmed the principle of individual ministerial responsibility by stating that, 'It will be for Ministers to judge how best to act in order to uphold the highest standards. They are responsible for justifying their conduct to Parliament. And they can only remain in office for as long as they retain the Prime Minister's confidence'.[467] The Government also refused to accept the recommendation regarding the acceptance of hospitality, stating that they did 'not believe that any useful purpose would be served by public records of such events [i.e. hospitality accepted by Ministers in their official capacity]'.[468] Roger Freeman, the Chancellor of the Duchy, announced in Parliament that the amended introductory paragraph was to have immediate effect (though the Government did not follow Nolan's recommendation of a free-standing code). Consequently, the Nolan Committee made a direct impact on the revision of *QPM* by compelling the Government to make an amendment to the text *before* the usual time for revision had come around, i.e., during the run-up to a general election or after the appointment of a new Prime Minister.

The implications for ministerial conduct of the Nolan reforms were wider than textual amendments to *QPM*. The other significant changes which have been implemented as a result of the Nolan Committee include the establishment, for the first time, of a formal code of conduct for Members of Parliament;[469] a Parliamentary Commissioner for Standards and a Committee on Standards and Privileges to enforce the Code and Register of Interests;[470] an independent Advisory Committee on Business Appointments[471] and a Commissioner for Public Appointments. All Members of Parliament now have to declare how much they earn from consultancies and what they do for the money, and are prohibited from advocacy, i.e., speaking on behalf of outside interests.[472]

Some of these broader changes are reflected in the new *Ministerial Code,* as Ministers are now instructed to seek advice from the independent Advisory Committee on Business Appointments about any posts they wish to take up within two years of leaving office ...'[473] They are also told, in a new paragraph, that 'In the event of a Minister accepting hospitality on a scale or from a source which might reasonably be thought likely to influence ministerial action, it should be declared in the House of Commons Register of Members' Interests (or Register of Lords' interests in the case of Ministers in the House of Lords)'.[474] This has established a clear ruling prohibiting Ministers from accepting undeclared 'cash-for-questions' — and with the machinery now in place, in Parliament, to enforce the Code of Conduct for MPs (which also prohibits cash-for-questions) and to maintain the Register of Members' Interests,[475] there is greater pressure on all politicians to avoid financial conflicts of interest and uphold high ethical standards.

To some extent, Parliament's approval and implementation of these wide-ranging reforms reflects the present political-cultural climate and is part of a wider process of code-creation, which David Willetts (the former Paymaster-General) has described as the 'great codification'.[476] Dawn Oliver notes that, 'these measures represent a further step in the progressive normativisation of public life which can also be detected in the use of codes on open government and in local government, in the professions, and in the charters promulgated under the Citizen's Charter.'[477] As performance is increasingly 'measured' against set standards and codes of conduct proliferate, the *Ministerial Code* has arguably become more important as the yardstick by which to assess the conduct of Ministers. Parliament has since adopted its own Code of Conduct subjecting its Members to a more formal system of self-regulation. In the post-Nolan environment, MPs will be concerned to uphold, and to be *seen* to uphold, the standards of this Code, and will continue to scrutinise ministerial behaviour very carefully against the *Ministerial Code*. Non-legal codes can only be effective if they are given weight and enforced — and in the post-Nolan and Scott political climate, these codes do appear to have been vested with significant status. For example, Jonathan Aitken has admitted that 'in the climate of the Nolan and Downey[478] investigations into MPs' conduct, he would have handled certain things differently'.[479] The November 1997 *Register of Members' Interests,* also indicates a change in behaviour as the numbers of Members with outside interests has fallen by two-thirds since the previous Register published in March 1996.[480]

Less than a year after the publication of the Nolan Report, another high-profile committee of inquiry, chaired by the Vice Chancellor, Sir Richard Scott, [481] published a lengthy report which criticised persistent breaches of a key paragraph in *Questions of Procedure for Ministers* relating to individual ministerial accountability. Sir Richard found, during his four-year investigation into the 'arms-to-Iraq' affair, that 'the Government statements made in 1989 and 1990 about policy on defence exports to Iraq consistently failed … to comply with the standards set by paragraph 27 of the *Questions of Procedure for Ministers* and, more important, failed to discharge the obligations imposed by the constitutional principle of ministerial accountability'.[482] He also commented on the wording of the new post-Nolan introductory paragraph in *QPM* which had received criticism in the Commons on the debate on standards in public life:[483]

> Ministers must not knowingly mislead Parliament and the public, and should correct any inadvertent errors at the earliest opportunity. They must be as open as possible with Parliament and the public, withholding information only when disclosure would not be in the public interest, which should be decided in accordance with established Parliamentary convention, the law and any relevant Government Code of Practice. [484]

The word 'knowingly' had been inserted to bring *QPM* in line with the Civil Service Code, but attracted much criticism for loosening the obligation on Ministers. A senior official privately commented that, 'I would have much preferred it to say, 'Ministers should tell the truth to Parliament. That places a much stronger positive obligation on Ministers. And I think that all the exceptions, for security reasons etc., are so well understood that they do not need to be included in a general statement of principle. They should not override the general principle that Ministers should be honest'.[485]

However, Sir Richard did not believe that it made 'any material difference to the substance of the obligation resting on Ministers not to mislead Parliament or the public.'[486] He was more concerned with the use of the phrase 'public interest', which could be interpreted widely to justify withholding information, and the rather vague reference to 'established Parliamentary conventions'. In his Blackstone Lecture, Sir Richard urged that there should be a 'comprehensive review' by both Parliament and the Government 'first, of the list of subjects on which the government's refusal to answer questions is still justifiable and, secondly, of the conventions governing the obligation of Ministers to provide or facilitate the provision of information to select committees'.[487]

Sir Richard distinguished 'accountability' from 'responsibility' in his report, but as Parliament was prevented from holding senior officials directly to account for operational issues, it was often difficult to obtain a satisfactory account indirectly through Ministers. Only a year before the Scott report was published, a dispute between the Home Secretary, Michael Howard, and the Director General of the Prison Service, Derek Lewis, had highlighted a growing difficulty in the operation of the traditional convention of ministerial responsibility/accountability since the establishment of 'Next Steps' agencies.[488] The distinction between policy and operations (Ministers being responsible for policy only) seemed to blur the lines of responsibility/accountability and allow Ministers to fudge the issue in order to escape blame.[489] As Dawn Oliver has stated, 'Accountability cannot be effectively imposed if the criteria against which conduct is to be measured in the process of calling to account are not made clear'.[490] The confusion over responsibility, coupled with damning revelations from Scott that Parliament had been consistently misled over the arms to Iraq issue, sparked a wider debate on ministerial accountability, and an investigation by the House of Commons Public Service Committee, which focussed particularly on how the duty to account had been defined by the Government in *QPM*.

The Public Service Committee noted in its report that *QPM* was 'the only guidance issued on how a Minister should discharge his duty of accountability'.[491] As this was a 'prime ministerial document', the Government were in effect setting the standards for their own conduct. Whilst the Committee accepted that, 'it is right that the Prime Minister should set out the standards that he expects Ministers to live up to', they added that, 'it seems extraordinary to us that the only explicit statement of how Ministers are expected to discharge their obligations to Parliament appears not in a Parliamentary document, but in a document issued by the Prime Minister.' In their opinion this, 'contribut[ed] to an illusion that the obligations on Ministers in relation to Parliament are derived from the instructions of the Prime Minister and not from Parliament itself'.[492] They therefore recommended that Parliament pass a Resolution 'which would state the obligation, how it is derived, and how far it extends'.[493] In addition, the Committee recommended that *QPM* be amended to remove the reference to 'Parliamentary conventions' as a means of determining which Parliamentary Questions Ministers can answer, and should insert a reference to the *Code of Practice on Access to Government Information*. These suggestions were accepted by the Government, but the proposal to strengthen the Prime Minister's position as the judge of Ministers' conduct was again rejected, as the Government continued to believe that the statement in *QPM* reflected an appropriate relationship between the Prime Minister and his colleagues.[494]

As a result of this report, the House of Commons passed the following Resolution on 'Ministerial Accountability to Parliament' on 19th March 1997, which expressed an agreed statement by all the main political parties in Parliament.[495]

Ministerial Accountability to Parliament

(1) Ministers have a duty to Parliament to account, and be held to account, for the policies, decisions and actions of their Departments and Next Steps Agencies;

(2) It is of paramount importance that Ministers give accurate and truthful information to Parliament, correcting any inadvertent error at the earliest opportunity. Ministers who knowingly mislead Parliament will be expected to offer their resignation to the Prime Minister;

(3) Ministers should be as open as possible with Parliament, refusing to provide information only when disclosure would not be in the public interest, which should be

decided in accordance with relevant statute and the Government's Code of Practice on Access to Government Information (Second Edition, January 1997);

(4) Similarly, Ministers should require civil servants who give evidence before Parliamentary Committees on their behalf and under their direction to be as helpful as possible in providing accurate, truthful and full information in accordance with the duties and responsibilities of civil servants as set out in the Civil Service Code (January 1996).

The new Labour Government has since amended the post-Nolan introductory paragraph in the *Ministerial Code,* by replacing the previous Government's statement on accountability with the verbatim text of the Resolution. Tony Blair also expressed a personal commitment to upholding the Resolution in his foreword to the *Ministerial Code,* by stating that he 'believe[d] the executive should adopt Parliament's judgement on how Ministers should account, and be held to account, by Parliament and the public'. Whilst a cynical observer might dismiss the reasoning given by the Prime Minister as nothing more than a 'PR stunt', the motive is less important than the result. A senior judge once made a private remark to the following effect, 'The Government desire to have a yardstick in order to defend themselves [whereas] Parliament want to hold the Government to account'.[496] But, at the end of the day, Ministers are now bound by a Code which is clear, authoritative and public, and which sets out the rules and principles of public office as agreed by the main political parties and influenced by two high-profile committees of inquiry and the House of Commons Public Service Committee.

Chapter Eight
TONY BLAIR AND THE RULE BOOK

Goodbye Cabinet government. Welcome the Blair presidency. The *Ministerial Code* ...
is the most revolutionary publication produced by the Government since the election.
It sets out in a formal code of conduct, to be obeyed by all ministers, the biggest centralisation of power seen in Whitehall in peacetime.

Peter Riddell [497]

Tony Blair was the first Prime Minister to enter Number 10 on a change of government, who had previously enjoyed public access to the current edition of
QPM whilst in Opposition. There was opportunity for him and members of his
party to review the document from the Opposition benches and to plan possible
alterations in preparation for government. Whilst it appears that they did not actually use this opportunity to draft specific amendments, many Labour MPs were
involved in the continuing debate about ministerial accountability and several
had made detailed criticisms of the wording of paragraph 27 in Mr Major's
QPM. A perceived lack of accountability to Parliament was a particular concern
for all Opposition parties after 18 years of Conservative power in an executive-
dominated system. Although the Government's majority was whittled away during John Major's final term,[498] the publication of the Scott Report confirmed
that the general approach of Government officials and Ministers when answering Parliamentary Questions, was to be economical with the truth in order to
avoid any political embarrassment. In a speech to Charter 88, the pressure group
for constitutional and democratic reform, Ann Taylor, then Shadow Leader of the
House of Commons, indicated that 'Labour will review the *Questions of Procedure
for Ministers,* [on the issue of ministerial accountability] to clarify it and tighten it.'
She went on to state that the word 'knowingly' would be excised from the paragraph on accountability.[499] As it turned out, the word was adopted in a Resolution of Parliament on Ministerial accountability, 19th March 1997, which has
been incorporated, verbatim, into the new *Ministerial Code.*[500]

Amending *QPM* was not high on Labour's list of priorities in the run-up to
the election. It was more important for the Party to concentrate their efforts on
securing an election victory. Even after the hard campaigning had paid-off in
May 1997, when Labour gained a 178-seat majority in the General Election,

there was little time to concentrate on the details of the Cabinet rulebook. The task of refining and implementing their ambitious plans for a package of substantial constitutional reforms was far more pressing. *QPM* was, nevertheless, an important issue for Tony Blair, and he did not want to approve the updated draft of the document, which would have been prepared by officials and presented to him on appointment, simply as a matter of routine. Instead he ordered an internal review of the document,[501] asking his Ministers in the meantime to abide by the principles enunciated in the 1992 edition of *QPM*.

It was reported in *The Times* that 'The Prime Minister believes that *Questions of Procedure for Ministers*, which were last updated in 1992, need[ed] rewriting and should make clear that ministers are expected to operate as team players. He also wishe[d] to ensure that the guidance takes note of all the concerns raised by Lord Nolan on standards in public life.'[502] However, despite these indications from Number 10 that the new Prime Minister had admirable intentions to tighten-up the rules of conduct and run an honest and collegiate Cabinet, the press speculated that the main impetus for his 'review' of the rulebook was 'to tighten [Prime Ministerial] control over his government', by centralising policy presentation to his Private Office.[503] Indeed, Mr Blair had himself remarked, before his appointment to the premiership, that 'People have to know that we will run from the centre and govern from the centre'.[504]

Whatever Blair's primary motives, the significance of the review was that it allowed an incoming Prime Minister, on a change of government, to initiate revisions at the start of his premiership, using foresight rather than hindsight. As the Chancellor of the Duchy, David Clark, stated in a speech given at the Queen Elizabeth Conference Centre, '*Questions of Procedure* is being reviewed to ensure that our administration is not undermined by abuses.'[505] Before May 1992, when *QPM* was first published, the document was usually amended *after* events had highlighted that an issue or a problem needed to be covered in the rulebook for future reference. The routine procedure of updating the confidential editions of *QPM* was explained to me by a former Cabinet Secretary:

> Revision will normally take the form of a Prime Ministerial Minute to Ministers and will *subsequently* be incorporated into *QPM*. Although a new edition of *QPM* may contain some new procedures it is very much a compendium of current practice. Thus when some new instruction or guidance is issued the Cabinet Secretary will ask himself, 'Is this sufficiently important and non-ephemeral to go into the next edition of *QPM*?'[506]

This process meant that on a change of government, senior officials in the Cabinet Office had a wider discretion to initiate amendments,[507] as the incoming Prime Minister would be unaware of recent issues and would generally approve the draft handed to them on appointment.[508] By contrast, although Tony Blair entered Number 10 with no experience of government office, he was well aware of the contents of Major's *QPM*. Consequently, he was able to take a fresh approach to the rulebook and consider the important issues and principles that 'should' be included in the guidance, without getting bogged down with the practical details that had arisen in the light of recent experience.

As the Labour Party had been so vocal during the accountability debate whilst in Opposition, it was felt to be essential that they were seen to be committed to improving accountability once in office. Tony Blair demonstrated this commitment by incorporating the terms of the Parliamentary Resolution of 19th March 1997, which expressed an agreed working definition of the obligation on Ministers to account to Parliament, into the new *Ministerial Code.* On paper, this looked impressive. The new Government tightened up the post-Nolan introductory paragraph by removing many of the perceived 'let-out' clauses which had attracted so much criticism.[509] However, the practical effect of the amendment was simply to bring the document in line with the Commons Resolution, by which Ministers[510] were already bound. And it seems unlikely that accountability will actually improve as a result of codifying a long-standing convention, without any increase in Parliament's powers to hold the government to account. At present, we have an executive-dominated system where the government-of-the-day is also the gatekeeper of information. As Parliament has frequently failed to hold Ministers to account, Diana Woodhouse concludes, that 'while the resolution is significant as a constitutional statement, in practice it may make little difference and its effects are likely to be further limited by Parliament's ability to police the operation'. She also comments on the text of the Resolution, believing that it 'still provides considerable opportunity for ministerial manoeuvring' as any assessment of when Parliament has been 'misled' is a subjective interpretation.[511]

The introduction of a Freedom of Information Act, which Labour pledged in their party manifesto,[512] has the potential to be far more significant to the issue of accountability. Depending on the specific provisions of the legislation, an FOI Act should provide Parliament with some of the necessary tools to enforce the Resolution, whilst also allowing the public direct access to a vast amount of material that is currently withheld. The Government proposals, set out in a white paper entitled 'Your Right to Know',[513] stated that the Act would extend to central government, local government, the health service and the wider public sector (including privatised utilities). The White Paper set out seven categories of exemption based on a test of 'substantial' harm. However, an appeals procedure, which would include an independent commissioner, accountable to Parliament, with the power to order disclosure, was further proposed. Finally, there would be no system of ministerial certificates to restrict or veto the Commissioner's decision. Although the publication of the White Paper was encouraging, the Home Secretary, Jack Straw, (who took over the ministerial lead on freedom of information when the Chancellor of the Duchy of Lancaster, Dr David Clark, was sacked in July 1998)[514] subsequently delayed the implementation of open government legislation until 2001. Furthermore, he ordered an internal review of the proposed legislation, sparking fears that the Government will attempt to weaken the provisions of the Bill, particularly the test of 'substantial harm'. David Clark has spoken out since his departure, criticising the delay as 'a great mistake'.[515] The final shape of the legislation is yet to be seen.[516]

Sleaze was another issue over which the Labour Party had expressed concern whilst in Opposition. The sleaze scandals which had plagued John Major's premiership had been the focus of strong criticism in Parliament and the media. The Labour leadership was naturally keen to distinguish its new administration from the previous Government. Just a week after the election victory, Blair had warned all Labour Members of Parliament that 'they were not there to enjoy the "trappings of power" but to uphold the highest standards [as] every one of them would be an ambassador for Labour and the Government'.[517] He also issued a very personal foreword to the *Ministerial Code,* in which he expressed his 'strong personal commitment to restoring the bond of trust between the British people and their Government' and acknowledged that 'openness is a vital ingredient to good, accountable government'.[518] The change of Government provided an opportunity to review the existing rules on Ministers' private interests. Although the substance of the rules and principles set out in *QPM* were considered to be tight enough, it was felt that the written expression was not sufficiently clear and could be open to misinterpretation. As a senior official remarked, 'we realised that words can mean different things to different people. We've been tagging on little bits to these sections over the years — and that's exactly what it looks like when you read it through'.[519]

The whole section dealing with private interests was extensively redrafted for greater clarity and coherence. The revised version clearly outlines at the beginning the general principles relating to private interests — which can be 'financial or otherwise' — before dealing specifically with financial interests. Senior officials have explained that the revision of paragraphs 114–123 on financial interests sought 'to bring together more clearly:

a. the way in which conflicts of interest (actual or perceived) can arise — i.e. by us-
    ing power or influence to add value to financial interests or by using knowledge
    gained in office to add value (e.g. dealing).
b. the risks of not avoiding conflict [such as the damage to] political reputation; legal
    challenge to validity of decisions [and] insider dealing legislation.
c. the kinds of financial interest capable of causing trouble.[520]

In addition, the section has been expanded to include quite detailed guidance on
alternative arrangements that could be made to avoid a conflict of interest if a
Minister is unwilling or unable to dispose of his or her interest. These options include setting up a bare trust (commonly known as a 'blind' trust) or power of attorney to deal with the interest. Alternatively, the Minister may seek to avoid
having any involvement in relevant decisions whilst in office. Whilst the underlying principles have not been changed, the rules now look tighter as they are
more explicit.

A new paragraph was also inserted to cover conflicts of interest arising out of
trade union membership. Again, this amendment was made in anticipation of
potential problems rather than in response to a particular case. It was by no
means a new issue though — previous Labour administrations in particular, had
considered whether and when associations with trade unions may create a conflict of interest. Ramsay MacDonald had ruled in 1924 that the same principles
applied to trade union membership, as applied to directorships[521] — and Attlee
decided in April 1946 that it would be inappropriate for unpaid Whips and junior Ministers to accept any direct payments from trade unions.[522] The issue arose
again in 1965 during Harold Wilson's premiership, sparking an adjournment debate on the Prime Minister's decision to allow Ministers to retain trade union
posts.[523] As a result, internal notes were drafted to clarify the position, which
stated that, 'It can be maintained that the holding of an office in a trade union
need not be inconsistent with the principle [to avoid conflicts of interest] if the
trade union office does not involve remuneration or, while the office holder remains a Minister, active participation in the union's affairs'.[524] Although these
long-standing rulings had never previously been incorporated into QPM, Tony
Blair's administration 'thought it better to put it into the Code, and give Ministers easy access to it, as they do have more Ministers [than Major's administra-
tion] who are also members of trade unions.'[525]

Once in office, however, Labour soon discovered that it was not easy to retain an image of honesty and propriety. A Government must not only avoid actual conflicts of interest — but also apparent conflicts of interest, which can
frequently arise. The sleaze issue reappeared within months of the first administration. The Labour leadership has, so far, taken a firm approach towards mis-

conduct within its own party, however. A Labour MP found to have falsely declared his interests in the House of Commons Register of Interests was suspended from the Commons and the PLP[526] and Labour Member for Glasgow
Govan, Mohammed Sarwar, was also suspended from the Party after an internal investigation suggested misconduct.[527] He later faced criminal charges for
election fraud.[528] However, the Prime Minister's reputation was damaged
when he was personally accused of accepting 'cash-for-influence' from Bernie
Ecclestone, the President of the Formula One Association. Although Mr Blair
publicly apologised for his handling of the tobacco sponsorship affair[529] and returned Mr Ecclestone's donation, it was widely felt that he was naive to think
that the announcement of a shift in policy to exempt Formula One motor rac-
ing from the tobacco advertising ban *after* accepting a party donation of £1m
from the President of the Formula One Association, would not be construed as
a conflict of interest.[530]

   The private financial affairs of two wealthy Ministers have also come under attack, as their complex financial arrangements have, almost inevitably, aroused suspicion of impropriety. Lord Simon was accused of creating a potential conflict of
interest by retaining his £2 million shareholding in BP whilst serving as Minister for Trade and Competitiveness in Europe. The former Paymaster-General,
Geoffrey Robinson, endured a lengthy campaign by Opposition parties to force
his resignation, which began with allegations of hypocrisy for placing his investments in offshore trusts in order to avoid tax. Although this in itself did not
breach any Parliamentary or Government rule, he was also accused of failing to
declare his offshore interests in the House of Commons *Register of Members' Interests* and failing to set up bare trusts for his investments, as required by the *Ministerial Code*. David Maclean (Conservative MP for Penrith and the Border) attacked
Robinson's Guernsey-based Orion trust in Parliament, stating that, 'The Pay-
master General is the minister responsible for corporate taxation and general accounting issues in the Treasury. It is not possible for him to avoid a conflict of interest so long as he is a discretionary beneficiary in an offshore tax haven'.[531] The
Prime Minister, however, strongly defended both Ministers, dismissing the allegations of impropriety and insisting that they did comply strictly with the *Ministerial Code*.[532]

   Although Geoffrey Robinson was initially cleared of breaking any Parliamentary rules by the Commissioner for Standards, Sir Gordon Downey and the
House of Commons Standards and Privileges Committee following two complaints by Conservative MPs[533] he faced a third investigation after a new complaint by the shadow Chancellor, Francis Maude. As a result, both the Commis-

sioner and the Commons committee found that Robinson had failed to register his shareholding in Stenbell Ltd until October 1997. Although Mr Robinson described this omission as an 'oversight', the Committee on Standards and Privileges found that during the period when Mr Robinson's interest in Stenbell was not declared 'the company acquired a rights issue of 9,805,550 shares in TransTec plc from him and sold it to the Orion Trust, an offshore trust of which he was a discretionary beneficiary'.[534] The report concluded with a recommendation that Mr Robinson make an apology to the House of Commons by means of a personal statement. Despite his brief apology, which lasted no longer than 54 seconds and simply fuelled further calls for his resignation, Mr Robinson survived in office for a few more months with the support of the Prime Minister.[535]

Aside from failing to register various financial interests, Mr Robinson was accused of several other alleged improprieties, including questions over his previous dealings with the discredited media business tycoon, Robert Maxwell, which led to the establishment of an investigation by the Department of Trade and Industry (DTI) into Robinson's business affairs under the Companies Act.[536] However, questions were also been raised over the extent of his generosity, both to the Party and to his fellow Labour colleagues in Government and Parliament. For example, it was discovered that Robinson funded the Smith Political Economy Unit, which advised the Chancellor of the Exchequer, Gordon Brown. In addition, he lent Tony Blair and his family his Tuscan villa for two summer holidays; lent the use of his Cannes apartment and his Park Lane penthouse in the Grosvenor House hotel to Gordon Brown and gave away free tickets for Coventry City Football Club, of which he owned a large part, to various Labour MPs.[537]

Mr Robinson's ability to cling on to ministerial office despite ongoing criticism gave rise to the appearance that he bought friends and influence within the Labour Party — an impression that was apparently confirmed by the revelation in *The Guardian* newspaper of a loan of £373,000 which he provided to Peter Mandelson in October 1996.[538] In an attempt to limit the political damage caused by the embarrassing scoop, Mandelson (Secretary of State for the DTI) swiftly tendered his resignation, which was accepted, leaving Robinson with few options. He resigned within hours of the announcement of Mandelson's departure.[539]

Peter Mandelson, who had been one of the most staunch critics of sleaze within the previous Conservative Government, was found to have accepted the loan from Robinson to help pay for his house in Notting Hill Gate, whilst he was an MP on the Opposition benches. However, he failed to declare or register

the loan at the time in the Commons *Register of Members' Interests*, and more importantly, failed to even mention it when he was appointed to ministerial office
in May 1997. Nothing was disclosed when he was moved to the DTI in 1998,
nor when his department began investigating Robinson under the Companies
Acts in September that year. Mandelson's initial response to the revelation of the
loan was to deny that he had done anything wrong. He further denied breaching
any rules. In his public statement, Mandelson said that:

> In the case of the register of members' interests and the ministerial code, you have to
> identify a potential conflict of interest before the need to declare a financial interest
> arises. In this case, I removed myself from any such conflict of interest and insulated
> myself from any of Geoffrey Robinson's affairs, and thereby removed the need for any
> declaration.[540]

However, Mandelson's statement was slightly contradictory. The fact that he had
felt the need to 'insulate' himself from any of Robinson's affairs suggests that he
did 'identify a potential conflict of interest' and therefore did need to declare his
financial interest in order to further protect himself from any actual conflicts of
interest from arising. The purpose of both the *Register of Members' Interests* and the
Ministerial Code is to avoid conflicts of interest through early disclosure rather
than to disclose interests *after* a conflict has arisen, as Mandelson's statement
seems to imply.

Although the *Ministerial Code* does not explicitly cover the situation of a
loan, the secrecy surrounding the substantial loan agreement between the Paymaster-General and the Secretary of State for the DTI was clearly in breach of
the spirit of the *Code*, which aims to uphold 'the highest standards of propriety'.[541] Following the extensive redrafting of the section on financial interests
at the beginning of the Labour administration in 1997, the *Code* sets out very
clearly the rules and principles relating to gifts and conflicts of interest generally. For example, paragraph 114 states that, 'Ministers must scrupulously avoid
any danger of an actual or apparent conflict of interest between their ministerial position and their private financial interests'. A loan on the scale of that
provided by Robinson to Mandelson clearly created an apparent conflict of interest, even if no actual conflict of interest ever arose. In any case, Ministers are
advised to consult their Permanent Secretary and to record their decision, 'in a
minute to the Permanent Secretary, on whether or not they consider any action necessary'.[542] In Mandelson's case, this advice was not followed until it was
too late. He informed his Permanent Secretary, Michael Scholar, and the Prime
Minister of the loan only after he was aware that the information would be
leaked to the public.[543] In relation to gifts, Ministers are advised not to accept

any gift, hospitality or services from anyone which would, or might appear to, place him under an obligation'.[544]

Despite Mr Blair's initial statements expressing a 'personal commitment' to upholding the highest standards in Government, he has, in practice, strongly defended any Minister who has been publicly accused of breaching the rules of public office. In his foreword to the *Ministerial Code*, Blair stated that he would 'expect all Ministers to work within the letter and spirit of the Code'. Yet he supported Robinson in his post of Paymaster-General throughout the twelve-month campaign of cumulative allegations of financial impropriety and Mandelson enjoyed his full support when the story of the £373,000 loan from Robinson first emerged. In the immediate aftermath of Mandelson's resignation, which appeared to be an exercise in damage limitation both for the Labour Government and the future of his own political career, he continued to act as the Prime Minister's 'personal representative' by keeping an engagement for high-level talks with the German Minister, Bodo Hombach.[545]

Whilst Ministers should not be forced to resign for every *apparent* conflict of interest, they should be seen to rectify the situation once suspicion has been aroused. The Prime Minister's strong defence of his colleagues is admirable, if indeed there has been no actual conflict of interest. However, the tendency of all Prime Ministers to offer a blanket denial of any impropriety, whether actual or apparent, in the face of allegations against Ministers raises the question of whether the Prime Minister (and his adviser on the rulebook, the Cabinet Secretary) is the best person to enforce the *Ministerial Code*. However, it is notable that Sir Gordon Downey was unable to enquire into any alleged breaches of the *Ministerial Code,* which remains a matter for the Prime Minister. As the leader of a political party, and head of a Cabinet team, one wonders whether the Prime Minister can always be an entirely impartial judge of the standards of his colleagues conduct. Any Prime Minister is always going to be primarily concerned with sustaining his government in office. The Hamilton and Aitken affairs have also shown that the Cabinet Secretary cannot, effectively, perform the role of internal investigator, as his working relationship with Ministers prevents him from challenging the validity of statements made to him by Ministers under investigation. This was highlighted particularly by Sir Robin Butler's internal investigation into the Aitken/Ritz affair which found no evidence of misconduct. Sir Robin had not called for witnesses and relied on documents and statements from Jonathan Aitken himself.[546]

Whether it would be feasible, or even desirable to introduce an independent element of investigation into the conduct of Ministers is debatable — and would involve the difficult question of who could perform such a role. Following the Mandelson loan affair, it has been suggested that the new Commissioner for Standards, Elizabeth Filkin,[547] should be empowered with a wider remit to investigate breaches of the *Ministerial Code*.[548] Parliament's new system of independent investigation into the standards of MPs conduct, operated by the Commissioner for Standards, has been largely successful and works as follows: complaints against Members of Parliament are investigated by the Commissioner, who reports his decision on whether the Commons rules of conduct have been breached to the Select Committee on Standards and Privileges (composed of MPs). The Committee then decides what sanctions, if any, should be imposed. Although criticism was made of the investigation into the allegations against Neil Hamilton, this complex and unique case can perhaps be regarded as an exception.

However, the likelihood of such a system working for Ministers has been doubted. Whilst one eminent judge believes that a Sir Gordon Downey-type figure for Cabinet could work,[549] a senior official privately remarked that, 'I don't think you can give the position of referee to an outsider. In an ideal world it might work, but the political significance of such a decision-maker would be immense'.[550] Lord Nolan also expressed doubts about the feasibility of such an idea, stating 'there is no independent source of authority which can determine whether the convention [of ministerial accountability] has been observed in any given circumstance'[551] and he has since added that 'The same principle applies to the conduct of Ministers more generally'.[552]

Alternatively, the rules of conduct could be placed on a statutory basis, as they have been in the Republic of Ireland,[553] enabling the courts to be the final judge. This would have huge constitutional implications though, as it involves a shift in the balance of power from Parliament to the courts, and is unlikely to be enacted in the near future. A senior official rejected the idea on the basis that Ministers are 'primarily political and they are ultimately accountable at the ballot box. The campaign against Neil Hamilton showed that if there has been misbehaviour in government, it is a relevant factor to the voter.'[554] Although the Law Commission have published a consultation paper on the issue of reforming the laws of bribery and corruption, they declined to take up the more specific issue of bribery of Members of Parliament, contrary to a recommendation in the first Nolan Report (paras. 2.103–2.104).[555] However, whilst the Nolan Committee would like to see clarity in the criminal law, they do not believe that it is appropriate for the courts to adjudicate on standards of conduct generally. The opinion of the Committee is that, 'cases of alleged ministerial misconduct are very rarely susceptible to a guilty/not guilty verdict'.[556]

Sir Richard Scott has suggested a compromise solution which is consistent with democratic accountability. Rather than appoint an independent officer to judge standards of conduct, he suggested to the Public Service Committee that Parliament should appoint an officer, with a role similar to the Ombudsman, to enforce Ministerial accountability.[557] He explained that this officer should have the power 'to call up all the documents which might bear upon the issue, in order to judge whether or not the Government's use of 'the public interest' as a reason for withholding information has been an acceptable use.'[558] A better informed Parliament and electorate could then decide, if the Prime Minister has not already done so, whether a Minister should retain his position in office. Although this may not, in practice, make a huge difference to the enforcement of the *Ministerial Code*, it certainly has the potential to improve the existing arrangements for regulating ministerial behaviour.

In addition to clarifying private interests, the new Government also wished to address the position of special advisers and unpaid advisers, as this was perceived to be another area in which problems could potentially arise. With the proliferation of advisers (paid and unpaid) under the new Government, a senior official explained that 'they saw this as a difficult area which might be misunderstood'.[559] While his predecessor, John Major, had also employed a high number of special advisers under his Government, the numbers did not rise above 40. In contrast, Tony Blair appointed a record number of 53 special advisers during the first few months of his administration.[560] Guidance on the position of special advisers,[561] who are paid from the public purse, was first included in the 1976 edition of *QPM*, following Wilson's second administration when he had 'introduced the general practice of appointing special advisers'.[562] In 1997, Tony Blair clarified their position in Government even further by drafting a model contract of employment, referred to in the *Ministerial Code*.[563] He also included guidance, for the first time, on the position of unpaid advisers — as these appointments would be more numerous. The new paragraph clearly states that they are personal appointments by Ministers and that 'there is no contractual relationship between such an adviser and the department'. Ministers are warned, however, that in making such appointments they 'must ensure that there is no conflict of interest between the matters on which the unpaid adviser will be advising and their unpaid contracts.' They are further required to seek the approval of the Prime Minister 'before commitments are entered into'.[564]

However, an unforeseen problem relating to Government contacts with lobbyists arose in July 1998, greatly damaging the reputation of the Labour administration. The Government was widely criticised through the media and in Parliament when it emerged that Derek Draper, a lobbyist working with GPC Market Access, had boasted about his contacts with the Government which he utilised to gain special access for clients paying lobbyist fees.[565] Journalists from *The Observer* posed as representatives of American energy companies to discover what Draper could offer in return for his fee. Draper stated that 'There are 17 people that count. To say that I am intimate with every one of them is an understatement of the century'. He asserted that he had special access to Downing Street and the Treasury and went on to give various examples of how his influence had achieved results for his paying clients, including the claim that he had pushed for the appointment of David Varney (chief executive of British Gas) to the Government's Welfare to Work Taskforce.[566] This raised questions as to the wider problems relating to modern professional lobbying and prompted the Government to issue new guidelines for civil servants.[567] The instructions detail some specific 'do's and don'ts' to highlight the sort of conduct that is unacceptable for a civil servant. For example, officials must not 'deliberately help a lobbyist to attract business by arranging for clients to have privileged access to Ministers or undue influence over policy'. In addition, they are prohibited from leaking sensitive or confidential material to lobbyists and are advised to consider carefully before accepting any hospitality from lobbyists. The guidelines inform civil servants that 'Provided that [they] are satisfied about the propriety of accepting, it may be legitimate to take modest hospitality from a lobbyist, but if [they] find this happening to [them] a lot, [they] should pull back quickly'.[568] It is likely that the essence of these guidelines will be incorporated into the next revised *Ministerial Code* for consistency.

The new *Ministerial Code* also codifies for the first time, the role of accounting officers, who are the permanent heads of department and chief executives of agencies. Although a senior official explained that this was included after it was noted by the Cabinet Office as a significant omission, it seems to be in keeping with Tony Blair's general desire to clarify the position and role of members of the Government (even though all accounting officers are civil servants). The new section reminds Ministers of the importance of the role of accounting officers, who are responsible for the 'propriety and regularity of the public finances for which he or she is responsible', and who are personally answerable to the Committee of Public Accounts.[569]

Perhaps the most significant amendment to emerge from Blair's internal review of the document, was the addition of a new paragraph dealing with the coordination of Government policy.[570] This incorporated the Prime Minister's Personal Minute on 'press handling', which was issued to Ministers on 21st May

1997, with a hand-written note from Blair urging Ministers that 'it is essential that we act on this'. The directive, which was leaked to the press, informed Ministers that, 'An interesting idea injected into the media will be taken as a statement of Government policy. All new ideas or statements of this sort must be cleared with No. 10'.[571] Political commentators have regarded this as further evidence of Blair's highly centralised and rather 'over-mighty' style of government, or as Peter Riddell describes it, the establishment of the 'Blair presidency'.[572] Although policy presentation has been increasingly important issue for post-war administrations, no Prime Minister before Tony Blair has gone as far towards formalising central control and coordination. The new paragraph states that,

> In order to ensure the effective presentation of government policy, all major interviews and media appearances, both print and broadcast, should be agreed with the No. 10 Press Office before any commitments are entered into. The policy content of all major speeches, press releases and new policy initiatives should be cleared in good time with the No. 10 Private Office, the timing and form of announcements should be cleared with the No. 10 Press Office. Each Department should keep a record of media contacts between both Ministers and officials.

Even Harold Wilson, who issued strict rules on policy presentation and collective responsibility in an attempt to control his more unruly Ministers,[573] did not formally require his colleagues to clear all new policy initiatives with the No. 10 Private Office. However, some senior officials have stated that the paragraph merely reflects current practice, and has not established a new regime. One remarked that, 'there has been a lot of nonsense talked about the directive on policy presentation in the press. This has not been a significant change — all Governments are concerned with the coordination of policy and Bernard Ingham [Mrs Thatcher's Press Secretary] kept a very strong control on departments during the 1980s for example. It was just seen as an opportunity to put this into the Code.'[574]

There had certainly been a noticeable trend towards greater centralisation of policy presentation before Mr Blair became Prime Minister. Mrs Thatcher did maintain a tight grip on policy presentation through the notoriously assertive Bernard Ingham. During the early 1980s, one of her Ministers, Francis Pym, observed that, 'increasingly, ministerial and inter-departmental press releases are channelled through Downing Street and suppressed or modified as necessary'.[575] In 1995, John Major appointed a special Cabinet Committee 'to consider the coordination and presentation of Government policy'[576] chaired by his Deputy, Michael Heseltine, who was also authorised to set up the CAB-E-NET computer link to coordinate all policy announcements. The electronic information system provided a diary of Government events with briefing and e-mail facilities.

However, some private comments from senior officials indicate that Blair has gone much further than his predecessors. One remarked to Peter Hennessy that, 'No one has *ever* governed through the press like this'.[577] In November 1997, the Labour Government announced the establishment of a central unit to coordinate departmental announcements.[578] The 'Strategic Communications Unit', which was recommended in the Mountfield Report on the Government Information Service, consists of a small group of civil servants and special advisers, based in Number 10, who work through the Chief Press Secretary.[579]

The inclusion of such a contentious paragraph as 88, apparently aimed at increasing the control of No.10, demonstrates that a determined Prime Minister still retains a high degree of autonomy over the contents of the rulebook if he or she can publicly defend their amendments and Ministers are prepared to acquiesce. However, it appears to be more important for Prime Ministers now to make sure in advance that their colleagues will not publicly object to a new edition of the rulebook. Failure to do so may lead to internal dissent and embarrassing leaks to the press which could be seen to undermine the Prime Minister's authority. A significant impact of the publication of *QPM* is that both Blair and his predecessor, John Major, felt the need to establish a degree of consultation with colleagues before publishing their updated versions of the rulebook. Although the final revised draft of the *Ministerial Code* was not submitted to the Cabinet for approval, or circulated to all Ministers in advance of publication, Tony Blair did appoint a special ministerial committee, outside the official Cabinet committee system, to consider the contents of his new Code. The committee consisted of a small group of Ministers who were appointed 'in order to pick up any major concerns that their colleagues may have had'.[580]

Despite making some bold amendments, Blair did not radically alter the form of the document, nor did he make any drastic cuts to the text of Major's *Questions of Procedure for Ministers*. Alongside the changes initiated by his own administration (following the internal review), the new Government also incorporated new instructions, which had been 'flagged-up' during Major's final term, in response to particular issues. For example, paragraph 82 on 'air miles' was drafted after the Cabinet Secretary, Sir Robin Butler, became concerned that some Ministers were collecting credits through official trips for their own personal use. It was reported in *The Independent* that Sir Robin sent a memorandum to all departments, warning Ministers not to use discounts for private travel. The article also stated that the new instruction would 'rank as part of *Questions of Procedure for Ministers*'.[581] The new paragraph 10, which relates to the preparation of business for Cabinet and Cabinet committees, is also an example of senior officials taking the opportunity to 'tidy up' and update instructions. This paragraph was expanded in order to pull together various pieces of advice that had been issued separately.[582] It now provides a comprehensive list of the considerations which Ministers need to take into account before submitting a proposal to Cabinet or a committee. Some amendments were also made directly in response to the various episodes which occurred during Major's last term in office. For example, paragraph 25 was revised following the furore over Lamont's legal expenses, and paragraph 85 reflects Michael Mates' error of judgement in offering a gift to Asil Nadir, the businessman who skipped bail to avoid fraud charges.[583]

Although it is too early to assess the full impact of the Blair administration on the rules and procedures of Cabinet government and standards of ministerial conduct, Mr Blair's eagerness to initiate immediate alterations to *QPM,* and to rename it as the *Ministerial Code,* indicates that he intends to utilise the document as a vehicle for asserting prime ministerial control over the workings of central government, in a similar fashion to Harold Wilson. Tony Blair has already demonstrated that, as Prime Minister, he can mould the public rulebook to suit his particular style of government. He has also shown, through his inclusion of a very personal foreword to the document, that he recognises the public relations potential of the published *Code.* It is, therefore, likely that his administration will continue to make certain strategic alterations, that are designed, primarily, to enhance or restore a positive public image. However, despite renaming the document with a title that is suggestive of a more formal status, there has been no indication that he will elevate the *Code's* traditional status as a guidance document, or issue a statement to enhance its 'informal' status. Similarly, there are no signs that the Blair administration will radically change the policing of the document by introducing an independent element of investigation into alleged breaches. So, although Blair is likely to be influenced, on occasions, by external pressures and recommendations for textual amendments, it seems that he will continue to make the final decision about what goes into the rulebook and how it is to be enforced.

Conclusion
THE SIGNIFICANCE OF THE CODE

Questions of Procedure for Ministers may now be taken as the defining constitutional document on Prime Minister and Cabinet.

Peter Madgwick & Diana Woodhouse [584]

The purpose of this study was two-fold — firstly, to trace the organic growth of *Questions of Procedure for Ministers* from its origins immediately after the First World War, to the very first edition of the *Ministerial Code,* issued in July 1997, and secondly, to assess the nature and importance of the document during its development. Having looked at what has driven the initial drafting, and subsequent revisions of, the document over the past eighty years, we can now turn to the important questions about its essential nature within the workings of government; what power and status *QPM* has had at any particular time and how it could be developed in the future.

If you posed the question — 'what is the *Ministerial Code?*' — the majority of people would probably reply that it is simply a guidance document. It is very difficult to describe it in any other terms as it has no formal status within the British constitutional framework. It is drafted and updated by the government, and issued on behalf of the Prime Minister, 'to give guidance [to Ministers] by listing the rules and precedents that may apply'.[585] However, several interesting findings have emerged from this study which indicate that the significance of the document goes far beyond guidance. Firstly, it is clear that, by the mid-1960s, *QPM* had acquired an 'informal' status within government as a permanent, non-party document which served as an important repository of guidance, precedents and prime ministerial instructions relating to the conventional practices, procedures and conduct of Cabinet government. Secondly, and more importantly, the developments that have occurred since it was first published in May 1992, indicate that the document has acquired a new, and constitutionally significant, role as a coherent code of ministerial conduct. Not only was the revamped *QPM* widely used by Parliament and the public as a yardstick of ministerial behaviour, but the document has also been revised in a way that appears to change its nature fundamentally.

There were several interesting stages of development in the document's history, before it was published, which have shaped its modern form. Its early formation was a crucial stage of development, as it was originally created for a limited purpose and lacked both status and permanence. The very first memorandum on procedure was drafted in 1917 by the Maurice Hankey, the first Cabinet Secretary, to establish certain ground rules within the Cabinet system for organising government business. The *Instructions to the Secretary,* as they were then called, simply set out the basic structure of the new Cabinet system, and, as it was a Cabinet Office creation, it was submitted to the full Cabinet for approval before reissue to a new administration. It was not until Attlee's premiership that *QPM* assumed its modern form and was firmly established as a prime ministerial document. Although the Cabinet Secretary's memo formed the basis of Clement Attlee's first edition of *Questions of Procedure for Ministers* in 1945, the new Prime Minister had a keen interest in procedural matters and issued numerous directives to establish his own way of doing business as the norm within Cabinet. In 1946, a consolidated version of these directives was amalgamated with the Cabinet Secretary's memorandum on procedure to create a single document, which was subject only to the Prime Minister's approval. The inter-war practice of submitting the memo on procedure to the Cabinet for approval had lapsed before the start of the Second World War, [586] leaving Attlee with a wide discretion to shape the new rulebook as he desired.

Attlee's treatment of the document as a prime ministerial rulebook that he could adapt to suit the particular needs of his Labour administration, suggests that, during the early stages of the document's growth, it was not anticipated that *QPM* would become a permanent, non-party reference manual for future administrations. The correspondence that flowed between the Cabinet Office and the Prime Minister's Private Office, shortly after the appointment of Churchill as Prime Minister in 1951, indicates that *QPM* may well have been abandoned, at least temporarily, if Churchill had refused to approve its reissue. The concerns that were expressed within the Cabinet Office, at that time, are very revealing of *QPM's* lack of status as a youthful document. However, after an 'edited' and more neutral version of *QPM* was finally issued by Churchill, the document slowly began to acquire a more authoritative standing as an apolitical, consolidation of prime ministerial directives on procedure by gaining the approval of successive Prime Ministers. Through periodic revision, during the run-up to a general election, or after the appointment of a new Prime Minister, *QPM* grew organically in the light of experience. Although existing text was often re-phrased and 'tidied-up', the substance of the rules and guidance has never radically changed during any single update since the 1950s. As a result, the practices within the text crystallised into continuing conventions, further increasing the importance of

QPM within government. The document became useful, not only to individual Prime Ministers as a vehicle for issuing instructions, but also to the Cabinet Office, as means of establishing some continuity of practice within the Cabinet system, through different political administrations.

The development of *QPM* since 1945 partly reflects the growing pressures of modern government — which highlight the increasing advantages for senior officials to maintain an up-to-date 'handbook' for the Cabinet system. During the post-war period, Government business has increased in complexity and volume, particularly at Cabinet level, making it essential to have written guidance of some form to ensure clarity, coordination and uniformity within the Cabinet system. As well as incorporating prime ministerial directives, senior officials would often include guidance to tackle internal administrative problems, such as the organisation of business during the frequent absences of Cabinet Ministers. By the 1960s written rules of conduct were also included, enabling permanent secretaries to offer clear and consistent advice to their Ministers. Although successive Prime Ministers had preferred to leave matters of conduct to the good sense of Ministers, only occasionally laying down a ruling through oral statement in the Commons, advances in media technology and the development of investigative journalism made it increasingly important to avoid incidents of misconduct, and the subsequent political damage that media coverage could cause. By the mid-1970s, *QPM* had become virtually indispensable to the smooth operation of Cabinet government, containing detailed guidance on such matters as the preparation and flow of business within the Cabinet system, security precautions, public appointments, coordination of policy presentation and rules of conduct.

However, this study has shown that the unique evolution and internal use of *QPM* created an important repository document consisting, not only of guidance, but more importantly, of a mixture of precedents and prime ministerial instructions. Whilst the various tips and guidance may have been discretionary, the precedents and instructions were clearly incorporated to create binding obligations. Consequently, *QPM* not only 'reflects' the development of the modern Cabinet system, but it has significantly shaped its operation and led to the formation of clear rules of conduct for Ministers. Although apparently motivated by practical necessity, the extension of *QPM's* parameters to include ministerial conduct was a significant development, which has led to a new growth area of the document. By incorporating Churchill's code on the conventional rules and principles relating to private interests, Macmillan established within *QPM,* a permanent and 'official' code of conduct for Ministers. Whilst the majority of 'prescriptive' instructions relating to practices and procedures could not easily be described as constitutionally important, for example, Churchill's instruction to Ministers intending to broadcast abroad,[587] the rules of conduct clearly dictated the constitutional behaviour of public office-holders. It could be argued, therefore, that the document began to develop a constitutional significance, even before it was published, as the main repository of precedents for Ministers relating to public conduct.[588] Although precedents do not create absolute obligations in themselves, they are generally expected to be followed — and the obligation to follow them is, arguably, strengthened by incorporation within the rulebook for Ministers.

In is interesting to observe how the document was simultaneously used as a prime ministerial rulebook. Although few of the post-war Prime Ministers showed any personal interest in *QPM*, preferring to leave the details of its revision to their senior officials, each revised draft was still subject to the Prime Minister's approval. Therefore, the well-known preferences and dislikes of individual Prime Ministers would have influenced senior officials who drafted and incorporated the revisions. However, the more bureaucratically-minded Prime Ministers (notably Attlee and Wilson), exercised a more direct influence over the shape of *QPM's* revision and manipulated the document in a number of subtle and interesting ways. For example, Harold Wilson used *QPM* to establish and 'legitimise' new procedures, such as his rule restricting the right of appeal from Cabinet committees to the full Cabinet; to assert Prime Ministerial control over the Cabinet system, by requiring Ministers to seek his approval on a number of issues; and even as a means of disciplining and controlling individual colleagues, such as Tony Benn, by reinforcing the obligation to comply with the doctrine of collective responsibility. Although it has always been labelled as a guidance document, *QPM's* role within government was far more complex. On the one hand, it offered practical advice on pension schemes and travel arrangements, and on the other, it incorporated the precedents and prime ministerial directives that were binding on Ministers.

The publication of *QPM* marks a watershed in the document's history. Since its release, the media and members of Parliament have not only used *QPM* as a strict code of conduct by which to judge and regulate ministerial behaviour, but pressure from various external bodies (most notably from the Nolan Committee, the Scott inquiry and Parliamentary select committees) have also led to significant amendments which has created, for the first time, a consolidated set of rules and principles governing the constitutional conduct of ministerial office.

Between May 1992 and July 1997, the succession of sleaze allegations against Ministers, and the findings of both the Nolan inquiry into Standards in Public

Life and the Scott inquiry into the 'arms to Iraq' affair, propelled *QPM* into the public arena as *the* authoritative set of rules and principles for ministerial office. Whilst the government continued to refer to the document as guidance, the public increasingly treated *QPM* as a quasi-constitutional document. Although academic and legal authorities have not regarded it as a *source* of the Constitution, members of Parliament and the public have, nevertheless, judged Ministers on the basis of the text and demanded resignations from those Ministers who were seen to breach the rules. As we have seen, allegations of non-compliance were, at least, a contributory factor to the resignation of one Cabinet Minister, David Mellor, and damaged the reputation of another, Norman Lamont.

However, the public's use of the text as a quasi-constitutional document has, consequently, led to revisions which have further developed its new, constitutional, role in the workings of government. External pressure to reform and tighten-up the rulebook where it has been found to be limited and inadequate, has led to significant amendments that appear to change the essential nature of the document by transforming its previous mould as a repository of government guidance and precedents, into a coherent code of conduct for Ministers. This dynamic process of transformation was initially set in motion by the Nolan Committee, who recommended, within their report into Standards in Public Life, that specific textual amendments be made to *QPM,* in order to draw out the ethical principles which underpinned the document. By accepting and implementing that recommendation, the Conservative Government created a consolidated and coherent code of public conduct which, in effect, confirmed *QPM's* evolving constitutional importance. The momentum for reform has continued under the Labour Government, which has made further, significant amendments to the document in response to the criticisms that were raised in the Scott report and the subsequent Parliamentary investigations and debates which all culminated in the passing of a Commons Resolution on ministerial accountability. The introductory paragraph of the new *Ministerial Code* now contains an important set of prescriptive, ethical principles governing ministerial conduct and includes the verbatim text of the Resolution of 19th March 1997.

Whilst the media and the public have used *QPM* as a quasi-constitutional document, however, the government have treated the published text quite differently, creating an underlying conflict between the 'public' and 'private'[589] importance of *QPM*. For the government, the published document has continued to function primarily as an internal guidance document, although it also continues to be used as a prime ministerial rulebook, and has notably, developed into a useful public relations exercise. As a result, the *Ministerial Code* has developed a dual, and arguably incompatible role, within the workings of government. On the one hand, the public seek to use the document to regulate ministerial conduct and call Ministers to account, whilst on the other, the government seek to project a positive public image in order to stay in office. The public, therefore, regard the document as mandatory and binding upon the whole government, including the Prime Minister, whilst the government appear to treat it as discretionary — something that can, at least in theory, be altered and redrafted by any Prime Minister. The former Cabinet Secretary, Sir Robin Butler, commented during a talk given to university students, that he '[did not] regard it as having a constitutional force at all.' He went on to explain that

> It would be perfectly possible for an incoming Prime Minister to scrap the whole thing and to devise new rules. The fact that it has been published, would, of course, lead to a debate about that and he would, no doubt, be questioned about the reasons for changes. But it is entirely at the discretion of the new Prime Minister to scrap this lot of rules and … deal with the administration in the way that he chooses.[590]

Although he later qualified that statement by adding that certain parts, such as the paragraph on ministerial accountability to Parliament, 'are not at the discretion of the Prime Minister to change', he confirmed that, in his opinion, 'the document itself has a discretionary status'.[591]

It is interesting to observe the extent to which the published *QPM* has become a promotional public relations exercise for the government, as this highlights the tension between the Executive's use of the document and the public's perception of its status and importance. The Major administration clearly anticipated that a published *QPM* could become a useful vehicle for presenting a positive public image, as they redrafted and extensively restructured the document in preparation for publication. Although the section on security procedures was removed for pragmatic reasons,[592] the extensive 're-phrasing' of the text was clearly designed to give the document a more neutral, formal appearance that implied strict internal regulation of conduct and procedures. Whatever Mr Major's motivations were for publishing *QPM,* he would, at least, have considered the public relations advantages of being the very first Prime Minister to de-classify the rulebook for Ministers and reveal the composition of Ministerial Cabinet committees. Similarly, his Government's acceptance of most of the recommendations of the Nolan Report in 1995, was partly intended to restore a positive image in the face of numerous sleaze allegations. In its report to the Cabinet, the ministerial committee set up to prepare the Government's response to the first Nolan Report, noted that the Government's handling of the report could be a 'unique opportunity … to rebuild public confidence'.[593]

Tony Blair has shown similar signs of mobilising the public relations potential of the document, most notably by his inclusion of a personal foreword which was clearly directed towards a public audience rather than his ministerial colleagues. However, his incorporation of the Parliamentary Resolution on accountability is likely to have also been influenced by the 'PR' advantage of projecting an anti-sleaze image to the public. The amendment did not create any additional obligations, as Ministers who sat in the Commons were already bound by the terms of the Commons Resolution. Overall, the revisions made by the Labour Government during the July 1997 update have significantly added to, and further entrenched, the dichotomous nature of the published *QPM*. Following the Government's internal 'review' of *QPM,* the Labour administration have simultaneously incorporated general guidance, a Parliamentary Resolution on the constitutional obligation to account to the House, the precedents relating to trade union membership and new prime ministerial instructions, most notably on the coordination of policy presentation. Consequently, the role and status of the new *Ministerial Code* within the political system appears to have become even more confused.

So what conclusions can we draw about the constitutional significance of the *Ministerial Code?* Whilst it clearly contains important constitutional obligations, that have been refined and drawn out more positively since its publication, one wonders whether it can properly be described, in Madgwick & Woodhouse's terms, as 'the defining constitutional document on Prime Minister and Cabinet', when it continues to be drafted and used by the government for non-constitutional purposes? It is clear from this study that *QPM* was not originally, nor has it subsequently been, intended as a 'defining constitutional document' for Cabinet government by any of the post-war Prime Ministers or senior officials who have been involved in the drafting and updating of the text. And since its publication, the successive members of the government have been reluctant to make any public statements about the document which would vest it with any constitutional significance. The Cabinet Secretary, Sir Robin Butler, and more recently, Sir Richard Wilson, [594] have insisted that it continues to be issued as a guidance document, and both have rejected the idea that it has become a constitutionally significant text.

However, despite the drafters' original purpose and intention, there is a strong case to support the argument that *QPM* has, nevertheless, developed a new role as an important 'constitutional player' in the British political system. Dawn Oliver has observed a 'progressive normativisation of public life which also be detected in the use of codes on open government and in local government, in the professions, and in the charters promulgated under the Citizens' Charter'.[595] I would add that it can also be detected in the amendments that have been made to *QPM* since May 1992, which have sought to 'normativise' the procedures and conduct of executive power.

As a result of the public's use of *QPM* as a quasi-constitutional document, it is, arguably, *becoming* a quasi-constitutional document. And the cycle of evolution appears to be self-perpetuating — the more frequently its used as the criteria of constitutional conduct, the greater the pressure will be to develop and reform the document to create a more comprehensive set of rules and principles. However, if *QPM* continues to be drafted internally, subject only to the approval of the Prime Minister, the Executive will continue to be, effectively, 'self-policing'. Although Members of Parliament are able to use the published *Code* as an instrument of accountability, they do not have the power to enforce compliance with the rulebook, nor can they impose sanctions for non-compliance. The formal power of Parliament to censure a Minister appears to be almost redundant within the modern executive-dominated system. Strict party discipline makes it virtually impossible for Opposition Parties to force a resignation against the wishes of the governing party and the Prime Minister. And indeed, resignation may not necessarily be the most appropriate sanction for every breach of *QPM* — depending upon the importance of the rule and the severity of the breach.

It will be interesting to see if the *Ministerial Code* develops a more tangible constitutional importance through the courts. Although it is not a legally binding document, a High Court judge privately suggested that the *Code* may become relevant to the legal doctrine of 'legitimate expectations'.[596] Lord Lester of Herne Hill Q.C, has expressed a similar view, specifically in relation to ministerial compliance with international human rights laws. In an article published in *Public Law,* Lord Lester observed that the Government 'ha[d] created a legitimate expectation' by publishing a Code which 'expressly places ministers and civil servants under a duty to comply with the law "including international law and treaty obligations"' [597] and by formally stating that, 'It is expected that ministers and civil servants will comply' with that Code.[598] If the courts do choose to increasingly refer to the *Ministerial Code* as evidence of 'expected' Ministerial conduct, it will have a significant impact upon the Government's own treatment of the document, and is likely to elevate the public's perception of the document's status. However, the courts are not likely to become directly involved in the enforcement or application of a document which contains Prime Ministerial instructions and general official guidance alongside the important precedents and constitutional obligations.

If the *Code* is going to function effectively, in either its public or private role, then clearly it needs to be reformed to remove the present dichotomy. The most sensible starting point would be to separate the existing text into two documents to clarify the separate, and logically very different, functions that the *Code* is currently used for. One document should contain the guidance, precedents and prime ministerial instructions relating to the internal practice and procedures of the Cabinet system, and the other should form a free-standing code of conduct. Whilst the first could continue to be drafted internally, in order to preserve the traditional flexibility of the Cabinet system, the latter should be drafted and enforced externally — either by Parliament, or a special independent body — and should be vested with a formal status. It is encouraging that the Labour Government has indicated an intention to introduce an independent advisory system to support Ministers in their application of the *Code,* and to investigate alleged breaches.[599] However, if this reform is introduced without any prior separation of the guidance and obligations within the *Ministerial Code* and without any clarification of the important status of the latter, then the *Code* will continue to be a discretionary executive document — and the role of any independent advisor can only be limited. To ensure effective and consistent regulation of ministerial conduct, there needs to be a free-standing code of conduct, that is independent of government, both in its drafting and policing. The underlying conflict that has developed between the government's use of the *Code* and Parliament and the public's perception, illustrates that the Prime Minister's document is no longer the appropriate location for the rules of constitutional conduct.

Footnotes

1 'Clement Attlee: A Private Secretary's View', Fifth Attlee Foundation Lecture (available from the Attlee Foundation, London).
2 Public Record Office (PRO), PREM 8/ 1330, 'Consolidation of directives; 1949'. Note by Edward Bridges to Attlee, 3rd August 1945
3 Attlee was Deputy Prime Minister between 1942–45. See C.R. Attlee, *As it Happened* (William Heinemann Ltd, 1954), pp. 151–4.
4 PRO, PREM 8/ 1330, 'Consolidation of directives; 1949'. Note by Edward Bridges to Attlee, 3rd August 1945.
5 Following the technological advances in media communication systems from the 1950s onwards, Ministers became increasingly concerned to observe rules of conduct in order to avoid public scandal, and would often the seek the advice of their Permanent Secretary. If there was no general ruling on the matter in question in *QPM*, then the Permanent Secretary would contact the Cabinet Office for further guidance and *QPM* would be amended accordingly during the next update. For other examples, see the correspondence in PRO, CAB 21/ 4334, 'Ministers of the Crown; acceptance of gifts, 1952–61 and PRO, CAB 21/ 4763, 'Cabinet ministers and heads of departments; company directorships and ministers of the crown holding shares in armament firms'. See chapter 3 also.
6 S. S. Wilson, *The Cabinet Office to 1945* (HMSO, 1975), p. 6.
7 The document was approved by the Cabinet on 1st November 1922, Cabinet 64 (22), Conclusion 2 [PRO/CAB 23/32]; January 1924, Cabinet 7 (24) Conclusion 1(b); 21/294 [PRO/CAB 21/ 294]; 12th November 1924, Cabinet 59 (24) Conclusion 1(a) [PRO/CAB 21/ 294]; and on 11th November 1931 [PRO/CAB 21/778 — see note from Hankey to MacDonald dated 21st June 1935].
8 When stock copies were exhausted in 1936, the opportunity was taken to revise the document. It is unclear if this revised draft was submitted to the Cabinet or not on this occasion. [PRO/CAB 21/778 — see note from Howath to Hankey dated 31.3.36]. However, when next revised in 1942 for the War Cabinet, the Cabinet Secretary, Sir Edward Bridges, did not submit the document for approval before circulation and even thought it unnecessary to show the revised proof to the Prime Minister [PRO, PREM 4/6/8 — see note from Bridges to Martin dated 21.3.42]. Churchill was, however, consulted when the document was revised again, a year later [PRO/PREM/4/6/ 8 — note from Bridges to Churchill dated 4.5.43].
9 Tony Blair submitted the first Ministerial Code to a small group of Ministers — but not to the full Cabinet — in July 1997. Private information.
10 Private information. See chapter 6.
11 PRO, PREM 4/6/8, 'Notes on War Cabinet Procedure, 1942–3'. Letter from E. E. Bridges to J.M. Martin dated 21st March 1942.
12 My italics. PRO, PREM 8/1330. Note from Brook to Rowan dated 26th April 1946.
13 This amendment, relating to House of Commons statements after Questions, was suggested by Lawrence Helsby, Attlee's Principal Private Secretary, and simply stated that 'A copy of the final text should in all cases be sent to the Speaker'. PRO, CAB 21/ 1624, 'Cabinet procedure; consolidated version of the Prime Minister's directives'.
14 The document was re-titled again in 1942 to become *Notes on War Cabinet Procedure*. In 1945 it was changed yet again to become *Questions of Procedure for Ministers*.
15 The quote was made to Kenneth Harris in an interview, see Peter Hennessy and Andrew Arends

'Mr Attlee's Engine Room: Cabinet Committee Structure and the Labour Government 1945–51' (1983), Strathclyde Paper No.26, p. 28.

16 'Lord Attlee on the Art of Being Prime Minister', *The Times*, 15 June 1957.

17 'THE MEMORANDUM', reprinted in Kenneth Harris, *Attlee* (Weidenfeld & Nicholson, 1982), pp. 589–93 and quoted in Peter Hennessy's Second Premiership Lecture, 7 November 1995, Gresham College.

18 Jerry H. Brookshire, 'Clement Attlee and Cabinet Reform; 1930–45', *The Historical Journal*, 24, 1 (1981), p. 184 & p. 187.

19 This quotation was used by Professor Peter Hennessy in his Second Premiership Lecture at Gresham College, 7 November 1995. It can be found in Sir Antony Jay (ed.) *The Oxford Dictionary of Political Quotations* (OUP, 1996) p. 19.

20 Harold Wilson, *The Governance of Britain* (Weidenfeld & Nicolson, 1976), p. 51.

21 In response to a question by Gwyneth Dunwoody, Tony Blair announced the following proposals: to merge the Office of Public Service with the rest of the Cabinet Office; to establish, firstly, a Performance and Innovation Unit and secondly, a Centre for Management and Policy Studies within the Cabinet Office; and finally, to place an emphasis on corporate management within the Civil Service as a whole. House of Commons, Official Report, 28th July 1998, Cols. 133–135w.

22 His first edition, issued in August 1945, contained 37 paragraphs including the annex of prime ministerial directives. The annex contained a selection of directives which had been issued on the authority of Churchill during the War, but which were approved by Attlee in 1945.

23 Attlee was Parliamentary Private Secretary to Ramsay MacDonald (1922–4); Under-Secretary for War (1924); Chancellor of the Duchy of Lancaster (1930–1); Postmaster-General (1931) Lord Privy Seal (1940–2); Secretary for the Dominions (1942–3); Lord President of Council (1943–5) and Deputy Prime Minister (1942–45). See David Butler and Gareth Butler, *British Political Facts, 1900–1994* (Macmillan, 1994), p. 71

24 Jerry Brookshire notes that 'In the decade of the 1930s and beginning when neither [Attlee] nor others suspected he would be a potential Prime Minister, Attlee became seriously concerned with the inadequate Cabinet procedures, and he emerged as the major Labour Party advocate for Cabinet reform'. During the Second World War, Attlee supported the establishment of the Machinery of Government Committee which was set up to examine internal structures and procedures and recommend reforms for post-war government. See Brookshire's article, 'Clement Attlee and Cabinet Reform 1930–45', *The Historical Journal*, Vol. 24, No.1, (1981), pp. 175–188. See also C. R. Attlee, *As It Happened* (William Heinemann, 1954), p. 151.

25 Harold Macmillan, *Tides of Fortune: 1945–55* (Macmillan, 1969), p. 50.

26 Kenneth Harris, *Attlee* (Weidenfeld & Nicolson, 1982), p. 403.

27 Paragraph 21 of the 1946 edition of *QPM*.

28 The review of the committee system was conducted in November — December 1945 by Sir Edward Bridges. The conclusion reached was that although 'the Cabinet itself is not being overworked … senior Departmental Ministers at the top of the list are being overworked'. PRO, CAB 21/4362, 'Cabinet procedure; ministerial committees'.

29 PRO, CAB 21/1624. C.P(46) 357 on 'Cabinet Committees' was circulated on 26 September 1946.

30 Paragraph 27 of the 1949 edition of *QPM*.

31 'Lord Attlee on the Art of Being Prime Minister', *The Times*, 15 June 1957.

32 Harold Macmillan, *Tides of Fortune: 1945–1955* (Macmillan, 1969), p. 486.

33 Quoted in Alistair Horne, *Macmillan: 1894–1956* (Macmillan, 1988), p. 287. For the original source see Harold Wilson, *A Prime Minister on Prime Ministers* (London, 1968), p. 291.

34 Paragraph 5 of the 1946 edition of *QPM*.

35 Professor Peter Hennessy in evidence to the Nolan Committee on Standards in Public Life. First Report of the Committee on Standards in Public Life (Cmnd. 2850–I) May 1995, p. 49.

36 For example, press articles written in 1946 regarding the future of the steel industry were kept by

the Cabinet Office as evidence of leaked information. See PRO, PREM 8/156, 'Cabinet Security: Future of the steel industry; leakage of information; 1946'.

37 Kenneth Harris, *Attlee* (Weidenfeld & Nicolson, 1995), p. 353. The italics appear in Harris' version.

38 Ibid., Again, the italics appear in Harris' version.

39 PRO, PREM 8/ 436, 'Cabinet (Security)'. See extract from the Cabinet Conclusions of 8th November 1945.

40 PRO, CAB 21/ 1624. See directive, C.P (45) 282, 'Secrecy of Cabinet Proceedings'. 9th November 1945.

41 PRO, PREM 8/ 156, 'Cabinet security: Future of the steel industry; leakage of information'.

42 Cited by Wade and Bradley, *Constitutional and Administrative Law* (Longman Group Ltd, 1986). p. 107. Original source is, Lady Gwendolen Cecil, *Life of Robert, Marquis of Salisbury* (Hodder & Stoughton 1921–32), vol. II, pp. 219–20.

43 PRO, CAB 21 /1624. See note from Helsby to Brook dated 9 February 1949.

44 House of Commons, Official Report, 3rd February 1949, col. 1853.

45 Paragraphs 9–12 of the appendix to the 1945 edition of *QPM*.

46 See paragraphs 31–41 of the 1946 edition of *QPM*.

47 Paragraph 39 of the 1946 edition of *QPM*.

48 Paragraph 41 of the 1946 edition of *QPM*.

49 PRO, CAB 21/1624, 'Cabinet Procedure: consolidated version of the Prime Minister's directives; 1949–59'. See directive, C.P (48) 271.

50 PRO, CAB 21/2778. See note dated 28 November 1951, by Sir Norman Brook recording Sir William Strang's (Permanent Secretary to the Foreign Office) request to dispense with the rule on the change of government.

51 Ibid.

52 PRO, CAB 21/ 1630, 'By-elections: Cabinet ministers and ex-ministers'.

53 PRO, CAB 21/1624. See note by Sir Norman Brook dated 30 March 1949.

54 Leslie Rowan was a senior official in the Treasury by that stage, having previously served as Principal Private Secretary to Attlee between 1945–47.

55 PRO, PREM 8/ 1135, 'Absence of Ministers from London & visits abroad: revision of C.P (40) 95'. See note from Rowan to Brook dated 21st July 1950.

56 I borrow the phrase 'good chaps' from Professor Peter Hennessy, though it was originally coined by Clive Priestley, Chief-of-Staff in the Prime Minister's Efficiency Unit under Lord Rayner. Sir Kenneth Stowe explained, in an interview with Professor Hennessy, that 'the "good chap theory" is shorthand for saying that there is a consensus among anyone with responsibility for the governance of the United Kingdom — that the Government shall be carried on in a certain spirit and an orderly way …' See Peter Hennessy, *The Hidden Wiring*, p. 61. Whilst Attlee attempted to introduce a more businesslike culture to central government, Churchill appeared to prefer the more traditional 'gentlemanly' culture that pervaded Whitehall before the Second World War.

57 Antony Jay (ed.), *Oxford Dictionary of Political Quotations* (OUP, 1996), p. 94.

58 This comes through strongly in Peter Hennessy's seventh Gresham Lecture, '"In History lie all the Secrets": Winston Churchill, 1951–55'.

59 The Conservative Manifesto 1951 focussed on the 'excesses of socialism' and harked back to 1945 when the War was won.

60 He was even suspicious of the senior officials which he inherited from Attlee, believing that they too were 'drenched in Socialism': John Colville, *The Churchillians* (Weidenfeld & Nicolson, 1981), p. 64.

61 Churchill had been familiar with the Cabinet Secretary's notes on procedure from his lengthy tenure in ministerial posts between 1917 and 1929 and then from 1939–45. He witnessed the creation of the Cabinet Secretariat and the very first rules of procedure which were drafted. Attlee's version of *QPM* was radically different from the minimalist notes of the Cabinet Secretary.

62   Sir David Hunt, interviewed by Peter Hennessy for the Wide Vision Productions/Channel 4 series *What Has Become of Us?*, August 1995.

63   Sir David Hunt, cited in a footnote by Harold Wilson, *The Governance of Britain* (Weidenfeld & Nicolson, 1976), p. 77. The original source of the quote is Sir David Hunt, *On the Spot: An Ambassador Remembers* (London 1975), p. 53.

64   Frederic James Marquis, Earl of Woolton, *The Memoirs of the Rt. Hon Earl of Woolton* (London, Cassell, 1959), pp. 376–7.

65   John Colville, *The Churchillians* (Weidenfeld & Nicolson, 1981), p. 186.

66   PRO, CAB 21/ 2778, 'Cabinet Procedure; consolidated version of the Prime Minister's directives.' See note from Marshall to Sinclair dated 24th March 1952.

67   PRO, CAB 21/ 2778, Note from Pitblado to Churchill, 24th April 1952.

68   PRO, PREM 11/4657, 'Questions of Procedure for Ministers'. See note to the Prime Minister from Sir Norman Brook dated 24th April 1952.

69   PRO, CAB 21/ 2778. Note from Brook to Pitblado, 2nd May 1952.

70   S. S. Wilson, *The Cabinet Office to 1945* (HMSO, 1945), p. 6.

71   Interview with Sir Robin Butler, 21st November 1995.

72   Paragraph 28 (b), 1949 edition of *QPM*.

73   Stanley Baldwin had also made use of radio broadcasts during his premiership, particularly during the General Strike. See Michael Cockerell, *Live From Number 10* (Faber & Faber, 1989), p. 3

74   Cited in Cockerell, *Live From Number 10*, p. 7.

75   See paragraph 32 of the 1949 edition.

76   PRO, PREM 8/ 1331, 'Television broadcast by Sir Hartley Shawcross with Mrs Roosevelt; supplementary directive by PM on general question of ministerial broadcasts over foreign wireless systems.' See directive, C.P.(51) 161, 'Broadcasts by Ministers over Foreign Wireless' issued June 1951.

77   Paragraph 33 of the 1952 edition of *QPM*.

78   Cockerell, *Live From Number 10*, p. 24.

79   A quote from Harold Macmillan's unpublished diaries, cited in Alistair Horne's, *Macmillan; 1957–86* (Macmillan London Ltd, 1989), p. 476.

80   David Dutton, *Anthony Eden; A Life and Reputation* (Arnold, 1997), p. 478.

81   Robert Rhodes James, *Anthony Eden* (Macmillan, Papermac, 1987), p. 439.

82   Dutton, *Anthony Eden; A Life and Reputation*, p. 478–9.

83   Ibid., p. 463.

84   Macmillan noted in a letter to his old friend, Lord Mills, that 'after the Suez debacle,' the government was faced with conditions 'at home and abroad, of incredible and sometimes baffling complexity'. PRO, PREM 5/ 375, 'Ministerial Appointments'. Macmillan to Mills, 15 July 1962.

85   He placed a sign on the door of the Cabinet Room which read 'Quiet, calm deliberation disentangles every knot'. Harold Macmillan, *Riding the Storm 1956–59* (Macmillan 1971), p. 198. The quotation comes from Gilbert & Sullivan, *The Gondoliers*.

86   A quote by Lord Kilmuir, cited in Anthony Sampson, *Macmillan: A Study in Ambiguity* (Allen Lane The Penguin Press, 1967), p. 127. The original source is: Viscount Kilmuir, *Political Adventure* (Weidenfeld & Nicolson, 1964) p. 308.

87   Alistair Horne, *Macmillan, 1957–86* (Macmillan London Ltd, 1989), p. 160.

88   Michael Cockerell, *Live From Number 10* (Faber & Faber, 1989), p. 28.

89   Sampson, *Macmillan: A Study in Ambiguity*, p. 156.

90   Ibid., p. 156.

91   Cockerell, *Live From Number 10*, p. 38–9.

92   See paragraphs 32–34 of the 1958 edition of *QPM*.

93   Macmillan decided that Ministers should consult the Minister without Portfolio in charge of government information (then William Deedes) if they were invited to appear in a magazine or feature programme. It would only be necessary to consult the Prime Minister himself in cases of 'spe-

cial difficulty or importance'. PRO, PREM 11/ 4657 'Questions of Procedure for Ministers'. See note from Woodfield to all Private Secretaries dated 31 October 1962.

94 Cockerell, *Live From Number 10*, pp. 51–2.

95 Ibid., p. 56.

96 For all the examples cited, see the correspondence in PRO, CAB 21/ 4763, 'Cabinet ministers and heads of departments; company directorships and ministers of the crown holding shares in armament firms, 1960–62'.

97 House of Commons, Official Report, Vol. 496, 25 February 1952, Cols. 702–3.

98 The existence of the Precedent Book was discovered by Peter Hennessy. Sir Robin Butler described the file as 'a loose-leaf collection of internal guidance notes, documents and precedents gathered together by the Cabinet Secretary's Private Office over the years and essentially for use within that office ... much of the Precedent Book consists of precedents derived from personal information about the affairs of Ministers and ex-Ministers ...' See Peter Hennessy, *The Hidden Wiring* (Victor Gollancz, 1995), p. 42.

99 House of Commons Official Report, Vol. 496, 25 February 1952, Cols 701–3.

100 H.C.G Matthew (ed.), *The Gladstone Diaries: With Cabinet Minutes and Prime Minister's Correspondence* (Clarendon Press, 1994), Vol. XIII.

101 Ibid., 14th August 1893, letter to Lord Rosebery.

102 Sandra Williams, *Conflict of Interest: The Ethical Dilemma in Politics* (Gower Publishing Co. Ltd, 1985), p. 48.

103 To take a few examples, Sir Henry Campbell-Bannerman re-stated the Gladstone principles on directorships in a reply to a Parliamentary Question on 20 March 1906. He stated that 'The condition which was laid down on the formation of the Government was that all directorships held by Ministers must be resigned except in the case of honorary directorships, directorships in connection with philanthropic undertakings, and directorships in private companies.' [HC Deb, Col. 234]. During the Commons debate on the Marconi Affair, Asquith laid down the general ruling that, '... Ministers ought not to enter into any transaction whereby their private pecuniary interests might, even conceivably, come into conflict with their public duty', which he expanded upon with a list of specific conflicts of interest to avoid [HC Deb, 19 June 1913, Cols. 556–7]. Sir Henry Campbell-Bannerman's rule was later refined in relation to private companies by Neville Chamberlain on 31 July 1939 [HC Deb, Cols. 1937–8].

104 House of Commons, Official Report, Vol. 496, 20 February 1952, Col.230.

105 House of Commons, Official Report, Vol. 496, 21 February 1952, Col.424.

106 PRO, CAB 21/ 4334, 'Ministers of the Crown: Acceptance of Gifts: 1952–61'. See note from Derek R.J Stephen to Sir Norman Brook dated 21st January 1959.

107 PRO, CAB 21/4334. Note from Derek Stephen to Sir Norman Brook dated 28th November 1958.

108 PRO, CAB 21/ 4334, Letter from Edward Heath to Sir Norman Brook dated 20th January 1959.

109 PRO, CAB 21/ 4334, Note by Sir Norman Brook dated 9th March 1961.

110 Following representations from the staff side of the Civil Service National Whitley Council, a committee of enquiry was appointed under the chairmanship of J.C Masterman, OBE 'to examine the existing limitations on the political activities (both national and local) which may be undertaken by Civilian Government staffs and to make recommendations as to any changes which may be desirable in the public interest'. See *Report of the Committee on the Political Activities of Civil Servants*, Cm.7718, (HMSO, 1949).

111 *Political Activities of Civil Servants*, Cm. 8783, (HMSO, 1953).

112 For the correspondence regarding the drafting of the white paper see PRO, PREM 11/ 344, 'Political activities of civil servants; White Paper following Report of the Masterman Committee in 1948; 1952–53'.

113 Paragraph 33, 1959 edition.

114 In the 1963 edition the following sentence was added to para.34. 'Ministers should refrain from

party controversy when making speeches on such occasions, though they may and should explain Government policy where appropriate.'

115 PRO, CAB 21/5199, 'Questions of Procedure for Ministers; 1961–5'. See note from E.M Abbott to A.L.M Cary dated 2nd November 1962.

116 PRO, PREM 11/ 2351, 'The Burden on Ministers'.

117 PRO, CAB 21/ 5199, 'Questions of Procedure for Ministers'. Directive C (57) 269, 'Transaction of Government Business', dated 26th November 1957.

118 PRO, CAB 21/ 1642, 'Duties of Parliamentary Private Secretaries and Junior Ministers, 1940–50', Directive C.P. (49) 81 on 'Parliamentary Secretaries' and Directive C.P. (51) 61 on 'Delegation of Responsibility to Junior Ministers and Parliamentary Secretaries'.

119 PRO, CAB 21/ 5199, 'Questions of Procedure for Ministers'. See note from Robertson to Martin dated 8th May 1962. See QPM, 1963 edition, paragraphs 46 and 47.

120 PRO, CAB 21/5199. See note from Brook to Helsby dated 8th May 1962. See also, the note from Robertson to Martin dated 8th May 1962, Helsby's reply to Brook dated 9th May 1962 and a note from Robertson to Brook dated 24th July 1962.

121 PRO, CAB 21/5199. Note from Brook to Helsby dated 8th May 1962.

122 Professor Peter Hennessy in evidence to the Nolan Committee on Standards in Public Life. First Report of the Committee on Standards in Public Life (Cmnd. 2850–I) HMSO, May 1995, p. 49.

123 For example, the Minister of Transport, Ernest Marples, was forced to make a personal statement to the House of Commons following accusations in the Press of a conflict of interest between his position as a senior partner to a firm of contractors and a government contract which he obtained, worth £250,000. House of Commons, Official Report, Vol.616, 1960, Cols. 371–73 and Cols. 380–1.

124 The 'Portland Spy Ring' (a group which had been supplying information from Britain's Underwater Weapons Establishment to the Soviets) was exposed in early 1961, leading to the the Portland trials and the establishment of a committee of inquiry under Sir Charles Romer. Shortly afterwards, George Blake, an MI6 officer, was found guilty and imprisoned for passing on secret information to the KGB. In the following year W. John Vassall, a ciphers clerk in the British Embassy in Moscow, was found guilty and imprisoned for passing on secret documents to the KGB. These are just a few examples to highlight the context of the Profumo Affair. For a good overall summary of the spies scandals during this period see, Alistair Horne, Macmillan, 1957–86 (Macmillan London Ltd, 1989), pp. 456–467.

125 Thomas Galbraith was then an Under-Secretary of State for Scotland, having previously served as a junior Minister at the Admiralty and once shared his private office with Vassall. Rumours and allegations spread in the Press that he had been involved in the Vassall spying scandal. See Horne, Macmillan, 1957–86, pp. 460–464.

126 PRO, CAB 21/ 5199. Douglas-Home issued a Directive on security — C (P) (64) 1 — which was inserted into QPM (paragraphs 28 and 35) during the run-up to the 1964 General Election.

127 D.R Thorpe, Alec Douglas-Home (Sinclair-Stevenson, 1997), p. 376.

128 PRO, CAB 21/ 5199, Letter from McIndoe to Trend dated 12th October 1964.

129 PRO, CAB 21/ 5199, Letter from McIndoe to Trend dated 23rd July 1964.

130 Ibid.

131 Ibid.

132 PRO, CAB 21/ 5199, Letter from McIndoe to Trend dated 12th October 1964.

133 Harold Wilson, The Governance of Britain (Weidenfeld & Nicolson, 1976), p. 58.

134 Harold Wilson, Labour Party Conference, Scarborough, 1st October 1963.

135 Wilson had consciously mimicked President Kennedy throughout the 1964 election. During a party political broadcast, he said, 'What I think we are going to need is something like President Kennedy had when he came in after years of stagnation. He had a programme of a hundred days of dynamic action'. See Michael Cockerell, Live From No.10 (Faber & Faber, 1989), p. 100.

136 D.R Thorpe states that 'The Press continually portrayed him as an antediluvian, inexperienced and anachronistic figure'. See Thorpe, Alec Douglas-Home (Sinclair- Stevenson, 1997), p. 324. For a gen-

eral overview of the General Election campaign of 1964 see chapter 14 of Thorpe's biography and chapter 7 of Cockerell, op. cit.

137 PRO, CAB21/ 5199, 'Questions of Procedure for Ministers', note from Trend to Wilson dated 16th October 1964.

138 Peter Hennessy, *Whitehall* (Secker & Warburg, 1989), p. 302.

139 PRO, PREM 8/ 1330, 'Consolidation of Directives, 1949', note from Bridges to Attlee dated 3rd August 1945.

140 Wilson, *The Governance of Britain,* p. 78.

141 Peter Hennessy, Fourth Premiership lecture at Gresham College, 6th February 1996.

142 Wilson, *The Governance of Britain,* p. 48.

143 Simon James, 'Relations between Prime Ministers and Cabinet', in R. Rhodes & P. Dunleavy (eds.), *Prime Minister, Cabinet and Core Executive* (St. Martin's Press, 1995), p. 65.

144 This was a further change he made to the first issue of *QPM* in 1964. See also the 'Note for the Record', dated 18th October 1964 which records the amendments Wilson desired to make. PRO, CAB 21/5199.

145 See paragraph 12 of the 1974 (Oct.) edition of *QPM*. By 1976, these two instructions were re-phrased in even more sharp terms (paragraph 9, 1976 edition of *QPM*), illustrating Wilson's determination to enforcing the procedure.

146 See paragraph 7 of the 1974 (Oct.) edition of *QPM*, and Wilson, *The Governance of Britain,* p. 48.

147 See paragraph 11, 1976 edition of *QPM*.

148 Wilson, *The Governance of Britain,* pp. 52–3.

149 Anthony King, '"Overload"; Problems of Governing in the 1970s', *Political Studies,* vol.22, nos. 2–3 (June – September 1975).

150 The annual number of ministerial Committee meetings has been estimated at around 300 during the 1970s, whereas there were only about 150 during the 1990s. The number of Cabinet papers circulated a year were around 130 during the 1970s, decreasing to less than 20 during the 1990s. And finally, the number of Cabinet Committee papers circulated in a year were around 250 during the 1970s, falling to around 150 during the 1990s according to unpublished statistics from the Cabinet Office. Peter Hennessy has estimated that Wilson established about 236 ad hoc groups between October 1964 and early 1969, and about 120 between April 1976 and April 1979. See Hennessy, *Cabinet* (Basil Blackwell, 1986), pp. 100–1.

151 For example, in *Ridge v. Baldwin* [1964] Ac 40, the House of Lords adopted a more intervention-ist approach to judicial review by applying the principle of natural justice to an administrative decision.

152 See paragraphs 30–1 of the 1969 version of *QPM*.

153 Paragraph 30, Ibid.

154 Wilson, *The Governance of Britain,* pp. 65–6.

155 Simon James, British Cabinet Government, (Routledge, 1992), pp. 69–70. James used R. Anderwag, 'The Netherlands: Cabinet Committees in a Coalition Cabinet' in Tom Mackie and Brian Hogwood's, *Unlocking the Cabinet,* pp. 138–54, as his source.

156 Wilson, The Governance of Britain, p. 65.

157 Richard Crossman, *The Diaries of a Cabinet Minister. Volume III* (Hamish Hamilton/ Jonathan Cape, 1977), p. 861. Diary entry for 17th March 1970.

158 Barbara Castle, *The Castle Diaries 1964–76* (Macmillan Papermac, 1990), pp. 270–1. Diary entry for 5th November 1968.

159 Diary entry for 5th November 1968, Ibid.

160 Richard Crossman, *Diaries of a Cabinet Minister; Volume II* (Hamish Hamilton & Jonathan Cape, 1976), p. 119. Diary entry for 10th November 1966.

161 PRO, CAB 21/ 5199, 'Questions of Procedure for Ministers; 1961–5'. See note from Woodfield to McIndoe dated 8th October 1964.

162 Paragraph 57 of the 1966 edition of *QPM*.

163 Ibid., paragraph 51.
164 Ibid., paragraph 56.
165 See paragraph 56 of the 1969 edition of *QPM* and paragraph 104 of the 1974 (Oct.) edition.
166 Paragraph 112 of the 1976 edition of *QPM*.
167 *The Sunday Times, 21* February 1965, editorial.
168 PRO, PREM 13/ 501, 'Appointment of Anthony Howard as Sunday Times Whitehall Correspondent; rules governing relations with press; circular to all ministers: January — June 1965'. Note from Derek Mitchell to Sir Lawrence Helsby, 24 February 1965.
169 Paragraph 56 of the 1966 edition of *QPM*.
170 PRO, PREM 13/ 501.
171 John Campbell, *Edward Heath; a biography* (Pimlico, 1993), p. 271.
172 PRO, CAB 171/ 4, 'C (PR) series; 1970 June – August, papers 1–2'. Covering letter to 1970 *QPM*.
173 Joe Haines was a journalist for the old, pre-Murdoch *The Sun* newspaper from 1964–68 before joining the Prime Minister's Press Office.
174 Campbell, *Edward Heath; a biography,* p. 503.
175 Ibid., pp. 503–4.
176 See Michael Cockerell, *Live From No.10* (Faber & Faber, 1989), pp. 174–6.
177 Ibid, pp. 175–6.
178 Ibid, p. 190.
179 Paragraph 110(a) of the 1971 edition of *QPM*.
180 Ibid., paragraph 113.
181 See paragraphs 80 and 91 of the 1969 edition of *QPM* — which were recent additions to the document.
182 Edward Short, *Whip to Wilson* (Macdonald & Co, 1989), p. 220.
183 Ibid., pp. 23–4.
184 Ibid., p. 90.
185 Paragraph 35(iv) of the 1969 edition of *QPM*.
186 Barbara Castle, *The Castle Diaries 1964–76* (Macmillan Papermac, 1990), p. 207.
187 Richard Crossman, *Diaries of a Cabinet Minister; Volume II* (Hamish Hamilton & Jonathan Cape, 1976), p. 120.
188 Short, *Whip to Wilson,* p. 91.
189 Paragraph 57 of the 1966 edition of *QPM*.
190 See Castle, *The Castle Diaries; 1964–76,* pp. 108–9.
191 Ibid., pp. 148–9.
192 Hugo Young, *The Crossman Affair* (Hamish Hamilton & Jonathan Cape, 1976), p. 194.
193 The Committee of Privy Counsellors on Ministerial Memoirs was appointed on 11th April 1975.
194 Report of the Committee of Privy Counsellors on Ministerial Memoirs, Cm. 6386, Session 1975–6 (HMSO, 1976).
195 They were both in favour of open government.
196 Tony Benn, *Against the Tide,* p. 501 and p. 549. Diary entry for 20th January 1976.
197 Ibid., p. 502.
198 Private information.
199 Tony Benn, *Diaries; Office Without Power,* p. 166. Diary entry for 8th May 1969.
200 Ben Pimlott, *Harold Wilson* (Harper Collins, 1992), p. 639.
201 Harold Wilson, *Final Term* (Weidenfeld & Nicolson, 1979), p. 33.
202 Harold Wilson, *The Governance of Britain* (Weidenfeld & Nicolson, 1976), p. 44.
203 This sentence was first inserted into the 1969 edition of *QPM*, paragraph 70.
204 Tony Benn, *Against the Tide: Diaries: 1973–76* (Arrow Books, 1990), p. 177. Diary entry for 17th June 1974.
205 Ibid., p. 235, n.2, 1974.
206 Ibid., p. 142. Diary entry for 25th March 1974.

207 Nevin Craig was the brother of Christopher Craig, the youth responsible, with Derek Bentley, for the shooting of a policeman in 1952. Longford has also visited Christopher during his sentence, but he was now out of prison.

208 29th March 1965. House of Commons, Official Report, vol.709, cols.1355–1364.

209 Edward Short, *Whip to Wilson* (Macdonald & Co, 1989), p. 126.

210 PRO, CAB 21/ 5200. 'Questions of Procedure for Ministers; 1964–5'. Note by Derek Mitchell circulated to all private secretaries, dated 12th February 1965.

211 Frank Pakenham, Earl of Longford, *The Grain of Wheat* (Collins, 1974), p. 136.

212 Edward Short, *Whip to Wilson*, p. 126.

213 PRO, CAB 21/5200, Draft minute from the Home Secretary to the Prime Minister, February 1965.

214 Ibid., Letter to Sir Charles Cunningham dated 2nd March 1965.

215 Ibid., Letter from Cunningham to Sir Burke dated 26th February 1965.

216 PRO, PREM 13/ 437, 'Attendance by Lord Privy Seal at wedding of Christopher Craig: PM suggested he should not go'. Note from Wilson to Longford dated 1 April 1965.

217 PRO, PREM 13/ 437. Note from Longford to Wilson dated 1 April 1965.

218 Frank Pakenham, Earl of Longford, *The Grain of Wheat*, p. 136.

219 Philip Ziegler, *Wilson; The Authorised Life of Lord Wilson of Rievaulx* (Weidenfeld & Nicolson, 1993), p. 313.

220 Ibid., p. 313.

221 *The Times*, 25 January 1974, p. 8.

222 Ziegler, *Wilson; The Authorised Life of Lord Wilson of Rievaulx*, pp. 472–3.

223 The reasons given for this amendment to *QPM* are speculative due to the lack of available information.

224 The Prime Minister was informed that 'While the Security Service have no evidence of the use of such girls as spies, they do represent a potential security risk …' He was told that 'no absolute ban was imposed on the employment of such girls, but it was discouraged; and we asked that, if anyone insisted on retaining such a girl in his employment, information about the girl should be given to the Security Service to carry out a check'. PRO, PREM 13/ 1789, 'Employment of foreign au pairs; advice to Ministers; Oct 1966–Mar 1967'. See note to the Prime Minister dated 27th October 1966.

225 PRO, PREM 13/ 1789. See note from Hall to Helsby dated 20 March 1967.

226 Paragraphs 32–38 of the 1974 (March) edition of *QPM*.

227 *QPM* was not revised on the appointment of Anthony Eden in April 1955, although interestingly, it was not revised after the General Election in May '55 either. The document was not revised immediately after Macmillan's appointment as Prime Minister in 1957, but a year later in 1958.

228 Private information.

229 Harold Wilson, *Final Term* (Weidenfeld & Nicolson, 1979), p. 86.

230 Paragraph 62 of the 1976 edition of *QPM*.

231 Ibid., paragraph 65.

232 House of Commons, Official Report, vol. 962, col. 244. The rule was inserted into paragraph 62 of the 1979 edition of *QPM*.

233 *Report of the Royal Commission on Standards in Public Life,* Cmnd. 6524 (HMSO, July 1976), p. 7.

234 Susan Crosland, *Tony Crosland* (Jonathan Cape, 1982), pp. 247–9.

235 Private information.

236 Paragraph 8 of the 1979 edition.

237 Lord Callaghan in a written reply (dated September 1997) to a written question from the author.

238 Edmund Dell, *The Chancellors: A History of the Chancellors of the Exchequer, 1945–90* (Harper Collins, 1996), p. 423.

239 James Callaghan, *Time and Chance* (Collins, 1987), p. 449.

240 John Stonehouse resigned the Labour Whip in April 1976 to become an Independent and James

Sillars (MP for South Ayrshire) and John Robertson (MP for Paisley) defected to the Scottish Labour Party in July 1976.

241 Clause 4 of the Bill was negatived in Standing Committee A on the 11th January 1977. House of
Commons, Official Report; Standing Committees, Session 1976–77,Vol.1, cols.173–226.

242 *The Times,* 18 January 1977, p. 2.Tony Benn, *Conflicts of Interest; Diaries 1977–80* (Hutchinson, 1990)
p. 6. Diary entry for 13th January 1977.

243 Ibid., p. 386. Diary entry for 6th November 1978.

244 Paragraph 39 of the 1979 edition of *QPM.*

245 *The Times,* 9th November 1978, p. 2.

246 *The Times,* 16th April 1986.

247 Nicholas Ridley, *My Style of Government, The Thatcher Years* (Hutchinson, 1991), p. 28.

248 Interview with Kenneth Harris, *Observer,* 25 February 1979.

249 Michael Heseltine, *Panorama,* BBC1, 13th January 1986.

250 Bernard Ingham, *Kill the Messenger* (Harper Collins, 1991), p. 167.

251 Ridley, *My Style of Government,* p. 39.

252 Ibid., p. 28.

253 K. C. Wheare, *Modern Constitutions* (Oxford University Press, 1951), p. 179.

254 Ibid., p. 179.

255 Private information.

256 Geoffrey Howe, *Conflict of Loyalty* (Macmillan, 1994), p. 459.

257 Simon James, *British Cabinet Government* (Routledge, 1992), p. 109–110. See also Howe, *Conflict of
Loyalty,* p. 459.

258 Private information.

259 The Conservative majority at the General Election 1979.

260 Geoffrey Howe mentions her 'recurrent sense of isolation in her own Cabinet' in his memoirs,
Conflict of Loyalty (Macmillan, 1994), p. 147. See also Anthony King, 'Margaret Thatcher: The Style
of the Prime Minister', in Anthony King (ed.), *The British Prime Minister* (Macmillan Education
Ltd, 1985), p. 103.

261 Sir John Hunt served as Secretary of the Cabinet for the first six months of Thatcher's first administration, retiring on 31st October 1979. Sir Robert Armstrong succeeded him.

262 Private information.

263 Jim Prior, *A Balance of Power* (Hamish Hamilton, 1986), p. 133.

264 PRO, CAB 171/ 11. Prime Minister's covering note to the 1979 edition of *QPM.*

265 *The Sunday Telegraph,* 7th October 1979, p. 40.

266 Nigel Lawson, *The View from No.11* (Bantam Press, 1992), p. 127.

267 PRO, CAB 171/12. Note by the Secretary of the Cabinet, dated 5 June 1980.

268 PRO, CAB 171/12. Note by the Secretary of the Cabinet, dated 24 September 1980.

269 The link between this incident and the amendment to *QPM* is speculative due to lack of information.

270 Henry Stanhope and Craig Seton, 'Services lose their own ministers in reshuffle', *The Times,* 30
May 1981, p. 1.

271 Paragraph 9 of the 1983 edition of *QPM.*

272 The Gallup Poll for May 1983 recorded that 50% of voters approved of the Prime Minister and
only 18% approved of the Leader of the Opposition, then Michael Foot. Mrs Thatcher had hit a
low in December 1981, when only 25% approved of her. See David Butler and Gareth Butler, *British Political Facts; 1900–1994* (Macmillan, 1994), p. 256.

273 Lawson, *The View from No.11,* p. 255.

274 Prior, *A Balance of Power,* p. 133.

275 Peter Hennessy, *Cabinet* (Basil Blackwell, 1986) p. 102.

276 Nigel Lawson speaking at an Institute of Historical Research symposium on 9 March 1994. 'Cabinet Government in the Thatcher Years', *Contemporary Record,* Vol.8, Winter 1994, No.3, p. 445.

277 The paragraph in the 1946 edition of *QPM* was slightly different to the paragraph quoted. The guidance was refined to assume its modern form in 1952.

278 Prior, *A Balance of Power,* p. 133.

279 Lawson, *The View from No.11,* p. 129.

280 See Peter Hennessy, 'The Solo Coalitionist; John Major 1990–' Premiership Lecture No.12 at Gresham College, 4 March 1997. See also Anthony Seldon, 'Policy-making and Cabinet', in Dennis Kavanagh and Anthony Seldon (eds.), *The Major Effect* (Macmillan Papermac, 1994), p. 161 and Sarah Hogg and Jonathan Hill, *Too Close to Call* (Little, Brown and Co, 1995), p. 13.

281 Ridley, *My Style of Government,* p. 36.

282 Paragraph 108 of the 1983 edition of *QPM.*

283 Paragraph 116 (d) of the 1983 edition of *QPM.*

284 Private information.

285 Paragraph 119 of the 1987 edition of *QPM.*

286 Jack Straw, the Opposition Spokesman on the Environment accused the Government of having 'outrageously abused the convention relating to party political propaganda in the MoD and the Prime Minister's Press Office.' *The Times,* 12 July 1984.

287 *The Times,* 12 July 1984.

288 See Committee of Enquiry into the Conduct of Local Authority Business, *Local Authority Publicity; Interim Report* (HMSO, 1985).

289 The memorandum was prepared by the Cabinet Office in April 1985 for submission to the Widdicombe Committee. See paragraph 119 of the 1987 edition of *QPM.*

290 Private information.

291 For a very readable account of the problems suffered by Lloyd's of London, and subsequent reforms, see Kathy Gunn, *Nightmare on Lime Street: Whatever happened to Lloyd's of London* (Smith Gryphon Ltd, 1992).

292 For a chronology of scandals between 1982–85 see, *The Economist,* 15 June 1985, p. 22.

293 Gunn, *Nightmare on Lime Street,* p. 20.

294 Paragraph 74 of the 1983 edition of *QPM.*

295 Ibid., Paragraph 75.

296 Ibid., Paragraph 76.

297 Ibid., Paragraph 77.

298 Gunn, *Nightmare on Lime Street,* p. 22.

299 See paragraphs 79–82 of the 1987 edition of *QPM.*

300 'Thatcher defends Oman lobbying', *The Times,* 16 January 1984, p. 22.

301 *The Times,* 18 and 19 January 1984, 13 April 1984.

302 'Heath calls for answers over Oman contract', *The Times,* 19 March 1984, p. 2.

303 '20 Labour MPs withdraw from Commons Register', *The Times,* 15 March 1984, p. 2.

304 Richard Dowden, 'Labour published Oman case', *The Times,* 13 April 1984, p. 1.

305 Paragraph 62 of the 1979 edition of *QPM.*

306 Paragraph 78 of the 1987 edition of *QPM.*

307 For a more detailed account of the unfolding saga see Diana Woodhouse, *Ministers and Parliament; Accountability in Theory and Practice* (Clarendon Press, Oxford, 1994), pp. 106–29.

308 Paragraph 25 of the 1987 edition of *QPM.*

309 *Government Response to the Third and Fourth Reports from the Defence Committee, Session 1985–6,* Cm. 9916 (HMSO, 1986).

310 For the full story see chapters four and five of Clive Ponting, *The Right to Know: The inside story of the Belgrano Affair* (Sphere Books Ltd, 1985).

311 Tam Dalyell was the Labour Member for West Lothian between 1962–83. Since 1983, he has been the Labour Member for Linlithgow.

312 Ibid., p. 131.

313 Ibid., p. 138.

314 Ibid., p. 149–153.
315 House of Commons, Official Report, written answer, 26 February 1985, Vol.74 (Session 1984–5) cols. 130–32.
316 *Seventh Report from the Treasury and Civil Service Committee* (1985–86), HC 92 (HMSO, 1986).
317 The Government's response to the TCSC report was published in *The Civil Service: Taking Forward Continuity and Change*, Cm 2748 (HMSO, 1995).
318 See the Prime Minister's covering note to the 1987 edition of *QPM*.
319 See paragraphs 27 and 28 of the 1991 edition of *QPM*.
320 *Taking Forward Continuity and Change*, Cm 2748, p. 1.
321 In 1983 there were approximately 92 applications for leave to apply for judicial review in civil matters against central government — a figure which rose to 602 by 1987 and 499 by 1989. See Maurice Sunkin and Andrew Le Seur, 'Can Government control judicial review?', *Current Legal Problems* (1991), p. 173.
322 Sir Michael Kerry, 'Administrative Law and the Administrator', *Management in Government* (1983) 3, pp. 170–171.
323 *R. Secretary of State for the Environment, ex parte Brent LBC* [1982] Q.B. 593.
324 *R. v. Secretary of State for Social Security, ex parte Cotton*, reported in *The Times*, 5 August 1985 and 14 December 1985.
325 *The Times*, Law Report, 5 August 1985.
326 *The Times*, Law Report, 14 December 1985.
327 *Council of Civil Service Unions v. Minister for Civil Service* [1985] A.C. 374.
328 The House of Lords held, dismissing the appeal, '(1) that executive action was not immune from judicial review merely because it was carried out in pursuance of a power derived from a common law, or prerogative, rather than a statutory source, and a Ministers acting under a prerogative power might, depending on its subject matter, be under the same duty to act fairly as in the case of action under a statutory power …'; [1985] A.C at 375.
329 It has been alleged that the possibility of eliminating judicial review altogether was also discussed, although not pursued. See Hugo Young, *The Guardian* 9 March 1988.
330 *The Judge Over Your Shoulder* (Cabinet Office, 1987).
331 Paragraph 23 (c) of the 1987 edition of *QPM*.
332 Paragraph 11 of the 1987 edition of *QPM*.
333 Paragraph 76 of the 1987 edition of *QPM*.
334 Sarah Hogg, 'Policy-making in Government', *The Sunday Times* Lecture, 7 March 1995.
335 John Major became the youngest Prime Minister since the appointment of the Earl of Rosebery in 1894. With only 11 years experience in the House of Commons (and 3 years in the Cabinet) he had the shortest experience of any Prime Minister of the Century, and had not been in Parliament long enough to see the Conservatives in Opposition. However, he had gained experience of the two most senior posts in Cabinet — Chancellor of the Exchequer and Foreign Secretary. See David Butler and Gareth Butler, *British Political Facts; 1900–1994* (Macmillan, 7th ed., 1994) and Dermot Englefield, Janet Seaton & Isobel White, *Facts About British Prime Ministers* (Mansell, 1995), pp. 350 and 396.
336 Jamie Dettmer, 'Major: the unknown Prime Minister', *The Times*, 28 November 1990.
337 David Butler and Gareth Butler, *British Political Facts; 1900–1994* (Macmillan, 7th ed., 1994), p. 127.
338 Colin Brown, 'Happy days are here again …', *The Independent*, 17 December 1990, p. 17. See also Anthony Seldon, *Major: A Political Life* (Weidenfeld & Nicolson, 1997), p. 148.
339 See chapter 15 of Anthony Seldon's biography, *Major: A Political Life*. See also, Anthony Seldon, 'Policy making and the Cabinet', in D. Kavanagh and A. Seldon (eds.), *The Major Effect* (Macmillan Papermac, 1994), p. 161; Colin Brown, 'Happy days here again …', *The Independent*, 17 December 1990, p. 17.
340 Sarah Hogg and Jonathan Hill, *Too Close to Call; Power and Politics – John Major in Number 10* (Little, Brown and Co., 1995), p. 13.

341 Anthony Seldon, 'Policy making and the Cabinet' in D. Kavanagh and A. Seldon (eds.), *The Major Effect,* p. 162.

342 Private information given to Peter Hennessy. See his Premiership Lecture, No.12, 'The Solo Coalitionist: John Major, 1990–', 4 March 1997, Gresham College.

343 Charles Powell continued to serve in the Prime Minister's Private Office as Private Secretary on Foreign Affairs until March 1991.

344 This quote from Sir Charles Powell appears in Penny Junor, *The Major Enigma* (Michael Joseph, 1993), p. 209.

345 Lord Wakeham, 'Cabinet Government', Brunel University, 10 November 1993. It is reproduced in *Contemporary Record,* vol.8, Winter 1994, pp. 473–483.

346 Article by Peter Hennessy, *The Times,* 21 October 1985, p. 4.

347 Paragraph 11 of the 1991 edition of *QPM.*

348 Sarah Hogg was Head of the Policy Unit between 1990–95. Jonathan Hill worked at No.10 between 1991–94, first in the Policy Unit, and then, from March 1992, as the Prime Minister's Political Secretary and Head of his Political Office.

349 Hogg and Hill, *Too Close to Call,* p. 14.

350 See Chapter 5.

351 Hogg and Hill, *Too Close to Call,* p. 60–1.

352 Paragraph 124 of the 1991 edition of *QPM.*

353 Paragraph 84 of the 1991 edition of *QPM.*

354 Philip Webster, 'Parkinson denies dealing rumours', *The Times,* 3rd November 1989; Richard Evans and Nicholas Wood, 'Parkinson named but not accused', *The Times,* 4 November 1989.

355 2nd November 1989.

356 *The Independent,* 3rd November, 1989; *The Times,* 3rd November 1989.

357 Richard Evans and Nicholas Wood, 'Parkinson named but not accused', *The Times,* 4 November 1989.

358 House of Commons, Official Report, 7th November 1989, Vol.159 (Session 1988–89), cols.515–7w. A Statutory Instrument [SI 1989/2164] was passed on 30th November 1989 to extend the definition of public servant for the purposes of section 2 of the Company Securities (Insider Dealing) Act 1985 to cover persons working within the Bank of England, Lloyd's and the Monopolies and Mergers Commission.

359 House of Commons, Official Report, 9th November 1989, Vol.159 (Session 1988–89), cols.723–4w.

360 See paragraph 54 of the 1958 edition of *QPM.*

361 Paragraph 84 of the 1991 edition of *QPM.*

362 Ibid., Paragraph 81.

363 Ibid., paragraph 82.

364 Ibid., paragraph 86.

365 Michael White & David Hencke, 'MPs ponder the "sleaze factor": Commons uproar revives row about conflicts of interest during the Thatcher years of lobbying and privatisation', *The Guardian,* 10 January 1990, p. 2

366 Colin Brown, '"Mr Nice" back at the centre of speculation and rumour. Cecil Parkinson; a profile', *The Independent,* 3rd November 1989, p. 6.

367 For an overall summary of such appointments up to 1990, see 'Nikki Knewstub traces the path from government to boardroom …', *The Guardian,* 27 August 1990, p. 7.

368 Alex Brummer, 'Time has come to think about Chinese Walls', *The Guardian,* 14 June 1990.

369 8th Report from the Treasury and Civil Service Committee, *Acceptance of Outside Appointments by Crown Servants,* H.C 302 (1983–4), App. 2.

370 Former Cabinet Ministers (Interests) Bill [176], Session 1989–90.

371 House of Commons, Official Report, 19 June 1990, Vol. 174, Cols. 793–794.

372 Paragraph 74 of the 1991 edition of *QPM.*

373 Paragraph 76 of the 1979 edition of *QPM.*

374 Paragraph 94 of the 1991 edition of *QPM.*

375 Paragraph 56 of the 1969 edition of *QPM*.

376 Paragraph 105 of the 1991 edition of *QPM*.

377 Paragraph 11 of the 1991 edition of *QPM*.

378 Lord Wakeham, 'Cabinet Government', *Contemporary Record,* vol.8, Winter 1994. See p. 482.

379 For example, in the case of *A-G v. Guardian Newspapers Ltd* (No.2), [1990] 1 AC 190, at 283, Lord Goff stated in his judgement that, 'I conceive it to be my duty, when I am free to do so, to interpret the law in accordance with the obligations of the Crown under the treaty [ECHR]'.

380 Between 1988, and January 1991, the UK Government appeared before the ECHR on two occasions in *Boyle v. UK* [1988] and *Soering v. UK* [1989]. In 1991, the UK was involved in a further two cases: *Observer and Guardian v. UK* [1991] and *Vilvarajah v. UK* [1991].

381 See Nicholas Grief, 'The domestic impact of the European Convention on Human Rights as mediated through Community Law', *Public Law* [1991], pp. 555–585.

382 *Reducing the Risk of Legal Challenge* (Cabinet Office, 1987).

383 See Chapter 5.

384 The injunctions restrained these newspapers from publishing information derived from Peter Wright during the course of his employment at MI5.

385 *Observer and Guardian v. UK* ECtHRR A 216 (1991) and *Sunday Times v. UK* (No.2) ECtHRR A .217 (1991). The case was reported in *The Guardian, The Independent* and *The Times,* on 27 November 1991.

386 Official Secrets Act 1989, Section 1. See also Richard Norton-Taylor, 'European judgement challenges Official Secrets Act; Spycatcher ban on papers ruled illegal', *The Guardian,* 26 October 1990.

387 Official Secrets Act 1989, see particularly section. 5. See also Peter Madgwick & Diana Woodhouse, *The Law and Politics of the Constitution of the United Kingdom* (Harvester Wheatsheaf, 1995), p. 269.

388 [1991] 1 AC 696.

389 Shiranikha Herbert, 'Law Report: Terrorist broadcasting ban not unreasonable', *The Guardian,* 8th February 1991.

390 For a summary of Lord Lester's arguments and the questions he put to the Government, see Lord Lester of Herne Hill, 'Government compliance with international human rights law: a new year's legitimate expectation', *Public Law,* Summer [1996], pp. 187–189.

391 Lord Lester, ibid., p. 188.

392 See Annex B of *The Government's Response to the First Report from the Committee on Standards in Public Life,* Cm 2931 (1995). Para.3 of the Civil Service Code states that Civil Servants are under a duty 'to comply with the law, including international law and treaty obligations, and to uphold the administration of justice.'

393 House of Lords, Official Report, W.A., cols. 44–45 (November 29, 1995).

394 House of Lords, Official Report, W.A., col. 57 (November 30, 1995).

395 Ministerial Code (July 1997, Cabinet Office), p. 2.

396 Sir Robin discussed Peter Hennessy's role and influence in a seminar chaired by Hennessy and which is reproduced in 'The Themes of Public Service Reform', *Policy Studies,* Autumn 1995, Vol.16, No.3.

397 Peter Hennessy published extracts of his correspondence with Number 10 in his 'Whitehall Watch' Column, *The Independent,* 25 November 1991.

398 Ibid.

399 *The Best Future for Britain,* Conservative Party Manifesto 1992, (Conservative Central Office, 1992).

400 Private information.

401 Private information.

402 Paragraph 22 of the 1991 edition of *QPM*.

403 Paragraph 18 of the first published version of *QPM*, (Cabinet Office, May 1992).

404 Ibid., paragraph 29(a).

405 Ian Aitken, 'No.10 press office quits party game.' 'Points of order', *The Guardian,* 18 October 1991, p. 6

406 Ibid., See also, 'Lobby decision', *The Independent,* 17 October 1991, p. 3.

407 This was added to paragraph 91(b) of *QPM* (May 1992).

408 This was added to paragraph 27 of *QPM* (May 1992).

409 See paragraphs 52 and 53 of *QPM* (May 1992).

410 Zai Bennett was a History/Politics undergraduate student at Queen Mary & Westfield College, University of London, when he used this phrase in an essay in March 1995. See Peter Hennessy, *The Hidden Wiring,* (Indigo, 1996), p. 187.

411 See Paragraph 1 of *QPM* (May 1992).

412 Ibid., paragraph 103.

413 Lord Nolan, 'Public Life; Public Confidence', The Richard Dimbleby Lecture 1997, 5th November 1997. This lecture was broadcast on BBC1 on 5th November 1997.

414 Private information.

415 Justice Parliament on CD Rom contains data of Parliamentary debates in the Commons and the Lords; written answers and Parliamentary Papers.

416 Excluding the tabloids.

417 This on-line search was conducted on 19th November 1997. As *QPM* is not often referred to by its full title, I searched for the following variations: 'procedure for Ministers', 'Ministerial rulebook', 'Ministers' rulebook' and 'Ministerial Code'.

418 For a detailed examination of the events leading to Mellor's resignation, see Diana Woodhouse, *Ministers and Parliament* (Clarendon Press, Oxford, 1994) pp. 77–86.

419 *QPM* (May 1992, Cabinet Office), para.126.

420 Lord Blake, 'Tough talk on gift guidelines; Diary', *The Times,* 24 September 1992, p. 12.

421 Colin Brown, 'Mellor quits amid Tory unrest', *Independent,* 25 September 1992, p. 1.

422 Lord Blake, op. cit.,

423 For a useful summary of 'John Major's Dwindling Majority 1992–7', see Anthony Seldon, *Major: A Political Life* (Weidenfeld & Nicolson, 1997), Appendix IV.

424 'Heseltine: I didn't break Cabinet rules', *Sunday Times,* 21 July 1996.

425 Paragraph 82 of the 1991 edition of *QPM.*

426 Lord Armstrong served as Secretary of the Cabinet from 1979–1987.

427 Quoted in 'Heseltine: I didn't break Cabinet rules', *Sunday Times,* 21 July 1996.

428 See Patrick Wintour & Richard Norton-Taylor, 'Whitehall defends Lamont deal', *The Guardian,* 30 November 1992, p. 3. See also, 'Lamont broke further rules over legal fees', *The Independent,* 2 December 1992, p. 2.

429 25th Report of the Public Accounts Committee; 'Payment of Legal Expenses incurred by the Chancellor of the Exchequer', HC 386, Session 1992–93, p. vi.

430 Ibid., p. viii.

431 *QPM* was retitled in 1997 to become the 'Ministerial Code' under Tony Blair's premiership.

432 My italics highlight the new text. See paragraph, 25, Ministerial Code (July 1997).

433 Private information.

434 Philip Webster, 'Major and Latimer sue two magazines for libel', *The Times,* 29 January 1993.

435 Michael White and Stephen Bates, 'Skids under Mates as support ebbs away', *The Guardian,* 22 June 1993, p. 2.

436 See paragraphs 79–81 and 126 of *QPM* (May 1992). See also Rodney Brazier, *Ministers of the Crown* (Clarendon Press, Oxford, 1997), p. 116.

437 Peter Riddell, 'Relieved Mates need not fall on his sword', *The Times,* 9 June 1993, p. 8.

438 House of Commons, Official Report, Vol. 226 (Session 1992–3), 8 June 1993, col.141.

439 Anthony Lester, 'A route through the moral malaise of public life', *The Guardian,* 11 October 994, p. 20. Lord Lester was referring to all the rules that existed (e.g. for Members of Parliament, civil servants and Ministers) — not just those contained in *QPM.*

440 Paragraph 85 of the Ministerial Code (July 1997) now states that, 'As a general rule Ministers should not offer gifts or initiate an exchange.'

441 Lord Nolan, 'Public Life: Public Confidence', The Richard Dimbleby Lecture, 5 November 1997.

442 First Report of the Committee on Standards in Public Life, Cm. 2850–I (HMSO, May 1995), p. 20.

443 Stephen Bates, 'Other Tories "would take cash for questions"', The Guardian, 11 July 1994, p. 2.

444 David Tredinnick and Graham Riddick both tendered their resignations on 10th July 1994.

445 Previously the Minister of State for Defence Procurement.

446 Peter Preston, 'The long corridor that led from 526', The Guardian (G2), 10 May 1994, p. 2.

447 The allegations against Hamilton and Smith first appeared in The Guardian, 20th October 1994. They were both accused of accepting money from a lobby firm, Ian Greer Associates, to ask questions on behalf of various clients, including the Harrods owner, Mohammed Al Fayed. Neil Hamilton was also accused of failing to declare a free 6–day stay at the Ritz Hotel, also owned by Mohammed Al-Fayed, which would have cost approximately £3,000. Tim Smith resigned immediately, but Hamilton clung on for 5 days before resigning on 25 October.

448 See Anthony Bevins and Chris Blackhurst, 'Sleaze; Major told he must clear Howard', The Guardian, 23 October 1994, p. 1.

449 See Stephen Castle, Paul Routledge and Brian Cathcart, 'Mark Thatcher accused; Sources say he got 12m pounds from arms deal signed by his mother', The Independent, 9 October 1994, p. 1.

450 Dale Campbell Savours brought an Early Day Motion (EDM 720) on 13th April 1989.

451 See the Seventh Report from the Committee on Standards and Privileges (Session 1997–8) HC 240 (HMSO, July 1997) and Eighth Report from the Committee on Standards and Privileges (Session 1997–8) HC 261 (HMSO, November 1997).

452 Luke Harding, David Pallister & Jamie Wilson, 'Revealed: Aitken's dirty tricks', The Guardian, 21st March 1997, p. 1

453 Andrew Pierce, 'Aitken is to offer himself for arrest', The Times, 17th March 1998.

454 Simon Jenkins, 'MPs need proper jobs', The Times, 17 May 1995.

455 The Richard Dimbleby Lecture, 1997, 'Public Life: Public Confidence', 5th November 1997.

456 For example, extracts of it were examined by the Royal Commission on Standards in Public Life, chaired by Lord Salmon in the mid-1970s. Cm.6524 (HMSO, 1976).

457 The Treasury and Civil Service select committee considered the published edition of QPM during their inquiry into the role of the Civil Service during the early 1990s, and criticised the document for being inadequate. However, the committee did not make any specific recommendations for amendment in their final report: 5th Report from the TCSC: Role of the Civil Service, HC 27–I (1993–94).

458 Private information.

459 First Report of the Committee on Standards in Public Life (Cm. 2850–I, HMSO, May 1995), para. 3.13.

460 Ibid., Recommendation 12, para. 3.13.

461 Ibid., Recommendation 13, para. 3.15.

462 Ibid., para. 3.16. These principles are also reproduced in Peter Hennessy's, The Hidden Wiring (Indigo, 1996), pp. 188–189.

463 Cm. 2850–I, Op. cit., Recommendation 13, para. 3.15. This was not implemented immediately, but the new Labour Government have re-named the document, Ministerial Code: A code of conduct and guidance on procedures for Ministers (July 1997).

464 Ibid., Recommendation 21, para. 3.41.

465 Government Response to the First Report of the Committee on Standards in Public Life (Cm 2931, HMSO, July 1995). See Annex A for the revised text.

466 Cm.2931, Ibid.

467 Cm. 2931, Ibid. This amendment has been incorporated into the new Ministerial Code (July 1997) by the new Labour Government.

468 Cm. 2931, Ibid.

469 This was passed as a Resolution of the House on 19 July 1995.

470 Parliament voted to appoint a Parliamentary Commissioner on Standards and a select committee

on Standards and Privileges on 6 November 1995 (see n 55). Sir Gordon Downey was appointed as Parliamentary Commissioner on 15 November 1995.

471 See *Guidelines on the Acceptance of Appointments outside Government by former Ministers of the Crown* (1995).

472 House of Commons Resolution of 6 November 1995. House of Commons, Official Report, Vol.265 (Session 1994–5), cols. 604–699.

473 Paragraph. 129, *Ministerial Code* (July 1997).

474 Paragraph. 128, *Ministerial Code* (July 1997).

475 The terms of reference of the Committee on Standards and Privileges are as follows:
   (a) to consider specific matters relating to privileges referred to it by the House;
   (b) to oversee the work of the Parliamentary Commissioner for Standards; to examine the arrangements proposed by the Commissioner for the compilation, maintenance and accessibility of the Register of Members' Interests and any other registers of interest established by the House; to review from time to time the form and content of those registers; and to consider any specific complaints made in relation to the registering or declaring or interests referred to it by the Commissioner; and
   (c) to consider any matter relating to the conduct of Members, including specific complaints in relation to alleged breaches in any code of conduct to which the House has agreed and which have been drawn to the committee's attention by the Commissioner; and to recommend any modifications to such code of conduct as may from time to time be necessary.

476 Peter Riddell, 'The politics of the small print', *The Times,* 29 July 1996.

477 Dawn Oliver, 'Standards of conduct in public life – what standards?', *Public Law* [1995] p. 502.

478 Sir Gordon Downey was appointed as the first Commissioner for Standards.

479 Kim Sengupta, 'Aitken admits to a lack of candour', *The Independent,* 12 June 1997, p. 4.

480 Sir Gordon Downey, Introduction to the Register of Members' Interests, (1997–8), HC291, 20 November 1997.

481 Sir Richard Scott was appointed Vice Chancellor in 1994.

482 *Report of the Inquiry into the Export of Defence Related Equipment and Dual Use Goods to Iraq and Related Prosecutions* (Scott Report) HC 115 (Session 1995–6), D4.63.

483 House of Commons, Official Report, 2 November 1995, Vol. 265, (Session 1995–6), cols.451–489.

484 The Conservative Government announced on 2nd November 1995, that the new paragraph took effect immediately and had been incorporated into the 1992 edition of *QPM.* However, to see the new text, refer to para. 1(iii), Ministerial Code, July 1997. The word 'knowingly' was inserted to bring *QPM* into line with the Civil Service Code. The word had originally been suggested by the TCSC report, *The Role of the Civil Service.* Recommendation 17 proposed that, 'any Minister who has been found to have knowingly misled Parliament should resign'.

485 Private information.

486 The Scott Report, op. cit., K8.5.

487 Sir Richard Scott, 'Ministerial Accountability', Public Law [1996] p. 424.

488 Following the Learmont enquiry into the Whitemoor and Parkhurst escapes, Derek Lewis was sacked for the operational failure of the Prison Services Agency. Lewis publicly complained of daily ministerial interference into operational matters. See 'My Life with Michael Howard', *The Independent,* 6 March 1996.

489 See Peter Riddell, *Parliament Under Pressure* (Gollancz, 1998), chapter on accountability.

490 Dawn Oliver, 'Standards of conduct in public life – what standards?', *Public Law* (1995), p. 497.

491 Second Report from the Public Service Committee, *Ministerial Accountability and Responsibility,* HC 313–I, (Session 1995–6), p. xxii, para.34.

492 Ibid., p. xxviii, para.53.

493 Ibid., p. xxix, para. 55.

494 First Special Report of the Public Service Committee, *Government Response to the Second Report from the Committee (Session 1995–6) on Ministerial Accountability and Responsibility,* HC 67 (Session 1996–7).

495 Although the Resolution was passed in the early hours of the morning, in a relatively empty Chamber, the Resolution was drafted after all-party talks. See Valerie Elliot, 'Talks on Ministerial Code', *The Times*, 18 January 1997.

496 Private information.

497 Peter Riddell, 'Tories should focus on what really matters', *The Times*, 1st August 1997, p. 8.

498 See Anthony Seldon, *Major: A Political Life* (Weidenfeld & Nicolson, 1997), Appendix IV.

499 Ann Taylor MP, Shadow Leader of the House of Commons, 'New Politics, New Parliament'. Speech to the Charter 88 seminar on Reform of Parliament, 14 May 1996.

500 Paragraph 1 (iii) of the *Ministerial Code* (July 1997).

501 Valerie Elliot & Andrew Pierce, 'Blair plans further tightening of the rules for ministers', *The Times*, 3 June 1997.

502 Ibid.

503 *The Times*, 3rd June 1997.

504 'Address by the Rt Hon Tony Blair MP, Leader of the Labour Party, to the Newspaper Society, London 10th March 1997', Labour Party Media Office, 10th March 1997.

505 Speech given by the Rt Hon Dr David Clark MP, Chancellor of the Duchy of Lancaster, 'The Civil Service and New Government', QEII Centre, 17 June 1997. The full text was issued as a press release.

506 Private information.

507 For example, in 1952, Attlee's departure created an opportunity for the Cabinet Office to remove an irksome ruling on consultation with the Law Officers (para.6, 1949). See 'note for the record' dated 28 November 1951, PRO, CAB 21/2778. Sir Alec Douglas-Home's resignation after the 1964 Election enabled officials to easily insert a paragraph, which they thought Douglas-Home may have objected to, dealing with the travel expenses of wives. See letter from W.J.M to Sir Burke Trend dated 12 October 1964, PRO, CAB 21/5199.

508 Seven General Elections in the post-war period have produced a new Prime Minister. Of those, six of the incoming Prime Ministers approved and issued an updated version of *QPM* in the first month of being in office.

509 See Chapter 7.

510 Who were appointed from the House of Commons.

511 Diana Woodhouse, 'Ministerial Responsibility: Something Old, Something New', *Public Law* (Summer, 1997), p. 205

512 *New Labour: because Britain deserves better.* The Government released their radical proposals for a Freedom of Information Act in a White Paper in December 1997, entitled *Your Right to Know: Freedom of Information* (Cm. 3818). For a review of this White Paper see, Maurice Frankel, 'Unlocking the Truth', *The Guardian* (G2 section), 16 December 1997, p. 17.

513 *Your Right to Know: The Government's proposals for a Freedom of Information Act* (1997– 8), Cm. 3818 (HMSO, December 1997).

514 Dr David Clark had set up a special unit in the Cabinet Office to handle the issue.

515 'Sacked minister hits out at information bill delay', Nicholas Watt, *The Guardian*, 18 November 1998.

516 David Hencke, 'Straw slows freedom of information legislation', *The Guardian*, 30 September 1998.

517 Philip Webster, 'Blair lays down the law on his MPs', *The Times*, 8th May 1997, p. 1.

518 *Ministerial Code* (July 1997).

519 Private information.

520 Private information.

521 House of Commons, Official Report (Session 1924), Vol. 169, 12 February 1924, col. 735.

522 PRO, PREM 13/ 434, 'Decision to allow Ministers to retain trades union posts'.

523 House of Commons, Official Report (Session 1964–65), Vol. 710, 5th April 1965, cc. 200–12.

524 PRO, PREM 13/ 434, Note, dated 31st March 1965, drafted by William McIndoe in preparation for Adjournment Debate of 5th April.

525 Private information.

526 'Bar on MP who failed to declare £6,000', *The Times,* 30 July 1997.

527 Jill Sherman, 'Bribery MP awaits party action', *The Times,* 13 June 1997, p. 11.

528 Shirley English, 'Suspended Labour MP appears in Court', *The Times,* 18 December 1997, p. 4.

529 BBC1, 'On the Record', 16 November 1997. See Michael White, 'Blair: I can still be trusted', *The Guardian,* 17 November 1997, p. 1.

530 For a summary of these events see Philip Webster, 'How Blair fell foul of donation fiasco', *The Times,* 14 November 1997, p. 13.

531 House of Commons, Official Report, 21st January 1998 (Session 1997–8), col.954.

532 Michael White & Roger Cowe, 'PM defends minister over £2m tax loophole', *The Times,* 31 July 1997. See also articles in *The Times,* 1 August 1997.

533 Tenth Report of the Committee on Standards and Privileges, *Complaints against Geoffrey Robinson.* Session 1997–98, HC 488. Eighteenth Report of the Committee on Standards and Privileges, *Complaints against Geoffrey Robinson* (No.2) Session 1997–98, HC 975.

534 Twentieth Report of the Committee on Standards and Privileges, *Complaints against Geoffrey Robinson* (No.3) Session 1997–98, HC 1190.

535 See *The Times* and *The Daily Telegraph,* 19th November 1998. See also 'Robinson put under renewed pressure', *The Times* 20th November 1998.

536 For an overall summary see 'Mandelson and the Millionaire', Caroline Merrell, *The Times,* 22nd December 1998.

537 'Robinson largesse aided key Labour players', David Hencke, *The Guardian,* 22 December 1998.

538 22nd December 1998.

539 See all national broadsheet newspapers on 24th December 1998.

540 Peter Mandelson's statement is reproduced in *The Guardian,* 22nd December 1998, p. 2. See also 'Government rules do not apply in this case, says minister', David Hencke & Ewan MacAskill, *The Guardian,* 22nd December 1998.

541 Foreword by the Prime Minister to the *Ministerial Code* (July 1997).

542 Paragraph 123, *Ministerial Code* (July 1997).

543 'Minister denies conflict over loan', Jill Sherman, *The Times,* 22nd December 1998.

544 Paragraph 127, *Ministerial Code* (July 1997).

545 'Tories stay on scent as Mandelson is cleared', Michael White, *The Guardian,* 9th January 1999.

546 See Richard Norton-Taylor and David Pallister, 'The Aitken Affair', *The Guardian,* 23 June 1997.

547 Elizabeth Filkin succeeded Sir Gordon Downey on his retirement in February 1999.

548 'Call to give MPs power to police ministers' conduct', David Hencke, *The Guardian,* 29th December 1998; 'MPs watchdog suggests extra remit for ministers', Jill Sherman, *The Times,* 30th December 1998.

549 Private information.

550 Private information.

551 Lord Nolan, 'The Executive', Second Radcliffe Lecture, 21 November 1996.

552 Letter from the Committee on Standards in Public Life, dated 24 April 1997.

553 The Ethics in Public Office Act was passed in 1995.

554 Private information.

555 Law Commission Paper 145, paras. 745–749. The Government is taking steps to review the law relating to bribery of, or receipt of bribes by MPs

556 This view was expressed in a letter from the Committee on Standards in Public Life, dated 24 April 1997.

557 Second Report from the Public Service Committee, *Ministerial Accountability and Responsibility,* Minutes of Evidence, HC 313–III, (1995–6), p. 72.

558 Conversation with Sir Richard Scott, 24th April 1997.

559 Private information.

560 James Blitz & George Parker, 'Whitehall's hybrid advisers arouse hostility', *Financial Times,* 3rd June 1997. See also *The Guardian* and *The Times,* 3rd June 1997.

561 For a summary of the role and function of special advisers, see Rodney Brazier, *Ministers of the Crown* (Clarendon Press, Oxford, 1997), pp. 141–3.

562 Ibid., p. 141.

563 Paragraph 48 of the *Ministerial Code* (July 1997).

564 Paragraph 49 of the *Ministerial Code* (July 1997).

565 Jonathan Freedland, 'Things can only get … worse?', *The Guardian,* 11 July 1998. See also David Hencke, 'Tough new code on lobbyists', *The Guardian,* 28 July 1998.

566 Gregory Palast, 'There are 17 people that count …' *The Observer,* 5 July 1998.

567 House of Commons, Official Report (Session 1997–98), 27 July 1998, col.4w.

568 For a summary of the new code on lobbyists see David Hencke, 'Tough new code on lobbyists', *The Guardian,* 28 July 1998.

569 Paragraphs 57–59 of the *Ministerial Code* (July 1997).

570 Paragraph 88 of the *Ministerial Code* (July 1997).

571 Sonia Purnell, 'Cabinet Big Guns Gagged by Blair', *Daily Mail,* 27 June 1997.

572 Peter Riddell, 'Tories should focus on what really matters, *The Times,* 1st August 1997, p. 8.

573 See chapter 4.

574 Private information.

575 Francis Pym, *The Politics of Consent* (Hamish Hamilton, 1984), p. 18.

576 The Ministerial committee on the co-ordination and presentation of Government policy (EDCP) was appointed on 20 March 1995.

577 Peter Hennessy, 'The Blair Style of Government: An Historical Perspective and an Interim Audit', Government and Opposition / Leonard Schapiro Lecture delivered at the London School of Economics, 2nd December 1997.

578 Ewan MacAskill, 'No. 10 tightens Whitehall grip', *The Guardian,* 27 November 1997.

579 *Report of the Working Group on the Government Information Service* (Cabinet Office; Office of Public Service, November 1997), recommendation 2.2.

580 Private information.

581 Patricia Wynn Davies, 'Ministers' air miles banned', *The Independent,* 25 February 1994, p. 9.

582 Private information.

583 See chapter 7.

584 Peter Madgwick and Diana Woodhouse, *The Law and Politics of the Constitution of the United Kingdom* (Harvester Wheatsheaf, 1995), p. 120.

585 Introductory paragraph to the 1992 edition of *QPM.*

586 This practice lapsed just before the start of the Second World War, and was never resumed; see chapter 1.

587 See paragraph 33 of the 1952 edition of *QPM* — which instructs Ministers to consult the Foreign Secretary before committing themselves to broadcasting abroad — and then to seek the permission of the Prime Minister. Whilst this clearly sets a prescriptive rule, it would not be regarded as significant to the constitutional framework of Cabinet government.

588 However, the main repository of precedents for the Cabinet Office continues to be the (unclassified) 'Precedent Book'.

589 I use the term 'private' here to indicate the government's private use and perception of *QPM.*

590 The talk was held at the Cabinet Office on 4 December 1992 for history undergraduate students at QMW college, University of London. See Peter Hennessy, *The Hidden Wiring* (Indigo, 1996), p. 33.

591 Ibid., p. 34.

592 Private information.

593 Anthony Seldon, *Major: A Political Life* (Weidenfeld & Nicolson, 1997), p. 556.

594 Talk for history undergraduate students at QMW college, University of London. The talk was held at the Cabinet Office on 20 February 1998.

595 Dawn Oliver, 'Standards of conduct in public life – what standards?', *Public Law* (1995), p. 502.

596 Private information.
597 Paragraph 1 of the *Ministerial Code* (July 1997).
598 Lord Lester of Herne Hill Q.C, 'Government compliance with international human rights law: a new year's legitimate expectation', *Public Law* (1996), pp. 187–189.
599 Valerie Elliot, 'Ministers may get own sleazebuster', *The Times,* 23 March 1998.

APPENDICES

C.P. (49) 95

29th April, 1949

CABINET

QUESTIONS OF PROCEDURE FOR MINISTERS

NOTE BY THE PRIME MINISTER

MY colleagues may find it convenient to have this consolidated and revised statement of the directives which I have issued from time to time on points of procedure and other similar matters. Special attention is drawn to the instructions in paragraph 40 regarding references in Ministerial speeches to Commonwealth affairs, which have not been included in any of my previous directives.

2. I should be glad if Ministers in charge of Departments would bring to the notice of Junior Ministers and officials such sections as concern them. For this purpose additional copies may be obtained from the Cabinet Office.

C.R.A.

10 Downing Street, S.W.1,

29th April, 1949.

I.—CABINET PROCEDURE

Preparation of Business for the Cabinet

1. The business of the Cabinet consists, in the main of—

(i) Questions of major policy which affect a number of Departments or engage the collective responsibility of the Government.

(ii) Questions on which there is a conflict of interest between Departments, which has not been resolved.

2. Except in cases of extreme urgency, questions falling under the second of these heads should not be referred to the Cabinet until all possible means of resolving the conflict have been exhausted, including personal correspondence or discussion between the Ministers concerned.

3. Similarly, it is the rule that matters falling under the first head should be thoroughly examined at the official level, if necessary interdepartmentally, before they are referred to Ministers, so that the policy decisions required may be clearly defined.

4. Proposals which involve expenditure, or affect general financial or economic policy; these should always be discussed with the Treasury—and, if Treasury agreement has not been secured at the official level, with the Chancellor of the Exchequer—before they are submitted to the Cabinet or to a Ministerial Committee. Full consideration must also be given to the probable cost in terms of man-power of any proposal involving new or extended administrative commitments. It is a standing instruction that any proposals submitted for consideration shall, if they would involve the employment of additional staff or would place a financial burden on the Exchequer, be accompanied by an estimate of—

(a) the man-power likely to be required by Government Departments (and also, where practicable, an estimate of the man-power required outside the Government service); and

(b) the cost to the Exchequer, whether direct or through grants-in-aid of local rates. An indication should always be given that the cost to the Exchequer has been discussed with the Treasury; and special attention should be drawn to proposals of whose potential man-power requirements the Treasury have not been informed.

5. These rules do not, of course, limit the right of Ministers to submit to the Cabinet memoranda setting out their views on general issues of policy.

6. Ministers should not hesitate to consult the Law Officers, as colleagues in the Government, on legal questions which arise in the formulation and administration of policy.

7. Matters which fall wholly within the Departmental responsibility of a single Minister and do not engage the collective responsibility of the Government need not be brought to Cabinet at all. A precise definition of such matters cannot be given and in borderline cases a Minister is well advised to bring the matter before his colleagues.

8. When a Minister wishes to raise a matter orally at the Cabinet, the Prime Minister's consent should be sought; and the earliest possible notice should be given to the Secretary.

Cabinet Memoranda

9. A Memorandum intended for consideration by the Cabinet, other than one commenting on a memorandum already circulated, must be circulated two clear days before the meeting at which it is to be considered. A precise formulation of this rule has been issued to all Departments by the Secretary of the Cabinet, who is responsible for seeing that it is strictly enforced. The permission of the Prime Minister is required for any exception to this rule and will be granted only in cases of extreme urgency.

10. Memoranda for the Cabinet should be as brief and as clear as possible. The model memorandum explains at the outset what the problem is, indicates briefly the relevant considerations and concludes with a precise statement of the decision sought. While it is sometimes useful to include a summary of the main points brought out in the body of the memorandum, such a summary should never exceed a few lines; any longer summary defeats its purpose and simply means repetition. So far as possible prefatory covering notes should be avoided. To facilitate reference in discussion, paragraphs should be numbered. Supporting data may often be relegated to an Appendix. If authority is sought to make a statement or despatch a telegram a draft may be attached. Time spent in making a memorandum short and clear will be saved many times over in reading and in discussion; and it is the duty of Ministers to ensure that this is done by personal scrutiny, and where necessary revision, of the memoranda submitted to them by their officials. In particular, the use of unnecessary neologisms and obscure technical terms should be avoided.

11. Cabinet memoranda (as distinct from memoranda for Cabinet Committees) are normally reproduced by the Cabinet Office, the text being sent by the originating Department to the Cabinet Office for the purpose. If, for any reason, a Cabinet memorandum is reproduced by the originating Department, all copies thus reproduced must be sent to the Cabinet Office, application being made to the Cabinet Office for any additional copies required by the reproducing Department. If an originating Department so wishes, a standing arrangement may be made, whereby the Cabinet Office will automatically supply a fixed number of additional copies of memoranda.

12. Subject to such special instructions in regard to any particular paper as he may receive from the Prime Minister or from the responsible Minister, the Secretary circulates memoranda and other documents prepared for their use to all members of the Cabinet and, where appropriate, to other Ministers whose Departments are affected.

13. In no circumstances, other than those provided for in paragraph 11 above, are Cabinet memoranda to be reproduced or copied in Departments. If a Department requires an additional copy or copies of a memorandum, application must in every case be made to the Cabinet Office.

Attendance at Cabinet

14. It is of assistance to the Secretary if Private Secretaries indicate, when asking for a subject to be placed on the Agenda, which Ministers, other than members of the Cabinet, are likely to be affected, so that arrangements may, if necessary, be made for their attendance.

15. Ministers summoned to meetings of the Cabinet for particular items will receive an Agenda Paper on which an approximate time will be set against each item. Every endeavour is made not to keep Ministers waiting, but the time at which each item will be reached cannot be forecast exactly. Cabinet meetings take precedence over other business. The utmost endeavours should be made by Ministers to be punctual and thus avoid wasting the time of their colleagues.

16. The Prime Minister's Private Secretary on duty at the Cabinet room is responsible for ensuring that the proceedings of the Cabinet are not disturbed. To assist him, Ministers should give general instructions that messages are not to be sent to them while in Cabinet, unless they are so urgent that they cannot wait until the end of the meeting.

17. If a member of the Cabinet, or a Minister summoned for a particular item, is unable, for any reason, to be present at a meeting of the Cabinet, he should notify the Secretary, who will inform the Prime Minister and will also consider whether any rearrangement of business is required.

18. The Secretary should also be informed of Ministers' out-of-town engagements, and also of their week-end and holiday arrangements, in order that, if some sudden emergency arises, he may be in a position to inform the Prime Minister at once which Ministers are immediately available.

Cabinet Conclusions

19. It is an instruction to the Secretary, in drafting Cabinet Conclusions, to avoid, so far as practicable, reference to opinions expressed by particular Ministers. The record in respect of each item will be limited to the decision of the Cabinet, together with such summary of the discussion as may be necessary for the guidance of those called upon to take action on the decision. Matters of exceptional secrecy may be recorded in a "Confidential Annex."

20. Copies of the Conclusions are circulated by the Secretary to Cabinet Ministers and Ministers of Cabinet rank. Copies of "Confidential Annexes" are sent only to the Ministers directly concerned.

21. Any suggested amendments to Cabinet Conclusions must reach the Secretary not later than the next day but one following that on which the Meeting was held. Thereafter the Conclusions will be sent to be printed in final form.

22. All Ministers are responsible for giving such instructions to their Departments as may be necessary to give effect to the Conclusions of the Cabinet, and for communicat-

ing to subordinate Departments or branches decisions of which they should be made aware. Where an urgent matter arises in Cabinet unexpectedly, and a decision is reached requiring immediate action by a Department not represented at the meeting, the Secretary will ensure that the Department concerned is notified forthwith.

23. Where a Department has to take action upon, or is otherwise directly affected by, a particular Conclusion, the actual decisions of the Cabinet on that matter may be copied in the Department, together with so much of the record of the discussion as is essential to a proper understanding of them and these extracts may be passed to responsible officers in the Department, as may be necessary. The distribution within a Department of such extracts from Cabinet Conclusions should be limited to the occasions on which it is strictly necessary for the efficient discharge of public business and care, should be taken to see that extracts are sent only to those officers of the Department who need be acquainted with the actual terms of the decision. Duplicate copies of the complete Conclusions are not issued for this purpose by the Cabinet Office save in exceptional cases. Where action has to be taken at once by a Department without waiting for the circulation of the full Conclusions, application may be made to the Secretary for an advance copy of the relevant Conclusions.

24. In this connection the position of the Parliamentary Secretary should not be overlooked. He may have to deputise for his Minister, at Cabinet or in the House, at short notice. Apart from any special responsibility assigned to him in a limited field, he should be fully informed of the work of the Department and kept in general touch with all Cabinet matters affecting it, so that when called upon to attend a meeting in place of the Minister he understands the subject and does not merely recite a brief. (On the work of Parliamentary Secretaries generally see C.P. (49) 31.)

Return of Cabinet Documents

25. Cabinet documents remain the property of the Crown. The normal practice is, therefore, that Ministers, on relinquishing office, return to the Cabinet Office all Cabinet, documents, with the exception of any immediately required for current administration, may be handed on to their successors. In order to facilitate this arrangement Ministers are asked to arrange for the return to the Cabinet Office during their tenure of office, say, at intervals of three to six months, of such Cabinet documents as are not required for current administration.

The provision above for handing on certain Cabinet documents to a Minister's successor, does not always apply on a change of Government: special instructions will be issued to cover such cases.

II. — COMMITTEES OF THE CABINET

Committee Procedure

26. The procedure outlined above applies *mutatis mutandis* to Ministerial Committees of the Cabinet.

27. While Committee meetings provide at times a useful forum for the discussion of policy and for enabling Ministers to ensure that their points of view are understood and to make a contribution to the formulation of policy, their prime object is the despatch of business and the making of decisions. Interdepartmental questions should be settled as far as possible between officials, or failing that between Ministers of the Departments directly concerned. They should not be allowed to drag on. Where colleagues have to be consulted, but only two or three are directly concerned, agreement can often be reached by correspondence or by personal meetings; much time can be saved by personal contact. Failing agreement recourse can be had to the Prime Minister, Lord President or Chancellor of the Exchequer. This will often make it unnecessary to take the matter to a Committee.

28. Particular points which the Prime Minister wishes the Chairmen of Committees to keep in mind are:—

(a) Care should be taken to prevent papers coming forward for discussion which could be settled otherwise; and Secretaries of Committees should be encouraged to submit Suggestions for reducing the amount of business to be transacted at full Meetings.

(b) Attendance should be restricted to the permanent members and other Ministers who have a major interest in the question under discussion. Ministers should not be required to sit through lengthy discussions, in case points affecting their Departments should be raised; nor should they insist on attending meetings, for the purpose of making Departmental points which have no important bearing on the main issues under discussion. Arrangements should be made for the attendance of one of the Law Officers at meetings at which legal issues are likely to arise.

(c) Discussion should be kept to the point; irrelevance or repetition should be checked.

(d) Conclusions should not be framed in a way which will require further discussion by Ministers, if that is not necessary. Once a policy decision has been taken, responsibility for its detailed working out and the supervision of its execution can usually be left to the Ministers departmentally concerned.

(e) The dilatory process of referring a question from one Committee to another should be avoided as far as possible.

(f) Much time is lost in the aggregate if meetings do not begin punctually at the appointed hour.

Secrecy of Cabinet Committees

29. While the collective responsibility of Ministers often calls for discussion between Ministers on some important question which falls wholly or mainly within the purview of a single Department, the normal course is for the resulting decision to be announced and defended by the Minister concerned as his own decision.

30. There may be rare occasions when it is desirable to emphasise the importance of some decision by stating specifically that it is the decision of His Majesty's Government. This, however, should be the exception rather than the rule. The growth of any general practice whereby decisions of the Cabinet were announced as such would lead to embarrassment. Thus, some decisions of Government would be regarded as less authoritative than others. It is contrary to accepted practice for Government decisions to be announced in terms which disclose or imply that they have been reached by a particular Committee of the Cabinet Critics of the decision reached by a particular Ministerial Committee would press for its review by some other Committee or by the Cabinet, while the constitutional right of individual Ministers to speak in the name of the Government as a whole would be impaired.

31. The underlying principle is, of course, that the method adopted by Ministers for discussion among themselves of questions of policy is essentially a domestic matter, and is no concern of Parliament or the public. The doctrine of collective responsibility of Ministers depends, in practice, upon the existence of opportunities for free and frank discussion between them, and such discussion is hampered if the processes by which it is carried out are laid bare.

III. — PRECAUTIONS AGAINST UNAUTHORISED DISCLOSURES OF INFORMATION

33. Disclosures in the Press of matters under discussion by the Cabinet or its Committees damage the reputation of the Government, impair the efficiency of its administration and assist its opponents.

The General Rule

34. Ministers who share the collective responsibility for the Government's programme must be generally aware of the development of important aspects of Government policy. But, outside this narrow circle, knowledge of these matters should be confined to those, whether Ministers or officials, whose duty it is to assist in the formulation of the particular policy concerned, but who need to know what is afoot because of its effect on other aspects of public business for which they are responsible.

35. Government policy should not be discussed with persons outside Government service unless this is necessary for the transaction of public business; and care should be taken to see that private discussions between Members of the Government are not held in places where they may be overheard. In particular, it is contrary to the doctrine of collective responsibility to make known the attitude of individual Ministers on matters of policy.

Points to be Kept in Mind

36. Ministers have a personal responsibility for ensuring that all members of their staffs understand the need for exercising the strictest discretion, and in particular for see-

ing that the appropriate precautions are strictly observed in their Departments. In this connection the following considerations should be borne in mind:—

(1) While it is within the discretion of Ministers to decide which of their advisers or subordinates should be shown Cabinet papers, the normal rule is that such papers, should not be seen by any save their immediate advisers concerned in the, formulation of policy. In particular, Cabinet should not be circulated as a matter of course to Information Officers or their staffs. It is important that these Officers should have enough background information to enable them to discharge their functions intelligently and to offer advice on matters within their province in time for it to be effective; and it is necessary for these reasons that they should be informed at once of some of the decisions of the Cabinet or its Committees, and, on occasion, of progress in the formulation of policy by the Cabinet or its Committees. Each Minister is, however, personally responsible for deciding how much of this information should be conveyed to his Information Officer; and it is preferable that the information should be imparted, with appropriate guidance, by the Minister himself.

(2) Ministers are expected to exercise a real measure of control in this matter, and must satisfy themselves from time to time that their instructions are being carried out.

(3) A Minister who is a Member of the Cabinet has responsibilities wider than those of his own Department, and will in that capacity receive some documents which are of no concern to any of his subordinates.

(4) A Parliamentary Private Secretary is not a member of the Government; and the information given to him should be correspondingly limited.

(5) Documents containing and reflecting the personal views of Ministers are in a special category, and their handling requires special care, if the collective responsibility of the Cabinet as a whole is to be preserved. This applies particularly to the Minutes of the Cabinet and its main Standing Committees; in the handling of which the procedure laid down in paragraph 2a above should be followed.

(6) If occasions arise on which it is necessary that any considerable number of officers should be consulted in particular issues arising out of Cabinet memoranda, this should be done by means of minutes addressed to the officers concerned, confined to, the, particular points on which they are required to advise, thus avoiding a wide circulation of the memoranda themselves.

(7) Experience has shown that leakages of information have often occurred as a result of the skilful piecing together, by representatives of the Press, of isolated scraps of information, each in itself apparently of little importance, gathered from several sources. The only safe rule is, therefore, never to mention such matters even in the form of guarded allusions, except to those who must be informed of them for reasons of State, until the time has come when disclosure, in whole or in part, is authorised. Reasons of State may require, in appropriate

cases, the confidential communication of some information to a responsible editor, lobby correspondent, &c., for purposes of guidance; but such communication is only justified where it can be ensured that the confidence and the terms on which it is made are respected.

Need for Discretion

37. Secrecy cannot, however, be secured, solely by rules, however carefully drawn, restricting the circulation of papers; public business cannot be transacted without a fairly wide dissemination of confidential information within Government circles; and the essential point is the observance of a high standard of discretion by all who acquire knowledge of such information in the Course of their duties — an attitude of mind which puts first the interests of the Government as a whole and subordinates everything to that end. It is the duty of Ministers to set this standard of discretion in regard to all confidential matters which come within their knowledge, to give an example to others, and to see that their example is followed.

Responsibility of the Lord Chancellor

38. The Prime Minister has asked the Lord Chancellor to assume a general responsibility for investigating unauthorised disclosures of information about the proceedings of the Cabinet or Cabinet Committees. Ministers are asked to notify the Lord Chancellor of any such disclosure which comes to their notice and to assist him in any investigation involving their Department.

IV. — MINISTERIAL SPEECHES, BROADCASTS, &c.

General

39. When addressing meetings Ministers must keep within the ambit of Government policy and not anticipate decisions not yet made public. They must be careful in dealing with matters within the responsibility of other Ministers not to embarrass them by statements at variance with Ministerial pronouncements. In all cases of doubt they should consult the Minister concerned.

40. The Foreign Office should invariably be consulted before any mention is made of matters affecting our relations with foreign powers or foreign affairs: and Ministers wishing to make reference to broad matters of defence policy should in all cases first consult the Minister of Defence. Ministers should also be specially careful in referring to matters affecting our relations with self-governing Commonwealth countries, or to the political aspects of Colonial affairs, e.g., self-government in certain Colonies, and should consult the Commonwealth Relations Office or Colonial Office respectively, except when the matter falls within their own responsibility.

41. In the present international situation care is needed as to what said by Ministers in conversations at social functions at Embassies. If matters of foreign policy are discussed

at such functions, a note should, be made afterwards of the salient points of the conversation and a copy sent to the Foreign Secretary.

Effect on Parliamentary Business

42. Unless they have first obtained the agreement of the Leader of the House of Commons, Ministers should avoid saying anything which might affect the programme of Government business in Parliament. Thus, they should not, without his agreement, promise White Papers, the publication of which might result in a demand for a special debate : and legislation should never be promised without the express approval of the Cabinet or the Legislation Committee. This is a matter in which special care is necessary, since statements made by Ministers are liable to be represented in the Press as foreshadowing early legislation.

Speeches at Parliamentary By-Elections and Local Government Elections

43. Members of the Cabinet should not normally speak at By-Elections; but other Ministers, including those of Cabinet rank, may do so. As a general rule Ministers above the rank of Parliamentary Secretary should not speak at local government elections. There may, however, be occasions on which a Minister may feel obliged to do so for special reasons, particularly in his own constituency.

Broadcasting Arrangements

44. Ministerial broadcasts should be kept to the minimum. All Ministers intending to broadcast should communicate with the Postmaster-General, who will be responsible for obtaining the Prime Minister's approval in all cases and for making the necessary arrangements with the B.B.C. In view of the fact that broadcasts by Ministers may be regarded by the B.B.C. or by the Opposition as controversial and therefore giving a claim to a reply, the subject of the broadcast must in all cases be given and the Prime Minister may require to see either an outline or the text of a broadcast before giving approval.

V. — PRESS ARTICLES AND INTERVIEWS BY MINISTERS

Press Articles

45. Ministers are precluded from journalism in any form; but this prohibition does not extend to authorship of writings of a literary, historical, scientific, philosophical or romantic character. For these there are abundant precedents.

46. This rule need not be interpreted as debarring Ministers from writing, on occasion, articles or letters to newspapers, in order to supplement the means already used for enlightening the public in regard to measures before Parliament and other administrative questions affecting the work of their Departments. (On replies to letters and statements in the Press, see paragraph 62 below.)

47. Should a Minister deem it necessary to write such an article, he should not accept payment if it is offered. In deciding whether to write an article he should bear in mind

his obligations to Parliament. For example, he should be careful not to discuss a Bill before it has received its Second Reading in the House of Commons.

48. These rules govern dealings with the foreign as well as the home Press.

Interviews

49. The granting of special interviews to individual Press representatives is a matter for the discretion of the Minister concerned. As a general rule, however, the same, considerations should apply as for written articles i.e., if granted, an interview should be confined to elucidating the policy or work of the Minister and Department concerned. The same considerations regarding obligations to Parliament also apply, and Ministers should bear in mind that an interview granted to a representative of a single newspaper or agency may arouse jealousy and thus hostility in the rest of the Press.

Contributions to Party Publications

50. The general prohibition on the writing of articles for the Press need not be regarded as debarring Ministers from contributing to the publications of the political organisations with which they are associated. Payment should not be accepted for such articles.

General

51. In general, Ministers should keep such activities to a minimum, and bear in mind that their relations with the Press are always liable to be the subject of Questions in Parliament. Ministers should refer to the Prime Minister in any case about which they are in doubt.

VI. — PARLIAMENTARY PRIVATE SECRETARIES

52. Parliamentary Private Secretaries occupy a special position which is not always understood by the general public, either at home or abroad. They are not members of the Government, and should be careful not to be spoken of as such. They are Private Members, and should therefore be afforded as great a liberty of action as possible; but their close and confidential association with Ministers necessarily imposes certain obligations on them, and has led to the generally accepted practice set out in the following paragraph.

53. Parliamentary Private Secretaries should not make statements in the House or put Questions on matters affecting the Department with which they are connected. They should also exercise great discretion in any speeches or broadcasts which they make outside the House, taking care not to make statements which appear to be made in an official or semi-official capacity, and bearing in mind at the same time that, however careful they may be to make it clear that they are speaking only as Private Members, they are nevertheless liable to be regarded as speaking with some of the authority which attaches to a member of the Government. Generally they must act with a sense of responsibility

and with discretion; and they must not associate themselves with particular groups advocating special policies.

VII. — ABSENCE OF MINISTERS FROM THE UNITED KINGDOM

54. It is the established practice for a Member of the Cabinet or a Minister in charge of a Department to obtain the King's permission to be absent from the United Kingdom, whether on duty or on leave, and to inform His Majesty of the arrangements which he proposes to make for the administration of his office during that time.

55. Any such arrangements must have the Prime Minister's prior approval and are subject to certain general limitations. In the absence of a Secretary of State, submissions to His Majesty must be made on his behalf by another Secretary of State. Submissions on behalf of the First Lord of the Admiralty may be made in his absence by the Senior Lord Commissioner. In the absence of other Cabinet Ministers, submissions may be made by the Parliamentary Secretary of the Department concerned, if he is a Privy Councillor; if not, by another Cabinet Minister.

56. Parliamentary Secretaries who wish to be absent from the United Kingdom should obtain the consent of the Prime Minister as well as of their own Minister.

VIII. – MISCELLANEOUS

57. Ministers may find it helpful to have available in this note a reference to instructions issued from time to time on other procedural and allied matters.

Statements after Questions

58. When Parliament is in session, important announcements of Government policy should be made, in the first instance, in Parliament. At the same time it is desirable to keep to the minimum the number of announcements made by way of statements at the end of Questions. Ministers are asked to conform with the following procedure:-

(a) Ministers proposing to make a statement after Questions, whether or not it is related to a Question on the Order Paper, should notify the Prime Minister's Private Secretary as early as possible and in any event not later than 10 a.m. on the day on which the statement is to be made. Particulars should be given of the subject matter of the proposed statement, the date on which it is desired to make it, and the grounds for making it on that date and adopting this method of announcement. It should also be stated whether the announcement has been approved by the Cabinet or one of its Committees.

(b) Copies of the draft statement should be sent, as soon as it is available, to the Prime Minister's Private Secretary and to the Leader of the House of Commons and the Chief Whip. These copies should arrive not later than 10 a.m. on the day on which the statement is to be made.

(c) It is at times desirable that a copy of such a statement should be shown to the

Opposition shortly before it is made. If this is desired, a copy of the final text should reach the office of the Chief Whip in the House of Commons not later than 10 a.m. on the day on which the statement is to be made.

(d) A copy of the final text should in all cases be sent to the Speaker.

(e) It may sometimes be expedient that a statement should be made simultaneously in the House of Lords. Ministers should, where necessary, consult the Leader of the House of Lords on this point.

Publicity Arrangements for White Papers

59. Care must be taken to avoid any possibility of an infringement of Parliamentary Privilege when publicity arrangements are made for White Papers. The accepted practice is for final revised proof copies of White Papers to be made available to Lobby Correspondents somewhat in advance of their being laid in the Vote Office and for Ministers to hold a Lobby Conference if they think it desirable. The Prime Minister has made his Adviser on Public Relations responsible for these arrangements generally and he should always be consulted by Departmental officials if there is any question of a wider advance distribution than this. Such wider distribution — e.g., to industrial correspondents — is to be avoided save in exceptional circumstances.

Signature on Subordinate Legislation

60. As a normal rule Ministers should themselves sign all statutory instruments (other than Orders in Council) which fall within the terms of reference of the Select Committee on Statutory Instruments, i.e., all instruments laid or laid in draft before Parliament, being instruments upon which proceedings may be, or might have been, taken in either House in pursuance of any Act of Parliament.

Crown Proceedings Act

61. Under the provisions of the Crown Proceedings Act, 1947, an order for the discovery of documents may be made against Government Departments. If, however, the appropriate Minister is of opinion that the production of a particular document would be injurious to the public interest, he may withhold production of that document. This right to withhold production of a document is of the greatest importance and should be exercised only after the most careful consideration. The Minister himself must personally consider the document in question and form his own judgment, with such advice as he thinks fit to take, whether or not the public interest would be injuriously affected by its disclosure.

Replies to Letters and Statements in the Press

62. Possible methods of dealing with letters and statements to the Press which are inaccurate or otherwise objectionable are set out in C.P. (47) 178. The general line to be taken was stated in the Prime Minister's reply to a question on 8th October 1946—

"It should be, I think, a general rule that, where the personal conduct of Ministers is concerned, the matter should be dealt with by the Minister himself." (*Hansard*, Vol. 427, Col. 25),

and the reply given by Mr. Churchill in the House on 22nd February, 1945—

"The best practice is that Ministers of the Crown should themselves expound all matters of Government policy, and that press interviews by officials should only be given on Ministerial responsibility and after due authorisation by the political chief. Such expressions of opinion by officials would usually have regard to technical aspects only. Of course, in an emergency, exceptions may be made. The principle of Ministerial responsibility to Parliament is paramount" (*Hansard*, Vol. 408, Col. 954)

63. Letters to the Press from Information Officers should be purely informative and must not enter into arguments on the merits of Government policy.

Consultation with the Trades Union Congress, &c.

64. Ministers should be careful to ensure that, wherever appropriate, the Trades Union Congress — and in suitable cases individual Trades Unions — are taken into consultation at an early stage. Hard and fast rules cannot be laid down and individual Ministers must judge cases on their own merits. The normal practice as regards consultation on matters of general industrial policy and principle and on appointments to Government bodies, &c., is outlined in C.P. (47) 46. Ministers should also bear in mind the desirability of including in the membership of Government Committees and other bodies, where appropriate, either an official representative of the Co-operative Movement or a member of the Co-operative Movement chosen in his personal capacity.

Employment of Judges

65. Ministers should not approach Judges for extra-judicial work without consulting the Lord Chancellor.

MINISTERIAL CODE

A CODE OF CONDUCT AND GUIDANCE ON
PROCEDURES FOR MINISTERS
FOREWORD
BY
THE PRIME MINISTER

In issuing this Code, I should like to reaffirm my strong personal commitment to restoring the bond of trust between the British people and their Government. We are all here to serve and we must all serve honestly and in the interests of those who gave us our positions of trust.

I will expect all Ministers to work within the letter and spirit of the Code. Ministers will find the Code a useful source of guidance and reference as they undertake their official duties in a way that upholds the highest standards of propriety.

I have decided to publish this document because openness is a vital ingredient of good, accountable Government. And we will extend openness further through a Freedom of Information Act.

I believe we should be absolutely clear about how Ministers should account, and be held to account, by Parliament and the public. The first paragraph of the Code sets out these responsibilities clearly, following the terms of the House of Commons Resolution, on Ministerial Accountability carried last March.

I commend the Code to all of my Ministerial colleagues.

TONY BLAIR

MINISTERIAL CODE

INDEX

ANNEX: MEMBERSHIP OF LLOYD'S

1. MINISTERS OF THE CROWN

1.   Ministers of the Crown are expected to behave according to the highest standards of constitutional and personal conduct in the performance of their duties. In particular, they must observe the following principles of Ministerial conduct:

i.   Ministers must uphold the principle of collective responsibility;

ii.   Ministers have a duty to Parliament to account, and be held to account, for the policies, decisions and actions of their Departments and Next Steps Agencies;

iii.   It is of paramount importance that Ministers give accurate and truthful information to Parliament, correcting any inadvertent error at the earliest opportunity. Ministers who knowingly mislead Parliament will be expected to offer their resignation to the Prime Minister;

iv.   Ministers should be as open as possible with Parliament and the public, refusing to provide information only when disclosure would not be in the public interest, which should be decided in accordance with relevant statute and the Government's Code of Practice and Access to Government Information (Second Edition, January 1997);

v.   Similarly, Ministers should require civil servants who give evidence before Parliamentary Committees on their behalf and under their directions to be as helpful as possible in providing accurate, truthful and full information in accordance with the duties and responsibilities; of civil servants as set out in the Civil Service Code (January 1996);

vi.   Ministers must ensure that no conflict arises, or appears to arise, between their public duties and their private interests;

vii.   Ministers should avoid accepting any gift or hospitality which might, or might reasonably appear to, compromise their judgement or place them under an improper obligation;

viii.   Ministers in the House of Commons must keep separate their role as Minister and constituency Member;

ix.   Ministers must not use resources for party political purposes. They must uphold the political impartiality of the Civil Service, and not ask civil servants to act in any way which would conflict with the Civil Service Code.

These notes detail the arrangements for the conduct of affairs by Ministers. They are intended to give guidance by listing the principles and the precedents which may apply. They apply to all Members of the Government (the position of Parliamentary Private Secretaries is described, separately in Section 4.) The notes should be read against the background of the duty of Ministers to comply with the law, including international law and treaty obligations, and to uphold the administration of justice, the general obligations listed above; and in the context of protecting the integrity of public life. Ministers must also, of course, adhere at all times to the requirements Parliament has itself laid down. For Ministers in the Commons, these are set by the Resolution carried on 19 March 1997 (Official Report, Columns 1946-47): the terms of the Resolution are repeated at ii to v above. For Ministers in the Lords, Official Report Col. 1057. It will be for individual Ministers to judge how best to act in order to uphold the highest standards. They are responsible for justifying their conduct to Parliament. And they can only remain in office for so long as they retain the Prime Minister's confidence.

2. MINISTERS AND THE GOVERNMENT

Attendance at meetings of the Privy Council

2.   Once a Minister has accepted a Summons to a meeting of the Privy Council this should take precedence over all other engagements. If a Minister is subsequently unable to attend because of illness, or an inescapable public duty, the Clerk of the Council must be informed immediately. If a Minister has a meeting immediately before a Council, the agenda should be arranged to leave ample time to reach the Palace. In no circumstances is it permissible for a Minister not to attend because an earlier meeting has overrun its time. The failure of a Minister to attend a Council after a summons has been accepted is not only discourteous to The Queen but could result in no quorum being present to transact essential Government business.

Cabinet and Ministerial Committee business

3.   Cabinet and Ministerial Committee business consists, in the main, of:

  a.   Questions which significantly engage the collective responsibility of the Government, because they raise major issues of policy or because they are of critical importance to the public;

  b.   Questions on which there is an unresolved argument between Departments.

Matters wholly within the responsibility of a single Minister and which do not significantly engage collective responsibility as defined above need not be brought to the Cabinet or to a Ministerial Committee unless the Minister wishes to have the advice of colleagues. A precise definition of such matters cannot be given; in borderline cases a Minister is advised to seek collective consideration. Questions involving more than one Department should be examined interdepartmentally, before submission to a Ministerial Committee, so that the decisions required may be clearly defined.

Ministerial Committees

4.   The Cabinet is supported by Ministerial Committees (both standing and ad hoc) which have a two-fold purpose. First they relieve the pressure on the Cabinet itself by settling as much business as possible at a lower level; or failing that, by clarifying the issues and defining the points of disagreement. Second, they support the principle of collective responsibility by ensuring that, even though an important question may never reach the Cabinet itself, the decision will be fully considered and the final judgement will be sufficiently authoritative to ensure that the Government as a whole can be properly expected to accept responsibility for it. When there is a difference between Departments, it should not be referred to the Cabinet until other means of resolving it have been exhausted, including personal correspondence or discussions between the Ministers concerned.

5.   If the Ministerial Committee system is to function effectively, appeals to the Cabinet must clearly be infrequent. Chairmen of Committees are required to exercise their

discretion in advising the Prime Minister whether to allow them. The only automatic right of appeal is if Treasury Ministers are unwilling to accept expenditure as a charge on the reserve; otherwise the Prime Minister will entertain appeals to the Cabinet only after consultation with the Chairman of the Committee concerned. Departmental Ministers should normally attend in person meetings of Committees of which they are members or to which they are invited; unless they make it possible for their colleagues to discuss with them personally issues which they consider to be important, they cannot—except where their absence is due to factors outside their control—expect the Prime Minister to allow an appeal against an adverse decision taken in their absence.

The priority of Cabinet meetings

6.   Cabinet meetings take precedence over all other business except of the Privy Council, although it is understood that Ministers may occasionally have to be absent for reasons of Parliamentary business. Requests by Cabinet Ministers for permission to be absent should be made only in the most exceptional circumstances, and should be made at the earliest opportunity and in writing to the Prime Minister. A minute is not necessary when the reason for absence from Cabinet is an overseas visit for which the Prime Minister's approval has already been obtained. As is indicated in paragraph 69(a) below, a copy of the letter seeking the Prime Minister's approval for the overseas visit or absence for any other reason should be sent to the Secretary of the Cabinet. (See paragraph 5 above for attendance at Cabinet Committees.)

7.   In order not to disturb the proceedings of the Cabinet and Ministerial Committees, Ministers should see that messages are not sent to them during meetings unless this is absolutely essential. A Minister invited to attend for a particular item will be called into the meeting by the Prime Minister's Private, Secretary (or the Secretary of the Committee) as soon as the item for which he or she is required has been reached.

Preparation of business for Cabinet and Ministerial Committees

8.   Guidelines on the conduct of Cabinet and Ministerial Committee business is set out in Cabinet Committee Business published by the Cabinet Office. In all cases the Secretary should be given at least seven days' notice of any business likely to require substantive policy discussion (including business to be raised orally) which a Minister wishes to bring before the Cabinet or a Committee. Memoranda should be circulated in sufficient time to enable Ministers to read and digest them, and to be properly briefed. Memoranda for Cabinet and Ministerial Committees should be circulated at least two full working days and a weekend in advance of the meeting at which they are to be discussed. If decisions; are urgently required, and an interval including a weekend is not possible, memoranda should be circulated as long before a meeting as possible, and at least two full working days before they are to be discussed. Where a Minister wishes to advise Cabinet of an issue on which no substantive policy discussion is expected, the Private Office should alert the Secretary of the Cabinet in the morning of the day before Cabinet.

9.   Ministers' Private Secretaries can help the Secretary by indicating where Ministers other than members of the Cabinet are likely to be concerned with a subject, so that arrangements may be made for their attendance.

10.   It is the responsibility of the initiating Department to ensure that proposals have been discussed with other interested Departments and the results of these discussions reflected in the memorandum submitted to Cabinet or a Ministerial Committee. Proposals involving expenditure or affecting general financial policy should be discussed with the Treasury before being submitted to the Cabinet or a Ministerial Committee. The result of the discussion together with an estimate of the cost to the Exchequer (or estimates, including the Treasury's estimate, if the Department and the Treasury disagree) should be included, along with an indication of how the cost would be met (e.g.. by offsetting savings). The estimate of the cost should identify any impact on other Departments. The list of other Departments to be consulted will depend on the proposal but, as a general guide, proposals involving legal implications, especially if there is a risk of successful legal challenge, should be cleared with the Law Officers. The Scottish Office, Northern Ireland Office and Welsh Office must be consulted where proposals have implications for their areas of responsibility. Memoranda should also include a regulatory appraisal where proposals affect business, charities or voluntary organisations; confirmation that the European Law Checklist has been followed if European requirements are being implemented; any significant costs or benefits to the environment; any change in local government responsibilities; consequences for European Union, European Court of Human Rights and other international obligations; and presentational aspects including, where appropriate, a draft statement or announcement. If, exceptionally, papers are circulated as minutes addressed to the Prime Minister, they are subject to the same requirements.

11.   These rules do not limit the right of Ministers to submit to the Cabinet memoranda setting out their views on general issues of policy.

12.   Memoranda for the Cabinet and Committees of the Cabinet should be as clear and as brief as possible. They should not normally exceed four pages at most, and the Cabinet Office may not accept an over-long memorandum for circulation. Time spent in making a paper short and clear is saved many times over in reading and in discussion; and it is the duty of Ministers to ensure that this is done and that, where necessary, papers submitted to them are revised accordingly. The model memorandum explains at the outset what the problem is, indicates briefly the relevant considerations, and concludes with a precise statement of the decisions sought. Paragraphs should be numbered for ease of reference. Detailed analysis and argument, together with supplementary detail, should be dealt with, where necessary, in annexes.

Cabinet Conclusions and Ministerial Committee minutes

13.   The record of Cabinet and Committee proceedings is limited to the conclusions reached and such summary of the discussion as is necessary for the guidance of those,

who have to take action. The Cabinet Office are instructed to avoid, so far as practicable, recording the opinions expressed by particular Ministers. Matters of special secrecy or political sensitivity may be recorded in a limited circulation annex.

14.   Any suggestions for amendment of Cabinet Conclusions or Committee minutes must reach the Secretary not later than 24 hours after the circulation of the minutes.

15.   Ministers are responsible for instructing their Departments to give effect to the conclusions of the Cabinet or of one of its Committees, and for telling subordinate Departments or branches about decisions affecting them. When immediate action is required by a Department not represented at the meeting, the Secretary will ensure that the Department concerned is notified forthwith. Where urgent action has to be taken by a Department, the Department may ask the Secretary for an advance copy of the relevant conclusions.

Collective responsibility

16.   The internal process through which a decision has been made, or the level of Committee by which it was taken, should not be disclosed. Decisions reached by the Cabinet or Ministerial Committees are binding on all members of the Government. They are, however, normally announced and explained as the decision of the Minister concerned. On occasions it may be desirable to emphasise the importance of a decision by stating specially that it is the decision of Her Majesty's Government. This, however, is the exception rather than the rule.

17.   Collective responsibility requires that Ministers should be able to express their views frankly in the expectation that they can argue freely in private while maintaining a united front when decisions have been reached. This in turn requires that the privacy of opinions expressed in Cabinet and Ministerial Committees should be maintained. Moreover Cabinet and Committee documents will often contain information which needs to be protected in the public interest. It is therefore essential that, subject to the guidelines on the disclosure of information set out in the Code of Practice on Access to Government Information, Ministers take the necessary steps to ensure that they and their staff preserve the privacy of Cabinet business and protect the security of Government documents.

18.   The principle of collective responsibility and the need to safeguard national security, relations with other countries and the confidential nature of discussions between Ministers and their civil servants impose certain obligations on former Ministers who are contemplating the publication of material based upon their recollection of the conduct of Government business in which they took part. They are required to submit their manuscript to the Secretary of the Cabinet and to conform to the principles set out in the Radcliffe Report of 1976 (Cmnd 6386) (see also paragraph 103).

Cabinet documents

19.　Ministers relinquishing office without a change of Government should hand over to their successors those Cabinet documents required for current administration and should ensure that all others have been destroyed. Former Ministers may at any time, and subject to undertakings to observe the conventions governing Ministerial memoirs, have access in the Cabinet Office to copies of Cabinet or Ministerial Committee papers issued to them while in office.

20.　On a change of Government, the outgoing Prime Minister issues special instructions about the disposal of the Cabinet papers of the outgoing Administration.

21.　Some Ministers have thought it wise to make provision in their wills against the improper disposal of any official or Government documents which they night have remained in their possession by oversight.

The Law Officers

22.　The Law Officers must be consulted in good time before the Government is committed to critical decisions involving legal considerations. It will normally be appropriate to consult the Law Officers in cases where:

a.　The legal consequences of action by the Government might have important repercussions; in the foreign, European Union or domestic field;

b.　A Departmental Legal Adviser is in doubt concerning

(i)　the legality or constitutional propriety of legislation which Government proposes to introduce; or

(ii)　the vires of proposed subordinate legislation;

or

(iii)　the legality of proposed administrative action, particularly where that action might be subject to challenge in the courts by means of application for judicial review;

c.　Ministers, or their officials, wish to have the advice of the Law Officers on questions involving legal considerations, which are likely to come before the Cabinet or Cabinet Committee;

d.　There is a particular legal difficulty which may raise political aspects of policy;

e.　Two or more Departments disagree on legal questions and wish to seek the view of the Law Officers.

By convention, written opinions of the Law Officers, unlike other Ministerial papers, are generally made available to succeeding Administrations.

23.　When advice from the Law Officers is included in correspondence between Ministers, or in papers for the Cabinet or Ministerial Committees, the conclusions may if necessary be summarised but, if this is done, the complete text of the advice should be attached.

24.   The fact and content of opinions or advice given by the Law Officers, including the Scottish Law Officers, either individually or collectively, must not be disclosed outside Government without their authority.

25.   Ministers occasionally become engaged in legal proceedings primarily in their personal capacities but in circumstances which may have implications for them in their official positions. Defamation is an example of an area where proceedings will invariably raise issues for the Minister's official as well as his private position. In all such cases they should consult the law Officers before consulting their own solicitors, in order to allow the Law Officers to express a view on the handling of the case so far as the public interest is concerned or, if necessary, to take charge of the proceedings from the outset.

26.   In criminal proceedings the Law Officers act wholly independently of the Government. In civil proceedings a distinction is to be drawn between proceedings in which the Law Officers are involved in a representative capacity on behalf of the Government, and action undertaken by them on behalf of the general community to enforce the law as an end in itself.

3. MINISTERS AND PARLIAMENT

Parliamentary statements and other Government announcements

27.   When Parliament is in session, Ministers will want to bear in mind the desire of Parliament that the most important announcements of Government policy should be made, in the first instance, in Parliament. Even when Government announcements are not of major importance their timing may require careful consideration in order to avoid clashes with other Government publications, statements or announcements or with the planned Parliamentary business. The Leader of the House of Commons, the Chief Whip and the No 10 Press Office should be given as long an opportunity as possible, and wherever possible at least two working days, to comment on the content and timing of all important Government announcements, whether in the form of a Written Answer or oral statement in Parliament, White Paper or press conference. Whenever possible they should also be shown the draft announcement in advance.

28.   If too many announcements are made by oral statement at the end of Questions, Parliamentary business could be hindered. Nevertheless, careful consideration should be given in the case of important or particularly sensitive issues to the desirability of making an oral statement rather than an announcement by Written Answer. Ministers proposing to make a statement after Questions (whether or not it is related to, a Question on the order paper) or to answer a Question by leave at the end of Questions or to make an important announcement by means of a Written Answer ate therefore asked to conform with the following procedure:

a.   As <u>much</u> notice as possible of the intention to make an announcement should be given to (i) the Prime Minister's Private Secretary; (ii) the Private Secretary to the Leader of the House of Commons; (iii) the Private Secretary to the Chief Whip; (iv) the No 10 Press Office. This notification should indicate the broad content of the proposed announcement; if necessary, why an oral statement is thought to be appropriate; and an indication whether the policy with which it is concerned has been approved by Ministers, including references to relevant discussions, in Cabinet or Cabinet Committees. If agreement in principle is given, a draft of the statement or answer should be circulated to the same recipients as soon as possible, having been approved in broad terms, though not necessarily in detail, by the Minister in charge of the Department. Draft statements or answers should be accompanied by background notes which identify the likely points of attack and suggest how these can best be met. Particular attention should be paid to the timing of Written Answers in this context. From Monday to Thursday an Answer to a Written Question may not be released before 3.30 p.m. (12 noon on Fridays) on the day before which the Question stands on the Order paper for reply. Where earlier release is required the Question may be tabled, by agreement with the Business Managers, one day earlier, the Answer being held back until the following morning;

b. In the case of announcements by Written Answer, particular care must be taken to avoid making a press announcement before the Written Answer has been delivered to the MP who tabled the Question;

c. Ministers should not give undertakings, either in or outside the House, of Commons, that an oral statement will be made to the House on any subject at a specific time or within a particular period until agreement has been given by the Private Secretaries; to the Prime Minister, the Leader of the House of Commons; and the Chief Whip, to the proposed timing and by the Ministers concerned to the terms of the statement;

d. Ministers will be conscious of the pressures of other Parliamentary business when deciding on the timing of statements. For example, on Thursdays a considerable amount of Parliamentary time after Questions is already pre-empted by discussion of the following week's business. It is also desirable, except in special circumstances, to avoid oral statements on Fridays;

e. Copies of the final version of such announcements should be sent to the Private Secretaries to the Prime Minister, the Leader of the House and the Chief Whip and to the No 10 Press Office as soon as they are available;

f. A copy of the text of any oral statement to be made at the end of Questions should usually be shown to the Opposition Parties shortly before it is made. For this purpose fifteen extra copies of the final text must reach the office of the Chief Whip in the House of Commons as early as possible and in any case not later than 2.45 p.m. (Monday-Thursday) on the day on which the statement is to be made and not later than 10.15 am in the case of statements made on a Friday;

g. A copy of the final text of an oral statement should in all cases be sent in advance to the Speaker;

h. The Leader of the House of Lords should be informed of a forthcoming oral statement in the House of Commons and consulted about the desirability of repeating it in the Lords;

i. A copy of any important Ministerial statement as actually delivered should be placed as quickly as possible in the Library of the House. This affords Members an opportunity of studying it in advance of publication in the Official Report. Depending on the importance, of the statement, Departments should also consider making copies available in the Vote Office;

j. Every effort should be made to avoid leaving significant announcements to the last day before a Recess.

Supply of Parliamentary publications

29.   A Minister in charge of an item of business in the House of Commons must ensure that reasonable numbers of copies of any documents published during the last two Sessions which may be needed for the debate are placed in the Vote Office and is responsible for supplying the House of Commons Library in advance with a list of all those older papers which the Minister considers relevant to the item. When any document is out of print the Minister should decide whether or not a reprint is required. Where any doubt exists about the need for any document to be available for a debate the Minister's Private Secretary should consult the Chief Whip's Private Secretary. Similar arrangements should be made with the Lord Privy Seal's office, for debates in the House of Lords

Money Resolutions

30.   All Money Resolutions are placed on the order paper in the name of the Financial Secretary, Treasury. But he or she is not responsible for seeing a Resolution through the House, of Commons. It has always been the practice (as for Civil Estimates) that, although Resolutions appear in the name of the Financial Secretary, the Minister having Departmental responsibility for the relevant Bill is also responsible for the Money Resolution in the House of Commons.

4. MINISTERS AND THEIR DEPARTMENTS

Changes in Ministerial responsibilities

31.   The Prime Minister is responsible for the overall organisation of the Executive and the allocation of functions between Ministers in charge of Departments. His approval should therefore be sought where changes are proposed that affect this allocation and the responsibilities for the discharge of Ministerial functions. This applies where the functions in question are derived from statute or from the exercise of the Royal prerogative, or are general administrative responsibilities.

32.   The Prime Minister's written approval should be sought where it is proposed to transfer functions:

    a.   between Ministers in charge of Departments (unless the changes are de minimis, can be made administratively and do not justify public announcement—but see paragraph 37 below);

    b.   within the field of responsibility of one Minister—e.g. by "hiving off" the discharge of some functions to a Non-Departmental Public Body where the change is likely to be politically sensitive or to raise wider issues of policy or organisation;

    c.   between junior Ministers within a Department when a change in Ministerial titles is involved (see also paragraph 38 below).

33.   In addition, his written approval should be sought for proposals to allocate new functions to a particular Minister where the function does not fall wholly within the field of responsibilities of one Minister, or where there is disagreement about who should be responsible.

34.   The Prime Minister will also determine questions where there is disagreement e.g. because one Minister has proposed a transfer of functions that is not accepted by the other(s) affected.

35.   In giving approval or in determining disputed issues, the Prime Minister may want to take the advice of the Head of the Home Civil Service. The Minister responsible should therefore ensure that the Head of the Home Civil Service is consulted, directly by the Permanent Secretary of the Department concerned or that the officials of the Machinery of Government Group in the Office of Public Service are approached so that they can bring the proposals to his or her attention, before proposals for a transfer or allocation of functions are submitted to the Prime Minister. The submission to the Prime Minister should be copied to the Head of the Home Civil Service.

36.   Responsibility for making a submission to the Prime Minister should normally he with the ceding Minister in the case of transfers of existing functions, and the principal receiving Minister in the case of allocation of new functions.

37.   Unresolved disputed issues concerning the allocation of functions should prefer-ably be referred to the Head of the Home Civil Service before a submission is made to the Prime Minister; and it may be appropriate for him to make the submission on behalf of the Minister concerned. ALL proposals for a transfer of functions, including those not considered to require the Prime Minister's approval, should be notified to the Machin-ery of Government Group in the Office of Public Service before they are implemented.

Ministers outside the Cabinet

38.   The Minister in charge of a Department is alone answerable to Parliament for the exercise of the powers on which the administration of that Department depends. The Minister's authority may, however, be delegated to a Minister of State, a Parliamentary Secretary or to an official; and it is desirable that Ministers should devolve on their jun-ior Ministers responsibility for a defined range of Departmental work, particularly in connection with Parliament. A Minister's proposal for the assignment of duties to junior Ministers, together with any proposed "courtesy titles" descriptive of their duties should be agreed in writing with the Prime Minister, copied to the Secretary of the Cabinet.

39.   Ministers of State and Parliamentary Secretaries will be authorised to supervise the day-to-day administration of a defined range of subjects. This arrangement does not relieve the Permanent Secretary of general responsibilities for the organisation and discipline of the Department or of the duty to advise, on matters of policy. The authority of Ministers out-side the Cabinet is delegated from the Minister in charge of the Department; the Perma-nent Secretary is not subject to the directions of junior Ministers. Equally, junior Ministers are not subject to the directions of the Permanent Secretary. Any conflict of view between the two can be resolved only by reference to the Minister in charge of the Department or, if the latter is absent and a decision cannot be postponed, by reference to the Prime Minis-ter or to a Minister whom he has nominated for the purpose.

Arrangements during absence from London

40.   The Secretary of the Cabinet should be informed of Ministers' out of town en-gagements, and also of their weekend and holiday arrangements, so that, if a sudden emergency arises, he can inform the Prime Minister which Ministers are immediately available.

41.   When a Minister will be unable to be contacted for a considerable period because of absence or illness a Minister of State will normally take Ministerial charge of the De-partment. On some occasions, it may be desirable that arrangements should be made for another member of the Cabinet to be available to oversee the Department and to repre-sent the Department's interests in discussions in Cabinet or Cabinet Committees. The Prime Minister's prior approval should be sought for the arrangements for superintend-ing the work of a Department when the Minister in charge will be absent.

42.   When one member of the Cabinet is acting in this way on behalf of another, spe-cial care must be taken over the exercise of statutory powers. Powers vested formally in

"the Secretary of State", as distinct from a specific Secretary of State, can be exercised by any Secretary of State in the absence of another. Otherwise the statutory powers of one Minister cannot formally be exercised in the Minister's absence by a colleague in charge of another Department, and a Minister who is acting for an absent colleague should be careful to avoid appearing formally to exercise powers which are expressed by statute as exercisable by that colleague. The powers of a Board or Council may, however, be exercisable in the absence of its principal member. There may also be statutory authority for formal documents to be signed on behalf of an absent Minister by junior Ministers or officials. Ministers should seek legal advice in cases of doubt.

43. There is no similar difficulty about submissions to Her Majesty. Submissions made in the absence of a Minister can however be made only by a junior Minister who is a Privy Counsellor or by another member of the Cabinet. Submissions on behalf of an absent Secretary of State must be made by another Secretary of State.

44. Parliamentary Private Secretaries are not members of the Government, and should be careful to avoid being spoken of as such. They are Private Members, and should therefore be afforded as great a liberty of action as possible; but their close and confidential association with Ministers imposes certain obligations on them. Official information given to them should generally be limited to what is necessary to the discharge of their Parliamentary and political duties. This need not preclude them from being brought into Departmental discussions or conferences where appropriate, but they should not have access to secret establishments, or information graded secret or above, except on the personal authority of the Prime Minister. While, as Private Members, they need not adhere to the rules on private interests which apply to Ministers, they should, as a general rule, seek to avoid a real or perceived conflict of interest between their role as a Parliamentary Private Secretary and their private interests.

45. Ministers choose and appoint their own Parliamentary Private Secretaries with the written approval of the Prime Minister. The Chief Whip should, however, be consulted about the choice of a Parliamentary Private Secretary; and in view of the special position which Parliamentary Private Secretaries occupy in relation to the Government, the Prime Minister's approval must also be sought before any such appointment is offered and announced.

46. Ministers should ensure that their Parliamentary Private Secretaries are aware of certain principles which should govern the behaviour of Parliamentary Private Secretaries in the House of Commons. Like other Private Members, Parliamentary Private Secretaries are expected to support the Government in all important divisions. However, their special position in relation to the Government imposes an additional obligation which means that no Parliamentary Private Secretary who votes against the Government may retain his or her position. Parliamentary Private Secretaries should not make statements in the House or put Questions on matters affecting the Department with which they are connected. Parliamentary Private Secretaries are not pre-

cluded from serving on Select Committees but they should not do so in the case of inquiries into their own Minister's Departments and they should avoid associating themselves with recommendations critical of or embarrassing to the Government. They should also exercise discretion in any speeches or broadcasts which they may make outside the House, taking care not to make statements which appear to be made in an official or semi-official capacity, and, bearing in mind at the same time that, however careful they may be to make it clear that they are speaking only as Private, Members, they are nevertheless liable to be regarded as speaking with some of the authority which is attached to a member of the Government. Generally they must act with a sense of responsibility and with discretion; and they must not associate themselves with particular groups advocating special policies.

47.   Parliamentary Private Secretaries making official visits in the United Kingdom may receive the normal Civil Service travelling and subsistence allowances in respect of absences on official (or Departmental) business, as would other MPs undertaking work for Government Departments. It is for the Minister concerned to decide whether or not the Parliamentary Private Secretary, when accompanying the Minister, is engaged on Departmental business. It may occasionally be useful for a Parliamentary Private Secretary to accompany the Minister on an official visit abroad but no such arrangements should be made without the prior written approval of the Prime Minister.

Special Advisers

48.   The employment of Special Advisers on the one hand adds a political dimension to the advice available to, Ministers, and on the other provides Ministers with the direct advice of distinguished "experts" in their professional field, while reinforcing the political impartiality of the permanent Civil Service by distinguishing the source of political advice and support. Cabinet Ministers may each appoint up to two Special Advisers ("political" or "expert"). All appointments require the prior written approval of the Prime Minister, and no commitments to make such appointments should be entered into in the absence of such approval. All such appointments should be made, and all Special Advisers should operate, in accordance with the terms and conditions of the Model Contract promulgated by the Prime, Minister on 19 May 1997.

Unpaid advisers

49.   The appointment of an unpaid adviser is a personal appointment by the Minister concerned, and there is no contractual relationship between such an adviser and the Department. Such appointments carry no remuneration or reimbursement from public funds. In making an appointment Ministers must ensure that there is no conflict of interest between the matters on which the unpaid adviser will be advising and their private concerns. The normal rules of confidentiality also apply. The prior written approval of the Prime Minister should be sought for all such appointments before commitments are entered into.

Royal Commissions, Committees of Inquiry

50.   The Prime Minister should be consulted in good time about any proposal to set up:

a.   Royal Commissions: these can only be set up with the sanction of the Cabinet and after The Queen's approval has been sought by the Prime Minister;

b.   Independent Committees of inquiry into, any aspect of public policy.

Submissions proposing either of the above should contain details of the proposed size and structure of the body. This requirement is separate from the provisions concerning appointments set out in paragraph 51 below. The Lord Chancellor should also be consulted where there is a proposal to appoint a judge or legal officer (e.g. a Law Commissioner) to, any of the above inquiries. Indeed it may be preferable, for the individuals concerned to be approached by the Lord Chancellor, rather than Departments.

Appointments by Ministers

51.   The Prime Minister should also be consulted in good time about the appointment or re-appointment of:

a.   The Chairman and other Members of Royal Commissions;

b.   The Chairman of

i.   Public Corporations

ii.   Nationalised Industry Boards

iii.   The most important Non-Departmental Public Bodies (both Executive and Advisory)

iv.   The more important Departmental committees, including those at 50(ii);

c.   Heads of Non-Ministerial Departments.

In all such cases the Prime Minister will need to be informed about the particular requirements of the post, the attributes essential for a candidate and the extent to which proposed candidates meet such requirements.

d.   Cases where the appointment is likely to have political significance. Ministers should take a wide view of what constitutes political significance. Even local or regional appointments may from time to time excite an unusual amount of public interest because of the circumstances surrounding the appointment or the background of the candidate. In all cases involving political considerations submissions to the Prime Minister by an appointing Minister should be copied to the Chief Whip. The Chief Whip should invariably be consulted before a Member of the House of Commons is approached about appointment to an office which would result in the vacation of a Parliamentary seat. A current list of individual public appointments on which the Prime Minister would expect to be consulted is held by the Public Appointments Unit (PAU) in the Office of Public Service. Departments may also choose to consult the Prime Minister in other cases, depending on circumstances.

52.   In all cases falling within paragraphs 50 and 51 on which a submission is to be put to the Prime Minister, Ministers should arrange for their Department to consult the PAU beforehand; and the submission to the Prime Minister should be cleared with the Head of the Home Civil Service in advance and should indicate that the PAU has been consulted and that any salary proposals have been agreed with the Treasury if necessary. No commitment should be made to any individual before the Prime Minister has been consulted. In the case of Royal Commissions, the Private Secretary to the Prime Minister as well as the Lord Chancellor (see paragraph 50) should be consulted before any informal soundings are undertaken. In other cases, any informal soundings should be made in such a way as to preserve freedom of action and avoid any appearance of commitment.

53.   Where there is doubt about the need for consultation with the Prime Minister, the PAU should be consulted.

54.   Subject to the above paragraphs and to the constitution of the body to which the appointment is made, public (non-Civil Service) appointments are the responsibility of the Minister concerned, who should appoint the person(s) he or she considers to be best qualified for the position. In doing so, the Minister should have regard to public accountability, the requirements of the law and (especially in the case of appointments to executive Non-Departmental Public Bodies or National Health Service (NHS) bodies to the Code of Practice for Public Appointments procedures set out by the Commissioner for Public Appointments. The process by which such appointments are made should conform to the principles in the Code—Ministerial responsibility, merit, independent scrutiny, equal opportunities, probity, openness and transparency, and proportionality; and to the procedures in the Commissioner's Guidance on Appointments to Executive Non-Departmental Public Bodies and NHS Bodies.

55.   In considering candidates for public appointments, Ministers should pay particular attention to securing, on merit, proper representation of women and members of ethnic minorities on public bodies. A Minister in each Department should be responsible for setting objectives to achieve this. All Ministers are asked to ensure, when shortlists of proposed candidates are submitted to them, that if no women candidates are proposed an explanation for this is given. Where the work of a body or committee will have a particular impact on ethnic minority communities or the disabled, the same procedure may be appropriate for ethnic minority or disability representation respectively.

5. MINISTERS AND CIVIL SERVANTS

56.   Ministers have a duty to give fair consideration and due weight to informed and impartial advice from civil servants, as well as to other considerations and advice, in reaching policy decisions; a duty to uphold the political impartiality of the Civil Service, and not to ask civil servants to act in any way which would conflict with the Civil Service Code; a duty to ensure, that influence over appointments is not abused for partisan purposes; and a duty to observe the obligations of a good employer with regard to terms and conditions of those who serve them. Civil servants should not be asked to engage in activities likely to call in question their political impartiality, or to give rise to the criticism that people paid from public funds are being used for Party political purposes.

The role of the Accounting Officer

57.   Heads of Departments and the chief executives of executive agencies are appointed as Accounting Officers. The essence of the role is a personal responsibility for the propriety and regularity of the public finances for which he or she is responsible; for keeping proper accounts; for the avoidance of waste and extravagance; and for the efficient and effective use of resources. Accounting Officers answer personally to the Committee of Public Accounts on these matters, within the framework of Ministerial accountability to Parliament for the policies, actions and conduct of their Departments.

58.   Accounting Officers have a particular responsibility to see that appropriate advice is tendered to Ministers on all matters of financial propriety and regularity and more broadly as to all considerations of prudent and economical administration, efficiency and effectiveness and value for money. If a Minister in charge of a Department is contemplating a course of action which would involve a transaction which the Accounting Officer considers would breach the requirements of propriety or regularity, the Accounting Officer will set out in writing his or her objection to the proposal, the reasons for the objection and the duty to inform the Comptroller and Auditor General should the advice be overruled. If the Minister decides nonetheless to proceed, the Accounting Officer will seek a written instruction to take the action in question and send the relevant papers to the Comptroller and Auditor General. A similar procedure applies where the Accounting Officer has concerns as regards the value for money of a proposed course of action. The procedure enables the Committee of Public Accounts to see that the Accounting Officer does not bear personal responsibility for the actions concerned.

59.   The role of Accounting Officers is described in detail in the Treasury memorandum, The Responsibilities of an Accounting Officer. There is also a Treasury handbook, Regularity and Propriety.

Civil servants and Party Conferences

60.   Ministers should not ask civil servants to attend, still less take part in, Party Conferences or meetings of policy or subject groups of any of the Parliamentary parties. It is an established principle in the public service that civil servants in their official capacity

should not accept invitations to conferences convened by, or under the aegis of, party political organisations. The situation is, of course, different when Ministers require officials to be in attendance at party political events in order to enable the Minister to carry out urgent Departmental business.

61.   If a Minister wishes to have a brief for a party political occasion to explain Departmental policies or actions, there is no reason why this should not be provided.

6. MINISTERS' CONSTITUENCY AND PARTY INTERESTS

62.   It is wrong in principle for Ministers to use for party or constituency work facilities provided at Government expense to enable them to carry out their official duties. This point of principle is reflected in the entitlement of Ministers to a Parliamentary salary in recognition of the time spent in attending to the interests of their constituents, and to the reimbursement of their secretarial expenses and the expenses of living away from home when attending to constituency business, within the limits prescribed by the relevant Resolutions of the House of Commons. Ministers should thus have their constituency work done at their own expense, as they would if they were private Members of Parliament.

63.   Government property should not generally be used for constituency work or party activities. A particular exception is recognised in the case of Nos. 10 and 11 Downing Street, Carlton House Terrace and other official residences where senior Ministers are required to live for the purposes of the job. Where Ministers host Party events in these residences or other Government property, it should, be at their own or Party expense with no cost falling to the public purse.

64.   Where Ministers have to take decisions within their Departments which might have an impact on their own constituencies, they should, of course, take particular care to avoid any possible conflict of interest.

Parliamentary Commissioner for Administration cases

65.   Ministers in the Commons who are asked by members of the public to submit cases to the Parliamentary Commissioner for Administration (PCA) should, where possible, act no differently from other MPs. Ministers should accordingly consider requests on their merits in deciding whether to refer complaints to the PCA, to take them up with the Minister of the Department concerned, to refer the case to another MP (where the complaint is not from a constituent of the Minister) or to decline to take action. Any Minister who has in mind the reference of a case to the PCA would naturally wish to inform in advance the Minister of the Department concerned.

66.   Where a complaint from a constituent is against the Minister's own Department the Minister will generally wish to investigate it personally unless he or she, or one of the other Ministers in the Department, has already been directly involved in the case. Where a Minister has been so involved, the PCA should be asked to investigate if the case is within his jurisdiction; and there may be other circumstances in which a Minister will prefer to refer a case to the PCA straight away.

Deputations

67.   Ministers are free to make their views about constituency matters known to the responsible Minister by correspondence, leading deputations or by personal interview provided they make clear that they are acting as their constituents' representative and not

as a Minister. Particular problems arise over views expressed on planning applications and certain other cases involving exercise of discretion by Ministers (e.g. on school or hospital closures, highway or power station inquiries) in which representations intended to be taken into account in reaching a decision may have to be made available to other parties and thus may well receive publicity. Ministers are advised to take particular care in such cases to represent the views of their constituents rather than express a view themselves; but when they find it unavoidable to express a view they should ensure that their comments are made available to the other parties, avoid criticism of Government policies, confine themselves to comments which could reasonably be made by those who are not Ministers, and make clear that the views they are putting forward are ones expressed in their capacity as constituency MPs. Once a decision has been announced, it should be accepted without question or criticism. It is important, in expressing such views, that Ministers do so in a way that does not create difficulty for Ministers who have to take the decision and that they bear in mind the Government's collective responsibility for the outcome. Ministers should also take account of any potential implications which their comments could have on their own Departmental responsibilities.

7. MINISTERS'VISITS

Ministers' visits overseas

68.   Overseas visits should not normally be made while Parliament is in session. Ministers should arrange such visits only in the Recess or, where appropriate, at weekends, except where the visit is in connection with the business of the European Union or there are other compelling reasons of Government business. In particular, overseas visits which are largely of a fact-finding kind should be reserved exclusively for the Parliamentary Recess. Moreover, in planning overseas visits Ministers should take account of paragraph 6 above, i.e. that Cabinet meetings take precedence, over all other business (other than meetings of the Privy Council). Sufficient Ministers must also be available during Recesses to ensure effective conduct of Government business, and it may be necessary for this reason to restrict or reconsider absences abroad.

69.   Any member of the Cabinet who wishes to be absent from the United Kingdom for any reason, except for visits to European Union countries on official business, or visits to member countries for NATO business should:

a.   seek the Prime Minister's written approval. This must be done before any commitment, even of an informal nature, is made. The reasons for the visit and a list of the countries to be visited should be given; where it is considered to be clearly in the public interest that a Minister be accompanied by his or her spouse at public expense the Prime Minister's permission should be sought. Copies of the letter should be sent to the Foreign and Commonwealth Secretary and to the Chief Whip: their views will be taken into account by the Prime Minister before reaching a decision. A copy should also be sent to the Secretary of the Cabinet;

b.   after the Prime Minister's approval has been obtained the Minister should, for all visits abroad other than visits to European Union or NATO or WEU countries on official business, seek The Queen's permission to leave the country. At the same time Her Majesty should be informed of the arrangements made for the administration of the Minister's Department during his or her absence.

70.   Other Ministers who propose to leave the United Kingdom whether on duty or on holiday must seek the approval of the Ministerial head of the Department concerned, the Foreign and Commonwealth Secretary and the Chief Whip. They need not obtain the Prime Minister's or The Queen's permission but the Prime Minister's written approval must be sought for official visits overseas by Ministers' spouses, special advisers and by Parliamentary Private Secretaries (paragraphs 47, 83 and 84).

71.   Ministers' Private Secretaries should not themselves approach diplomatic posts direct nor should they make tentative preparations for overseas visits (other than those to EU countries on official business) before telling the Foreign and Commonwealth Office:

arrangements for official Ministerial visits should invariably be put in the hands of the diplomatic post concerned.

72. Ministers should make it their personal responsibility to approve the size and composition of any Ministerial delegation for which their Department is responsible. (Where a delegation includes a Foreign and Commonwealth Office Minister the concurrence of the Foreign and Commonwealth Secretary in the size and composition of the delegation should also be obtained.) Each Minister in charge of a Department should ensure that the Department draws up and maintains a comprehensive and central record of travel by Ministers in the Department. This record should contain details of the numbers and costs of all Ministerial delegations whose travel has been at public expense, including visits to EU countries for the purpose of attending meetings of EU Councils. The record should be maintained in such a way that an up-to-date list of visits and costs of such visits can be made, available by Departments at short notice in the event of Departmental Ministers being asked to account for travel undertaken by Ministers in their Departments. Ministers should give a lead in keeping down the size of parties of visitors, by keeping their own parties as small as possible.

Relations with other governments

73. Ministers should remember the importance of sending to the Foreign and Commonwealth Secretary a note of the salient points of any discussions which they may have with representatives of foreign or Commonwealth countries. This applies to informal discussions as well as those held in the course of official business.

Visits by Commonwealth or foreign Ministers

74. Ministers should inform the Foreign and Commonwealth Secretary before extending invitations to Ministers in other governments to pay official visits to this country; and in any case of doubt or difficulty, they should consult him. Departments should also inform the Foreign and Commonwealth Office about all visits which become known to them, whether private or official, by Ministers in other governments or by any other person of equivalent status potentially at risk, so that the security implications can be considered at the earliest possible stage.

75. Ministers should not overlook the possible foreign policy implications of such day-to-day matters as offering hospitality to prominent political figures visiting this country, accepting social commitments of a similar kind, giving public support for petitions, open letters, etc. Such actions may be construed as significant by foreign observers of the United Kingdom. In any case of doubt Ministers should consult the Foreign and Commonwealth Secretary before making commitments. In addition the Foreign and Commonwealth Secretary should be consulted whenever a Minister intends to make a speech touching on matters affecting foreign and Commonwealth affairs.

Entertainment overseas

76.   If it is thought that a Minister may need to provide entertainment while overseas, the advice of the Foreign and Commonwealth Office should be sought both on the desirability and on the form of such entertainment.

Ministers recalled from abroad

77.   If a Minister is abroad with permission and is called home, for Ministerial or Parliamentary reasons—including to vote—the cost of the extra journey back and forth may be met by public funds.

Ministers' visits in the United Kingdom

78.   Ministers who are planning official visits to Scotland, Wales and Northern Ireland should inform the Secretary of State concerned and the Chief Whip. It is also customary to inform the Home Secretary of prospective visits to the Channel Islands and the Isle of Man. In addition, Ministers wishing to visit a Government establishment not sponsored by the Department in which they are a Minister (e.g. the barracks of a unit of the Armed Forces) should advise the sponsor Department in advance.

79.   It is the custom for a Minister when preparing to make a visit within the United Kingdom to inform the Members for the constituencies to be included within his itinerary. Special care should be taken not to overlook this courtesy. Ministers cannot, of course, invite Members to accompany them to functions organised by a third party, but adequate notice to the relevant constituency MP will enable them to ensure that they have an opportunity to request invitations from local organisers to functions of an official nature, should they wish to attend. It will also enable them to make suggestions to the Minister about the inclusion in the itinerary of places which it would be helpful to visit.

Expenses on travel and hospitality

80.   In using official cars and travelling by rail or air, Ministers must always make efficient and cost-effective travel arrangements. When Ministers travel on official business, their travel expenses should normally be borne by the Departmental Vote. When any expenses are not met in this way, Ministers will wish to ensure that no undue obligation is involved.

81.   Accepting offers of free travel can be misinterpreted. However, an offer to a Minister on official business to accompany a representative of a host foreign government may be acceptable, provided it creates no undue obligation, and if it offers a saving of official time or provides an opportunity to conduct official business. Offers of transport from other organisations should not normally be accepted, except where provided as an integral part of a tour of inspection. In exceptional cases such an offer may be accepted if this would represent a saving of official time and there is no risk of an undue obligation being created. In these cases, if the journey is of any significant distance, the organisation

concerned should be reimbursed from the public purse to the value of a scheduled business class ticket. In any cases of doubt, the Prime Minister should be consulted.

Air Miles

82.   Air Miles and other benefits earned through travel paid for from public funds, other than where they are de minimis (for example, access to special departure lounges or booking arrangements which go with membership of regular flier clubs), should be used only for official purposes or else foregone. However, if it is impracticable to use the benefits for Government travel, there is no objection to Ministers donating them to charity if this is permissible under the terms of the airline's scheme and the charity is one chosen by the airline.

Travelling expenses of spouses

83.   The expense of a Minister's spouse when accompanying the Minister on the latter's official duties may occasionally be paid from public funds, provided that it is clearly in the public interest that he or she should accompany the Minister. In the case of official visits overseas, the Prime Minister's prior assent should be obtained on each occasion (see paragraph 70). For official visits within the United Kingdom, this is at the discretion of the Minister in charge of the Department concerned who should consult the Permanent Secretary. The Prime Minister's prior written approval is however required for any arrangement whereby a Minister's spouse may regularly travel at public expense within the United Kingdom; Ministers should arrange for the Treasury to be consulted about such arrangements before submitting them to the Prime, Minister.

Travelling expenses of Special Advisers

84.   If necessary, a Minister may take a Special Adviser on an overseas visit at the public expense, but when an unpaid adviser whose salary is not met from public funds accompanies a Minister on Government business, any additional expenditure which may be incurred should not normally fall on public funds. The written approval of the Prime, Minister should be obtained before a Special Adviser or an unpaid adviser accompanies a Minister overseas.

Offers of hospitality, gifts, etc.

85.   Detailed rules on the acceptance of gifts, services and hospitality can be found at paragraphs 126-128. While these paragraphs make clear that no Minister or member of their family should accept a gift from anyone which would, or might appear to, place him or her under an obligation (see paragraph 126), there may be difficulty in refusing a gift from another government (or governmental organisation) without the risk of apparent discourtesy. On the other hand the acceptance of a gift or the knowledge that one will be offered may in some, countries and in some circumstances entail the offer of a gift in exchange. As a general rule Ministers should not offer gifts or initiate an exchange. In deciding whether to accept gifts from or offer gifts to members of other governments (or

governmental organisations) Ministers should wherever possible consult their Permanent Secretaries who will be able to advise them of the rules applicable in such circumstances.

Foreign decorations

86.   It is a well-established convention that Ministers should not, while holding office, accept decorations from foreign countries.

8. MINISTERS AND THE PRESENTATION OF POLICY

87.   Official facilities financed out of public funds can be used for Government publicity and advertising, but may not be used for the dissemination of material which is essentially party political. The conventions governing the work of the Government Information Service are set out in a guidance note issued simultaneously with the Code and placed in the Library of the House.

Co-ordination of Government Policy

88.   In order to ensure the effective presentation of government policy, all major interviews and media appearances, both print and broadcast, should be agreed with the No 10 Press Office before any commitments are entered into. The policy content of all major speeches, press releases and new policy initiatives should be cleared in good time with the No 10 Private Office; the timing and form of announcements should be cleared with the No 10 Press Office. Each Department should keep a record of media contacts by both Ministers and officials.

Press conferences

89.   In order to explain policies or to announce new policies a Minister may decide to hold a press conference. This will be convened by the Chief Information Officer of the Department. All press conferences are on the record and open to any representative of the home and overseas media. It is often the practice of Ministers to give separate radio and TV interviews afterwards in order to secure the most effective presentation of their views or announcement. Where a Minister wishes to seek an invitation to address the Lobby the No 10 Press Office should be consulted both about the desirability of such a briefing and the method of organising it. This paragraph applies to the overseas as well as to the home media.

Publication of White and Green Papers

90.   Before publishing a White or Green Paper, Departments should consider whether it raises issues which require full collective Ministerial consideration, and, after consulting the Cabinet Office as necessary, seek clearance through the appropriate Cabinet Committee. Any Command Paper containing a major statement of Government policy should be circulated to the Cabinet before publication. This is usually done at the Confidential Final Revise (CFR) stage and should be done under cover of a letter from the Minister's Private Secretary. This rule applies to Papers containing major statements even when no issue requiring collective consideration is required.

91.   Except where such Papers are of a routine character or of minor importance, the timing of their publication is governed by similar considerations to those applying to announcements made in Parliament. Ministers are therefore asked to apply to White Papers the procedure laid down in paragraph 28(a) above. From time to time, White Papers are laid before Parliament in the name of the Prime Minister. In all such cases, the lead De-

partment on the policy issues concerned takes responsibility for the processing and distribution of the White Paper. This should be handled in close consultation with the Parliamentary Clerk at No 10.

92.   Care should be taken to avoid infringing Parliamentary privilege when publicity is being arranged for White Papers and similar documents. A procedure is available whereby Confidential Final Revise proof copies (CFRs) of White Papers can be made available under embargo to the Lobby and Upper Gallery, and with discretion to members of other organised groups of correspondents, a short time before copies are laid in the Vote Office (i.e. before publication). In some cases (for instance, where commercially sensitive information is involved, or where the disadvantages of any breach of an embargo are thought to outweigh the benefits of making advance copies available to the media) no copies should be made available to the media before publication. Where it is considered that the balance of advantage favours the issue of advance copies to the media under embargo, so, as to enable their representatives to digest the contents of a White Paper before general publication, the interval between issue of CFRs under embargo and publication should not normally exceed a few hours: for instance, where a White Paper is to be published in the afternoon, CFRs should be issued under embargo during the morning of the same day. Only in special circumstances—for instance, if a White Paper is particularly long or technical—should CFRs be issued under embargo overnight. Any proposal to issue CFRs under an embargo of longer than 24 hours must be cleared with the Chief Press Secretary at No 10. CFRs may be given only to representatives of the media and then only under strict embargo. Any breach of an embargo is a serious matter and should be reported immediately by the Chief Information Officer of the Department to the Minister in charge of the Department and to No 10.

Speeches

93.   Ministers cannot speak on public affairs for themselves alone. In all cases other than those described in paragraph 67 they speak as Ministers and the principle of collective responsibility applies. They should ensure that their statements are consistent with collective Government policy and should not anticipate decisions not yet made public. Ministers should exercise special care in referring to subjects which are the responsibility of other Ministers. Any Minister who intends to make a speech which deals with, or makes observations which bear upon, matters which fall within another Minister's responsibilities should consult that Minister.

94.   The Prime Minister should always be consulted before any mention is made of matters which either affect the conduct of the Government as a whole or are of a constitutional character. The Foreign and Commonwealth Secretary should always be consulted before any mention is made of matters affecting foreign and Commonwealth affairs, relations with foreign and Commonwealth countries and the political aspects of the affairs of dependent territories. Ministers wishing to refer in a speech or any other public statement to economic policy or to proposals involving additional public expenditure

or revenue costs should in all cases consult the Chancellor of the Exchequer or the Chief Secretary. Ministers wishing to refer to defence policy should in all cases first consult the Secretary of State for Defence. Ministers wishing to discuss or refer to Northern Ireland should in all cases first consult the Secretary of State for Northern Ireland.

95.   Ministers should use official machinery for distributing texts of Ministerial speeches only when such speeches are made on official occasions and deal with Government as distinct from Party policy. Speeches made in a party political context should be distributed through the Party machinery.

96.   Ministers should not accept payment for speeches of an official nature or which directly draw on their responsibilities or experience as Ministers, either on their own or their Department's account, or with a view to donating the fee to charity.

Broadcasts

97.   The provisions of paragraphs 87–89 apply to Ministerial broadcasts as well.

98.   Radio and television broadcasts by ministers are of four types: party political; Budget; special broadcasts by Ministers; and interviews with Ministers for news and feature programmes:

a.   Party political broadcasts on radio and television within the Government's quota are arranged through the Chief Whip acting on behalf of the Prime Minister;

b.   Budget broadcasts (by the Chancellor of the Exchequer and a member of the main Opposition Parties in reply) constitute a special series of party political broadcasts. These are arranged through Parliamentary channels and agreed by the Chancellor of the Exchequer;

c.   The broadcasting authorities may provide opportunities within the regular framework of their programmes for Ministers to give factual explanations of legislation or policies approved by Parliament, or to seek the cooperation of the public, on matters where there is a general consensus of opinion. The Opposition have no automatic right of reply. The British Broadcasting Corporation (BBC) may also provide the Prime Minister or a senior Cabinet Minister designated by him with an opportunity to broadcast to the nation to explain events of prime national or international importance or to seek public co-operation over such events. These are traditionally known as "Ministerial" broadcasts. The Opposition have the right to make an equivalent broadcast in reply. In this event the BBC will arrange as soon as possible for a broadcast discussion of the issues involved. A member of the Cabinet, a senior member of the opposition, and, if they so desire, representatives of third, parties with appreciable electoral support would be invited to participate. The Independent Television Commission (ITC) is not obliged to relay either type of special broadcast, but if they transmit a "Ministerial" broadcast they must also take any Opposition reply and arrange a third stage, the discussion programme. Proposals for a special broadcast of either type should be referred as soon as possible to the Chief Press Secretary at No 10. The Leader of the House of Commons and the Chief Whip should also be consulted. No approach should be made to the BBC or to the ITC for a broadcast of either type without the approval of the Prime Minister.

99. Ministers invited to broadcast on radio and television in a private and not a Ministerial capacity will wish to consider if such a broadcast would have a bearing on another Department's responsibility in which case they should clear the matter with the colleague concerned before agreeing to the invitation. Ministers invited to take part in programmes to be broadcast outside the United Kingdom should consult the Foreign and Commonwealth Secretary and any other Minister who may be concerned with the subject of the broadcast. Ministers invited to broadcast while on a visit to another country should seek the advice of Her Majesty's Representative in that country. Ministers will wish to use their discretion as to whether the nature of any such invitation at home or abroad is such that they should consult the Prime Minister before agreeing to broadcast.

100. Ministers should not accept payment for official broadcasts on radio or television, either on their own or on their Department's account or with a view to donating the fee to charity.

Press articles

101. Ministers may contribute occasionally to a book, journal or newspaper (including a local newspaper in their constituency) for the purpose of supplementing other means of informing the public about the work of their Department provided that publication will not be at variance with their obligations to Parliament and their duty to observe the principle of collective Ministerial responsibility. Any Minister wishing to practice regular journalism, including the contribution of weekly or fortnightly articles to local newspapers in their constituencies, must have the prior approval of the Prime Minister. In cases of doubt, and in all cases where a Minister is contemplating the contribution of an article going beyond the strict confines of his or her Departmental responsibility, the Prime Minister should be consulted, before work has begun and in any case before any commitment to publish is entered into. In all cases where an article contains material which falls within the Departmental responsibility of another Minister, that Minister must be consulted. Ministers should not accept payment for writings, either on their own or on their Department's account, or with a view to donating the fee to charity.

102. Ministers are advised not to engage in controversy in the correspondence columns of either the home or the overseas press. Ministers may however see advantage in correcting serious errors or misstatements of fact which lead to false conclusions. Such letters should be brief and confirmed to the exposition of facts.

Books

103. Ministers may not, while in office, write and publish a book on their Ministerial experience. Former Ministers are required to submit their manuscript to the Secretary of the Cabinet and to conform to the principles set out in the Radcliffe Report of 1976 (Cmnd 6386) (see paragraph 19 above). Ministers may not receive payment for a book written before becoming a Minister if the decision to publish was taken afterwards.

Party and other publications

104. The rule in paragraph 101 does not debar Ministers from contributing to the publications of the political organisations with which they are associated. However, in all cases where an article contains material which falls within the Departmental responsibility of another Minister, that Minister must be consulted. Payment should not be accepted for articles which draw on Ministerial experience or which have been prepared with any assistance from public resources.

105. The prohibition of the practice of journalism by Ministers above, does not extend to writings of a literary, sporting, artistic, musical, historical, scientific, philosophical or fictional character which do not draw on their Ministerial experience. While payment for the occasional piece is acceptable, regular payments are not.

106. Ministers are sometimes asked to give interviews to historians or to other persons engaged in academic research or in market opinion surveys, or to fill in questionnaires at the request of such people or organisations. Ministers should bear in mind the possibility that their views may be reported in a manner incompatible with their responsibilities and duties as members of the Government. Careful consideration should therefore be given to such invitations before they are accepted; in cases of doubt, the Prime Minister should be consulted.

Complaints

107. Ministers who wish to make a complaint against a journalist or a particular section of the media either to the Press Complaints Commission or to the Broadcasting Complaints Commission must have the authority of the Prime Minister. The nature of the complaint and the case for referring it to the appropriate body should be set out in a letter to the Chief Press Secretary at No 10, copied to the Secretary of the Cabinet.

Royal Commissions

108. The Prime Minister should be consulted if any Minister is invited to address a Royal Commission or Committee of Inquiry.

9. MINISTERS' PRIVATE INTERESTS

109. Ministers will want to order their affairs so that no conflict arises or is thought to arise between their private interests (financial or otherwise) and their public duties. They should normally make their own decisions on how best to proceed but in many cases, as is shown below, there are established precedents. Where there is a doubt it will almost always be better to relinquish or dispose of the interest but Ministers should submit any such case to the Prime Minister for his decision.

110. Where it is proper for a Minister to retain any private interest, it is the rule that he or she should declare that interest to Ministerial colleagues if they have to discuss public business in any way affecting it, and that the Minister should remain entirely detached from the consideration of that business. Similar steps may be necessary should the matter under consideration in the Department relate in some way to a Minister's previous private interests such that there is or may be thought to be a conflict of interest.

Public appointments

111. When they take up office Ministers should give up any other public appointment they may hold. Where it is proposed that such an appointment should be retained, the Prime Minister must be consulted.

Non-public bodies

112. Ministers should take care to ensure that they do not become associated with non-public organisations whose objectives may in any degree conflict with Government policy and thus give rise to a conflict of interest. Hence Ministers should not normally accept invitations to act as patrons of or otherwise offer support to pressure groups, or organisations dependent in whole or in part on Government funding. There is normally no objection to a Minister associating him or herself with a charity (subject to the points above) but Ministers should take care to ensure that in participating in any fund-raising activity, they do not place, or appear to place, themselves under an obligation as Ministers to those to whom appeals are directed (and for this reason they should not normally approach individuals or companies personally for this purpose). In any case of doubt, the Prime Minister should be consulted before a Minister accepts an association with such bodies. Ministers should also exercise care in giving public support for petitions, open letters etc.

Trade unions

113. There is, of course, no objection to a Minister holding trade union membership but care must be taken to avoid any actual or perceived conflict of interest. Accordingly, Ministers should arrange their affairs so as to avoid any suggestion that a union of which they are a member has any undue influence; they should take no active part in the conduct of union affairs, should give up any office they may hold in a union and should receive no remuneration from a union (a nominal payment purely for the purpose of protecting a Minister's future pension rights is acceptable).

Financial interests

114. Ministers must scrupulously avoid any danger of an actual or apparent conflict of interest between their Ministerial position and their private financial interests. Such a conflict, or the perception of it, can arise:

a.   from exercise of powers or other influence in a way that does or could be considered to affect the value of interests held; or

b.   from using special knowledge acquired in the course of their Ministerial activities in ways which bring benefit or avoid loss (or could arouse reasonable suspicion of this) in relation to their private financial interests.

115. Apart from the risk to the Minister's reputation, two legal obligations must be born in mind:

a.   any exercise or non-exercise by a Minister (including a Law Officer) of a legal power or discretion or other influence on a matter in which the Minister has a pecuniary interest could be challenged in the courts; and, if the challenge is upheld, could be declared invalid. The courts interpret conflict of interest increasingly tightly;

b.   Ministers are bound by the provisions of Part V of the Criminal Justice Act 1993 in relation to the use or transmission of unpublished price-sensitive information obtained by virtue of their Ministerial office.

116. These risks attach not only to the Minister's personal interests, but. to those of a spouse or partner, of who are children who are minors, of trusts of which the Minister or a spouse or partner is a trustee or beneficiary, or of closely associated persons. They relate to, all kinds of financial interests, including not only all kinds of financial instrument but also such interests as partnerships, unincorporated businesses, real estate etc.

117. It is not intended to inhibit the holding of Ministerial office by individuals with wide experience, whether of industry, a profession or some other walk of life. In order to avoid the danger of an actual or perceived conflict of interest, Ministers should be guided in relation to their financial interests by the general principle that they should either dispose of any financial interest giving rise to the actual or perceived conflict or take alternative steps to prevent it.

118. If for any reason the Minister is unable or unwilling to dispose of a relevant interest, he or she should consider, with the advice of the Permanent Secretary of the Department and, where necessary, of external advisers, what alternative measures would sufficiently remove the risk of conflict. These fall into two types: those relating to the interests themselves, and those relating to the handling of the decisions to be taken or influenced by the Minister.

119. As regards steps other than disposal which might be taken in relation to interests, the Minister might consider placing all investments (including derivatives) into a bare

trust, i.e. one in which the Minister is not informed of changes in investments or of the state of the portfolio, but is still fully entitled to both the capital and income generated. This course would normally be useful only in the case of a widely-spread portfolio of interests. Alternatively a power of attorney may be suitable. However, this is a complex area and the Minister should seek professional advice because, among other things there may be tax consequences in establishing this kind of arrangement. Ministers should re-member that Part VI of the Companies Act 1985 allows companies to require informa-tion as to the true owners of its shares, which could result in the fact of a Minister's in-terest becoming public knowledge despite the existence of a trust. It should also be re-membered that even with a trust the Minister could be assumed to know the contents of the portfolio for at least a period after its creation, so the protection a trust offers against conflict of interest is not complete. Another step which (perhaps in conjunction with other steps) might provide a degree of protection would be for the Minister to accept an obligation to refrain from dealing in the relevant shareholdings etc for a period.

120. Unless adequate steps can be taken in relation to the financial interests themselves, the Minister must seek to avoid involvement in relevant decisions. The extent to which this can be done depends on the specific powers under which the Minister would be re-quired to take decisions. For example:

    a.   in the case of a junior Minister, it should be possible for the Ministerial head of the Department to take the decision or for the case to be handled by an-other junior Minister in the Department;

    b.   in the case of the Ministerial head of Department or the holder of a specific office in whom powers are vested, it will normally be possible without risk of legal challenge to pass the handling of the matter to a junior Minister or ap-propriate official in the Department, or, exceptionally, to another Secretary of State. In such cases, legal advice should always be sought to ensure that the relevant powers can be exercised in this way.

121. In some cases, it may not be possible to devise such a mechanism to avoid actual or perceived conflict of interest, for example because of the nature or size of the investment or the nature of the Department's work. In such a case, or in any case where, after taking legal advice and the advice of the Permanent Secretary, the Minister is in doubt whether adequate steps have been or can be taken, he or she should consult the Prime Minister. In such a case it may be necessary for the Minister to cease to hold the office in question.

122. In addition to this general guidance:

    a.   Partnerships. Ministers who are partners, whether in professional firms, for example solicitors, accountants etc, or in other businesses, should, on taking up office, cease to practise or to play any part in the day-to-day management of the firm's affairs. They are not necessarily required, however, to dissolve their partnership or to allow, for example, their annual practising certificate to lapse. Beyond this it is not possible to lay down precise rules applicable to every case; but any continuing financial interest in the firm would make it necessary for the Minister to take steps to avoid involvement in relevant decisions, as described in paragraph 120 above. Ministers in doubt about their personal position should consult the Prime Minister;

b. Directorships. Ministers must resign any directorships they hold when they take up office. This applies whether the directorship is in a public or private company and whether it carries remuneration or is honorary. The only exception to this rule is that directorships in private companies established in connection with private family estates or in a company formed for the management of flats of which the Minister is a tenant may be retained subject to the condition that if at any time the Minister feels that conflict is likely to arise between this private interest and public duty, the Minister should even in those cases resign the directorship. Directorships or offices held in connection with charitable undertakings should also be resigned if there is any risk of conflict arising between the interests of the undertakings and the Government.

123. In all cases concerning financial interests and conflict of interest Ministers may wish to consult financial advisers as to the implication for their (or their families') affairs of any action which they are considering to avoid any actual or potential conflict of interest. They should also consult the Permanent Secretary in charge of their Department, who is the Minister's principal adviser and who also, as Accounting Officer, has a personal responsibility for financial propriety and regularity. It is in the end for Ministers to judge (subject to the Prime Minister's decision in cases of doubt) what action they need to take; but they should record, in a minute to the Permanent Secretary, whether or not they consider any action necessary, and the nature of any such action taken then or subsequently to avoid actual or perceived conflict of interest.

Membership of Lloyd's

124. Any Minister who is a member of Lloyd's should abide by the guidance set out in the Annex to this document.

Nominations for international awards, etc.

125. From time to time, the personal support of Ministers is requested for nominations being made for international prizes and awards, e.g., the annual Nobel prizes. Ministers should not sponsor individual nominations for any awards, since it would be inevitable that some people would assume that the Government was itself thereby giving its sponsorship.

Acceptance of gifts and services

126. It is a well established and recognised rule that no Minister or public servant should accept gifts, hospitality or services from anyone which would, or might appear to, place

him or her under an obligation. The same principle applies if gifts etc are offered to a member of their family.

127. This is primarily a matter which must be left to the good sense of Ministers. But any Minister in doubt or difficulty over this should seek the Prime Minister's guidance. The same rules apply to the acceptance of gifts from donors with whom a Minister has official dealings in this country as to those from overseas (paragraph 85 above), that is:

a. Receipt of gifts should, in all cases, be reported to the Permanent Secretary;

b. Gifts of small value (currently this should be put at up to £140) may be retained by the recipient;

c. Gifts of a higher value should be handed over to the Department for disposal, except that

(i) The recipient may purchase the gift at its cash value (abated by £140)

(ii) If the recipient wishes to reciprocate with, and pay for, a gift of equivalent value, the gift received may be retained

(iii) If the Department judges that it would be of interest, the gift may be displayed or used in the Department

(iv) If the disposal of the gift would cause offence or if it might be appropriate for the recipient to use or display the gift on some future occasion as a mark of politeness, then the gift should be retained in the Department for this purpose for a period of up to five years;

d. Gifts received overseas worth more than the normal travellers' allowances should be declared at importation to Customs and Excise who will advise on any duty and tax liability. In general, if a Minister wishes to retain a gift he or she will be liable for any tax or duty it may attract.

128. In the event of a Minister accepting hospitality on a scale or from a source which might reasonably be thought likely to influence Ministerial action, it should be declared in the House of Commons Register of Members' Interests (or Register of Lords' Interests in the case of Ministers in the House of Lords).

Outgoing Ministers: acceptance of appointments outside Government

129. On leaving office Ministers should seek advice from the independent Advisory Committee on Business Appointments about any appointments they wish to take up within two years of leaving office, other than unpaid appointments in non-commercial organisations or appointments in the gift of the Government, such as Prime Ministerial appointments to international organisations. Although it is in the public interest that former Ministers should be able to move into business or other areas of public life, it is equally important that there should be no cause for any suspicion of impropriety about a particular appointment. If therefore the Advisory Committee considers that an

appointment could lead to public concern that the statements; and decisions of the Minister, when in Government, have been influenced by the hope or expectation of future employment with the firm or organisation concerned, or that an employer could make improper use of official information to which a former Minister has had access, it may recommend a delay of up to two years before the appointment is taken up, or that for a similar period the former Minister should stand aside from certain activities of the employer.

10. MINISTERIAL PENSIONS

Participation in the Parliamentary Contributory Pension Fund

130. Ministers who have accrued pension rights in another pension scheme may, if they elect to participate in the in respect of their Ministerial salary, and if the rules of the other scheme permit, also to have the value of those accrued rights transferred to the Fund. The Fees Office will advise on the additional benefits which will be secured by such a transfer payment.

Participation in other pension schemes

131. Ministers with accrued pension rights in another pension scheme who do not (or cannot) elect for a transfer payment may leave these as "frozen" rights in the other scheme, with no further contributions being payable during their tenure of office. Alternatively, if the rights are secured by an insurance policy (and assuming that the rules of the other scheme, and the policy itself so permit) the policy could be transferred to them, either on a paid-up basis or with the right to continue payment of the premiums themselves.

132. Ministers who expect to resume their former employment on ceasing to hold Ministerial office and who, elect not to participate in the Parliamentary Fund in respect of their Ministerial salary may remain in active membership (that is, with continued payments of contributions, and with their period of office counting as continued pensionable employment) of any pension scheme relating to that employment provided that this can be done under the rules of the scheme. In these circumstances the continued contributions may be paid by the Ministers alone, or by the former employer alone, or jointly, depending on the rules of the other scheme.

133. It must be emphasised that any arrangements made under paragraph 131 must not go outside the terms of the particular pension scheme. There would be no objection to a general alteration of the rules of a scheme when this is necessary to permit such arrangements; but approval could not be given for the addition to the scheme of a special provision relating only to the tenure of a Ministerial Office. If Ministers have any doubts about the propriety of any arrangements they intend making, the Prime Minister's Private Secretary may be consulted.

134. Ministers who elect not to participate in the Parliamentary scheme in respect of their Ministerial salary, and who make no arrangements of the kind set out in paragraph 131, may be entitled to claim tax relief on premiums paid under a "retirement annuity contract" or "personal pension scheme" to provide additional pension etc, benefits for themselves or provision for their families in the event of death. Such contracts are issued subject to the limitations and conditions laid down in the Tax Acts. Relief is normally limited to 17.5 per cent of the Ministerial salary excluding, for a Minister in the Commons, the difference between a Minister's reduced salary as a Member and a Member's pensionable salary. Higher limits apply to those aged over 50 (in the case of retirement annuity contracts) or aged over 35 (with personal pension schemes).

135. The taxation effects of arrangements such as are mentioned in the paragraphs above may vary according to the Minister's particular circumstances. The Controller, Inland Revenue Pension Schemes Office, PO Box 62, Yorke House, Castle Meadow Road, Nottingham, NG2 1BG, will be willing to explain the effects for tax purposes of any proposed arrangements under paragraph 131; he will also give, on request, further information on the legislation and reliefs available in respect of retirement annuity contracts or personal pension schemes.

ANNEX

MEMBERSHIP OF LLOYD'S

1.   A Minister holding office as Prime Minister, Chancellor of the Exchequer or as President of the Board of Trade (Secretary of State for Trade and Industry), or a Minister holding office as a Minister in the Treasury who is responsible under the Chancellor of the Exchequer for taxation matters relating specifically to Lloyd's, or as a Minister in the Department of Trade and Industry responsible under the Secretary of State for Trade and Industry for insurance matters relating specifically to Lloyd's, should not become an underwriting member of Lloyd's. Such a Minister, if already a member of Lloyd's on appointment, should cease underwriting during tenure of that office.

2.   Apart from those Ministers covered by the specific requirements of paragraph 1 above, any Minister who is an underwriting member of Lloyd's should not take an active part in the management of the affairs of syndicates of which he/she is a member, and should on appointment as a Minister withdraw from any such active participation in management. Ministers who are underwriting members of Lloyd's should arrange their syndicate participation solely through a Members Agent Pooling Arrangement (MAPA). This requirement will operate from the 1995 year of account, or from the first year of account after appointment for newly appointed Ministers, subject to time being available for the procedures for joining a MAPA.

3.   No Minister who is a current underwriting member of Lloyd's should take part in any Departmental or collective discussions or decision affecting Lloyd's whether directly or indirectly (e.g. the Secretary of State for Transport in relation to questions concerning marine, aviation and transport insurance, the Secretary of State for Employment on questions concerning employers' liability insurance, Treasury Ministers on tax issues affecting Lloyd's).

4.   Some Ministers may have ceased underwriting but still have, open syndicate commitments in respect of past membership. Such Ministers should take no part in those Departmental or collective discussions or decisions affecting Lloyd's (whether directly or indirectly) if their continuing benefits or liabilities in respect of the period before cessation might thereby be affected, and might therefore make them vulnerable to reasonable suspicion of exerting or being in a position of undue influence.

5.   A Law Officer who is an underwriting member of Lloyd's, or who still has open syndicate commitments in respect of past membership, should not tender advice on the formulation, application or enforcement of legislation relating to Lloyd's, or take part in any collective discussion or decision on any matters affecting Lloyd's and should, as far as is practicable, avoid taking enforcement decisions relating to Lloyd's.

6.   Where a Minister is contemplating investing in a corporate entity at Lloyd's, or has made such an investment prior to Ministerial appointment, the provisions of paragraphs 109-123 apply.

7.　A Minister in whom powers under legislation relating to Lloyd's are vested should not delegate the exercise of those powers to any other Minister who is an underwriting member of Lloyd's or who still has open syndicate commitments in respect of past underwriting.

8.　Every Minister is required, on first appointment to Ministerial office, to obtain the Prime Minister's written permission before continuing a connection with Lloyd's, however nominal. Any Minister wishing to establish or re-establish any such connection during his term of appointment should likewise obtain the Prime Minister's permission to do so. Before granting permission, the Prime Minister will need to be satisfied that the conditions indicated above will be met.

9.　In addition, the Secretary of the Cabinet is required to keep a list of Ministers who are members of Lloyd's. He will ask all Ministers on appointment for the first time to Ministerial office whether they are a member of Lloyd's and if so whether they propose to continue or to suspend underwriting while they hold that office. He will also ask those Ministers who are members of Lloyd's and who are appointed to a subsequent Ministerial office whether they propose to continue or suspend underwriting while they hold that office.

10.　Where a Minister has a shareholding in an investment trust or any other entity which holds a corporate membership of Lloyd's, that shareholding should be treated on the same basis as any other by a Minister (see paras 109–123).